"*By Their Side* is a moving ar[...] directly to the caregivers, friends, a[...] disorder. Having a support network that understands the core issues and complexities plays a significant—yet often overlooked—role in lasting recovery, and Lara Lyn Bell's strong voice offers guidance and solidarity throughout the journey."

—Kirsten Haglund, global business development and digital director for Eating Disorder Hope; Miss America 2008; political analyst and host for Fox, MSNBC, and CNN; founder and president of the Kirsten Haglund Foundation

"Sharing their stories in one powerful voice as Lara Lyn Bell, the contributors to *By Their Side* stand united as allies for anyone battling an eating disorder. By speaking together, these recovered advocates, families, friends, and professionals turned their most humbling challenges into a source of healing, and they are a poignant reminder that together is always stronger than alone."

—Brian Cuban, best-selling author, attorney, eating-disorder recovery advocate

"Having worked with many of the courageous contributors to this book, I have no doubt their collective knowledge will be an invaluable education for caregivers as they work to help their loved ones heal. Enabling caregivers with the necessary coping skills, self-awareness tools, and self-care resources is critical, and the combination of the book and workbook empowers them to be fully engaged in the recovery process."

—Melody Moore, PhD, E-RYT, licensed clinical psychologist; founder of Embody Love Movement Foundation; author and speaker

"The incredibly honest stories in *By Their Side* offer more than perspective; they offer a roadmap to equip readers to better support loved ones recovering from eating disorders. Having devoted my career to helping others rebuild a healthy body image and a healthy relationship with food that is built on inner trust, I believe the diverse—yet universally familiar—experiences shared in this book are a vital resource for those fighting the shame, secrecy, and stigma that is often at the heart of their struggle."

—Elyse Resch, MS, RDN, CEDRD-S, Fiaedp, FADA, FAND, originator and coauthor of *Intuitive Eating: A Revolutionary Program That Works*, 3rd ed.; author of *The Intuitive Eating Workbook for Teens*

"The contributors to *By Their Side* are selflessly courageous, and their stories are unforgettable examples of transparency, perseverance, and, above all, grace. For those walking alongside someone they love on the long road to recovery, the book will resonate, and the workbook turns this resonance into action with a hands-on approach to reconnecting with hope and faith. This is an incredible resource that will bless so many."

—Tova Sido, pastor, author, and podcast host, "The Remedy with Tova Sido"

"This is a must-read for anyone whose family has been affected by an eating disorder. The book delivers invaluable insights and will resonate with families and caregivers who are feeling alone, afraid, and totally overwhelmed."

—Stephanie Setliff, MD, CEDS-S, regional medical director, Eating Recovery Center of Dallas

"This book is thoughtful and insightful. After nearly two decades in the field, it is wonderful to have a resource that gives such a direct and candid look at the diverse experiences of treating and recovering from eating disorders. This collected work will guide you through the path taken by so many others and show that you are not alone in the darkness."

—Tyler Wooten, MD, medical director,
Eating Recovery Center of Dallas

"Equal parts raw, poignant, emotional, and powerful. The stories, advice, and solutions in the book are excellent and potent because they do not come from an eating disorder 'expert' but from the real experts on the frontlines—moms, families, and loved ones."

—Eddie Coker, singer-songwriter,
founder of the Wezmore Project

"Dearest family, friends, acquaintances, and strangers, this book is for you . . . For anyone who loves someone struggling."

—A mom

"A great read for caregivers of loved ones with an eating disorder. Families and parents supporting their children with eating disorders are some of the strongest people that I know. Parents and families can be incredible allies to their children in recovery."

—Jennifer Rollin, MSW, LCSW-C

"Research shows putting our feelings into words actually produces therapeutic effects in the brain. Journaling takes the healing process to a deeper level. In addition to reading *By Their Side*, working simultaneously in the companion workbook will be one of the caretaker's greatest assets in their journey. It will put them steps ahead in the therapeutic process as they walk toward health and healing."

—Bethany Haley Williams, PhD, LCSW,
founder and CEO, Exile International

"The entire family struggles when their loved one battles an eating disorder, and support for family and friends is vital to the healing process. *By Their Side* delivers that support through firsthand experiences from an array of warriors, because knowing you're not alone is the beginning of healing. The book offers hopeful solutions for an extremely complicated and terrifying illness, and hope is the key to sustaining the team effort that's necessary for recovery."

—Terry Bentley Hill, criminal defense attorney,
Presidential Citation Award, Mental Health
of America's Carmen Miller Michael Prism
Award for Mental Health Advocacy

BY THEIR
SIDE

BY THEIR SIDE

A Resource for Caretakers and Loved Ones Facing an Eating Disorder

Lara Lyn Bell

Written by a collection of families, friends, and healed advocates.

BROWN BOOKS
PUBLISHING GROUP

By Their Side
A Resource for Caretakers and Loved Ones Facing an Eating Disorder

Brown Books Publishing Group
16250 Knoll Trail Drive, Suite 205
Dallas, Texas 75248
www.BrownBooks.com
(972) 381-0009

A New Era in Publishing®

Publisher's Cataloging-In-Publication Data

Names: Bell, Lara Lyn, author.
Title: By their side : a resource for caretakers and loved ones facing an
    eating disorder / Lara Lyn Bell ; written by a collection of families,
    friends, and healed advocates.
Description: Dallas, Texas : Brown Books Publishing Group, [2019]
Identifiers: ISBN 9781612543123
Subjects: LCSH: Eating disorders. | Eating disorders--Patients--Care. |
    Eating disorders--Patients--Family relationships. | Caregivers.
Classification: LCC RC552.E18 B45 2019 | DDC 616.85/26--dc23

ISBN 978-1-61254-312-3
LCCN 2019938212

Printed in the United States
10 9 8 7 6 5 4 3 2 1

For more information or to contact the author,
please go to www.ByTheirSideBook.com.

This book is dedicated to . . .

The child whose struggle became our window to the world,
uniting a family with a bond that cannot be broken.

The sister and brother who felt alone at times but
purposefully chose love. The risk of loving won.

The mom and dad who fought beyond reason and would
do it all over again to save the life of their child.

The extended family who opened their home and those
who showed up and held the foundation in hand when
others were exhausted, confused, or scared.

The wingman who loved us just as we were.

The friends and mentors who offered comfort without judgment.

The young man who believed in the light and goodness of our child's soul.

The neighbors who supportively held our village strong.

The professionals who have chosen to dedicate their lives
to the health and well-being of our children.

And the honest people who have chosen to share their hearts in this book.

A special thanks to all the wonderful
people at Brown Books Publishing Group.

*A portion of the proceeds from this book will be
dedicated to help those who cannot afford treatment.*

You will be tested; you will be pushed to what you think
is your limit. At times, you will break. Motherhood isn't
a job; it is a part of who you are. I'm a mom.

You will stumble and, at times, want to run away, but you won't.
You will find you're resilient . . . And yes, you will second-guess
your wisdom. "Am I doing this right? Am I equipping this special
child with what they need to address this ever-changing world?"

As time passes, you'll realize it's not about molding your child into the
person you think they should become; it's about finding out who they are,
encouraging their strengths, and loving them through their weaknesses.

You'll be surprised at how different the child from your womb seems,
and those differences can cause you immeasurable anxiety. But you'll
come to realize that your child is like you. And it's through the eyes
of that child that you will learn about yourself and about life.

—A mom

Contents

Section 2: Getting Grounded and Preparing Yourself for the Journey Ahead

Section 3: Treatments and Therapies

Section 4: The Bigger Picture? Deepening Your Essential Purpose

Foreword

You have an eating disorder.

Or maybe you're not the one with an eating disorder—maybe it's your daughter, your son, your husband, your wife, your grandchild, your parent, your best friend, or your roommate. This book, written by individuals who have experienced the complex challenges faced by those who struggle with eating disorders, will be a valuable resource no matter who is the focus of treatment.

You may know firsthand how all-encompassing and potentially life threatening these disorders can be. And those who love you, who are in the trenches with you, battling the eating disorder as best they can for and with you, experience their own pain as they watch you in the midst of your suffering.

Everyone who comes in contact with an eating disorder struggles for control. Control over body. Control over food. Control over feelings. Control over others. The desire for control is not limited to the person with the disorder; family members and friends may also desperately feel a need for the person in question to "just eat," "just quit exercising so much," "just quit purging," "just quit lying to us."

The authors of this book have chosen to speak as one voice. All have been deeply impacted by their loved ones' various eating disorders, and they wish for you to have the wisdom they have gained through experience. They want you not to have to start at square one when you hear a professional say, "I think your child (or you or a family member) has an eating disorder." They want you not to feel alone as you start on the journey toward recovery—often a very long and arduous journey that can feel confusing, overwhelming, circuitous, and never ending.

Each chapter in this book stands on its own, so you may read them in the order presented or pick and choose based on what you need help with most urgently. The testimonials at the end of each chapter give a candid glimpse into the lives of those who have personally been affected by an eating disorder. If you are a parent or caretaker for someone who is struggling to recover from an eating disorder, this book has been lovingly written to provide you support, understanding, resources, care, and concern.

As a psychologist specializing in the treatment of eating disorders for over thirty-five years, I can attest to how much effort is required by everyone involved to help someone with such a disorder heal. *By Their Side* offers each reader hope for a recovered future.

—Betty K. Armstrong, PhD, clinical psychologist

The Purpose of *By Their Side*

How do we love and support someone suffering from an eating disorder without losing ourselves? How do we best care take our loved one while maintaining a clear and sound mind? Where do we find practical answers based in experience, medical advice, and research? The trickle-down effect is inevitable, so how do we balance our lives? This book will help answer those questions and many more.

Who Is This Book For?

You, the reader. This unique book is for anyone who loves someone suffering from an eating disorder. Most likely, you picked up this book because someone you love is fighting one, and you are likely frustrated, scared, and looking for answers. We deeply understand your concerns. In this book, you will learn how to best support your loved ones and yourself during this treacherous fight. So, whether you are a mom, dad, sibling, friend, mentor, partner, or family member, this book is for you. *By Their Side* is full of important, insightful, and life-changing information caretakers should know about eating disorders as they continue to learn about themselves and their loved one who is struggling.

By Their Side was created with you, *the reader*, in mind. It is not just another person's story. It is your story; it is all of our stories; and it will likely feel familiar. We hope that with the knowledge gained from this book, you will have an opportunity to redirect your own story.

Who Wrote This Book?

This detailed project was birthed from the lives of several families and individuals who have endured long struggles with eating disorders. It began as a project of love and of giving back, as we believe it is our human responsibility to pay forward what one learns from life's challenges. Many professionals have also provided their expertise, knowledge, research, and science.

The author's name, Lara Lyn Bell, is an acronym representing the thirty-two anonymous contributors to this book. It invites you to recognize and react to your own personal role in healing your loved one. We chose to speak collectively, in one powerful voice, writing from the most vulnerable, raw place in our hearts in hopes that our honesty will help you to never feel alone in this battle and to believe that full and comprehensive healing is real.

You are Lara Lyn Bell. We are all Lara Lyn Bell. Our lives are mirrored as you connect with the familiar struggles and successes of mothers, fathers, brothers, sisters, aunts, uncles, extended family members, friends, and fully recovered loved ones who share how they felt with an eating disorder and how they ultimately healed. We want to share our successes and our failures and, in doing so, help you to understand that this is life; we've got to come together and face the challenges.

> *When it comes to the people we love, there is a common thread that resides in all of us. Our hopes, dreams, and prayers for our loved ones are universally the same.*
>
> *—Lara Lynn Bell*

What's in the Book?

Answers, proactive suggestions, new data, and hope. *By Their Side* offers suggestions with affirmation, so as you read the pages of this book, make the book about you. See yourself in the familiar threads, answer questions honestly, educate yourself, and be openhearted to learning about yourself, your loved ones, and the complexity of eating disorders.

This intelligent book of hope includes new, up-to-date information from the fields of education, medicine, and science, with recommended suggestions for healing as well as instructional information, personal diary entries, experienced suggestions, testimonials, innovative thoughts, professional advice, and many resources. What makes *By Their Side* unique is that you will hear from children who have recovered from an eating disorder and speak directly to caretakers. You will read sibling-to-sibling interactions; you will hear from other parents who are steps ahead of you in the process, as well as from professionals in the field; and you will learn from new research regarding eating disorders. Hope will be shared from recovered families who, today, are healed in the light and out of the darkness of a once debilitating disorder.

The Companion Workbook, *Working by Their Side*

One of the most important aspects differentiating this book from others in the market is its companion, *Working by Their Side*. This accompanying workbook is a guided journal that will enhance your education by providing opportunities to answer questions, record thoughts, explore uncertainties, and take notes as you learn about being a caretaker for a loved one who is struggling with an eating disorder. The companion is not just freehand journaling; it is designed to answer specific questions posed throughout this book. *Working by Their Side* follows *By Their Side* chapter by chapter, prompting us with reflective questions and enhancing our knowledge of the topics discussed in this book.

How to Use This Book

Make it personal. *By Their Side* can be read cover to cover or modularly depending on where you are in the journey. You can pick and choose what works for you or read it from beginning to end.

While reading, we suggest you take notes and answer questions honestly in the accompanying workbook, *Working by Their Side*. Use the advice and knowledge from the author, contributing writers, and professionals to direct your journey to recovery. Then take this journal—full of answers, research, and questions—to an eating-disorder professional, and get help for yourself and your family. You will be many steps ahead in therapy and knowledge.

In the appendix, you will find referrals, answers, and tangible places to start or further your education. Additionally, this material is intended to help you decipher, identify, and manage your discomfort. The hard work toward healing is worth it, we know!

Why This Book Was Created

Hope in full and comprehensive healing. This book was created to remind us all that, even in the darkest of times, it is crucial we vigorously believe there is hope for whole and comprehensive healing.

What does that really mean? It means that if you're willing to do the work—reading this book is a great start—true recovery for your loved one and your family is attainable.

Recovery is not about perfection, becoming the perfect person, or having a perfect relationship with food. Perfection is nonexistent. Recovery is about allowing yourself to be human—imperfect and free from the lies of an eating disorder. Recovery is about developing into the person you want to be. Worthy. Purposeful. Validated. Knowledgeable. Connected. Loved and loving.

Please allow us to help you help yourself, as we are made stronger together in the knowledge that you and your loved ones are worthy of the effort.

—Lara Lyn Bell

Introduction

> If, when I was thirteen, you had told me where I would
> be now, at twenty-six . . . I wouldn't have believed you.
> I wouldn't have believed that I would appreciate and
> be abundantly grateful for my body and all that it can
> do. I wouldn't have believed that exercise would be an
> option for pleasure rather than a ritual necessary for
> bodily control. I wouldn't have believed that I could
> walk into any room knowing that I matter and that I
> have something to offer this world. I wouldn't have
> believed that I would be able to enjoy dessert on a
> date. I wouldn't have believed that I could stop calorie
> counting. I wouldn't have believed that I would care more
> about others' well-being than their perception of me.

In the depths of an eating disorder, it is incredibly hard to imagine that true recovery is possible or that it even really exists. I remember being told by multiple professionals, "You will live with this the rest of your life. You simply have to learn how to manage the disordered thoughts." Well, I am here to tell you that your loved one does not have to simply "learn how to endure this horrible disease." I believe that with the right tools and resources, they too can experience full freedom and recovery.

I am not promising perfection or ease; I am simply telling you that there is hope for your loved one—and there is even the possibility that this horrific struggle will end up making them into an even more whole, happy, and confident human in the long run. I am speaking from experience here. Once someone who thought I would never be capable of loving myself, I am now standing on the other side of my battle, strong, confident, and truly happy. This takes time, effort, and true dedication. Healing is a process, and

it takes an extreme amount of patience and work both from the one struggling with an eating disorder and from their family. This is not a disease that
can be fought individually; to conquer this, a true team effort is critical. In
the following pages, please listen to those who have fought this battle before
you, and please know that there is no perfect path to recovery.

It is critical to understand that we need the wisdom of all members
dedicated to the patient's healing. We need the instinctive intuition of a
mother, the protective nature of a father, the loving perspective of a sibling,
the inquisitive disposition of a friend, the professional attentiveness of a
therapist. No matter the role, we need the support of our community in
order to heal.

My family was monumental in my recovery. They always showed up
and continued to believe in me, even when I didn't believe in myself. They
attended family therapy sessions, listened to me when I needed to be heard,
and were always willing to adjust their actions to aid in my recovery. No
matter what, they loved me with their entire ability. This unconditional love
acted as the single most important influence in my healing process. I no longer wanted to get better only for myself but also for them. In my experience,
recovery can be fueled not only by an individual's need to heal but by their
desire to be "whole" for their collective family or community. We need others
outside of ourselves to support us, believe in us, and cheer us on.

Furthermore, the help of a professional is also critical to the recovery
process. The assistance that therapy provides in unraveling the reasons and
motivations behind the eating disorder is monumental in creating lasting
change. As survivors, we need the third-party perspective and encouragement to be capable of moving forward. There is no way I would have been
able to truly heal without the intense use of talk therapy. I would highly
encourage anyone participating in this journey of healing to participate in
therapy.

The collective wisdom in this book is meant to equip you with the
knowledge needed to give yourself or your loved one the best chance for
comprehensive healing. The healed advocates, friends, and families who share
their experiences here are all rooting for you. We know that hope exists, and
our prayer is that you take comfort in knowing that recovery is truly possible.

—A recovered advocate and promoter of comprehensive healing

How Does Your Loved One Really Feel?

This life isn't about me. But that's not what I'm told by the million messages that unfold on TV. I am a soul . . . I have a body. Yet *tuck, nip, trim, diet, starve* led me to think perfection should be my new hobby. For "never enough, never enough" is what the media whispers in my ear . . . through the self-medicated self-abuse that leads to an inability to hear truth. Caught up in lies, I run to the arms of the culture . . . desperate for an affirmation of love. If I can change this, or if I alter that, will it be enough?

—Diary of a teen in the depths of an eating disorder

1 When You Suspect Your Loved One Has an Eating Disorder

> Listen to your intuition; it is trying to tell you something.
> There is knowledge in one's own intuition, most especially
> when you just simply know something is not right.
> Intuition knows right from wrong and sometimes requires
> doing the hard thing, like making painful decisions for
> the betterment of your loved ones and yourself.

Begin by asking yourself, "Is there a problem?"

If you believe there is a problem, what makes you think that your loved one has an eating disorder?

Below is an email sent to a psychologist regarding a teenage child's unfamiliar behavior and the mom's worry. You can feel the mother's concern; it seems almost all mothers, as well as fathers and siblings, can identify with the idea that "something just is not right!" We can't always find the words, but we know the gut feeling.

There is a very steady pattern that happens when she drops to a certain weight (as she presently has). This monster comes at her like a wicked demon. She is irrational, obsessive, and irritable . . . cries a lot, easily frustrated, cannot sleep, is not engaged in the present, and she fights herself. She fights me. She tends to make logic out of illogical situations or thoughts, and yet she can fool most anyone with her poise. Of course, her family sees it daily, and just recently, through tears of frustration, she admitted to the

5

power this monster has over her right now but still cannot hear with a clear mind. Since birth, her personality has been packed with emotions; it is what makes her a passionate, compassionate person. I understand she is thirteen, with all the hormones and such, but as her mom, I know the difference. There is something terribly wrong, yet I cannot identify the exact problem. I think she is in trouble, and we need to consider a concentrated treatment plan. What are your thoughts?

—An email to a therapist from a mom

Are there moments when you look at your loved one and do not recognize them—not only in a physical sense but also behaviorally? Do you feel like they do not hear you? Or that your conversations often get convoluted? Do you know they need help but find yourself unable to identify exactly what's wrong?

As her mom, I know she needs more professional help versus confiding in me; lately it ends up in a tremendously frustrating place for us both. I am not even sure how that happens! I keep wondering what I did wrong. Perhaps she needs to be put in treatment or you can advise us on how much she needs to see you on a regular schedule. I will work it out with her school . . . She needs more help, we need more help—can we please talk this afternoon? By this email I'm sure you can tell my level of frustration. I have watched too many mothers pretend their child is perfect and look the other way. Or just write the behavior off as a "phase." We are not willing to pretend everything is "perfect" with our precious child. We need help and your suggestions. Please consider seeing [our child] several times over the next week, and then, will you please meet with my husband and me?

—An email to a therapist from a mom

If you have experience with an eating disorder—whether the victim is a loved one or yourself—we urge you to move forward in getting help and dealing directly with the issue at hand.

If you do not have experience with an eating disorder, now is the best time for an education. You are not alone, and you need to take this illness very seriously. According to the National Eating Disorders Association, up to thirty million people in the United States suffer from eating disorders; worldwide, the figure is up to seventy million.[1] But sadly, only one in ten seeks and follows through with treatment. Statistics prove that the earlier the treatment, the higher the possible probability of full recovery and healing.

Pause and Write

Before proceeding, please answer the first set of questions for this chapter in *Working by Their Side*.

Next Steps to Take Now:
Putting One Foot in Front of the Other

Please read through the suggestions below. We hope they help you recognize and better understand the behaviors and symptoms you are witnessing in your loved one. You are most likely reading this book because you are concerned for a loved one and want help either in deciphering whether what they are experiencing is an eating disorder or, if you know it is, then in gathering facts and necessary knowledge. If you have been on this journey a long time and are well educated about eating disorders, feel free to move to the next chapter.

---

1   Libby Lyons, "Eating Disorders on the Rise All Around the World: An Overview," *Eating Disorder Hope*, March 1, 2017, https://www.eatingdisorderhope.com/blog/eating -disorders-world-overview.

Address the Serious Nature of an Eating Disorder

Eating disorders are very serious illnesses:

> Eating disorders are serious, potentially life-threatening conditions that affect a person's emotional and physical health. They are not just a "fad" or a "phase." People do not just "catch" an eating disorder for a period of time. They are real, complex, and devastating conditions that can have serious consequences for health, productivity, and relationships.[2]

Early intervention is key to providing the best possible chance of healing.

Learn the Behavior and Characteristics of an Eating Disorder

There is an obvious change in the behavior of a person with an eating disorder. If you are this person's parent or have another kind of close relationship with them, your emotional radar will warn you that something is not right. Eventually, you will find the behavioral changes shocking, as the person you felt you knew so well now confuses you. For a period of time, your loved one can hide these traits, but eventually, they will surface. Those suffering from an eating disorder most often adopt these behaviors as a means to cope with the psychological struggles they are going through. Keep in mind that the first six characteristics on the following list are also often used to hide symptoms.

These are characteristics of the disease, not of your loved one. The core of your precious child, your sibling, or your friend is still there. A good rule of thumb: fight the disease, not the person.

- Withdrawn: Less social. Pensive. Pushes friends, parents, and loved ones away.
- Manipulative: Attempts to control situations so they get their way. Twists stories and situations to hide their disordered behaviors.
- Avoidant: Finds excuses for why they can't be with others. Avoids questions or confrontations with those who question activities and behaviors.

---

2   "Health Consequences," National Eating Disorders Association, 2018, https://www.nationaleatingdisorders.org/health-consequences.

- Controlling: Manipulates situations in order to contain/control their world and structure it the way they want.
- Dishonest: Lies. Does not reveal full truths. Hides the truth. Manipulates the truth.
- Sneaky: Secretive.
- Short tempered: Agitated. Irritable. Replies with short answers to get you off their back.
- Disrespectful: Rude in both actions and verbal responses. Ill mannered. Unnaturally impolite. Flippant.
- Emotional: Temperamental. Reactionary outside of typical sensitivity.
- Volatile: Quick to anger. Emotionally and physically abusive.
- Teary: Quick to cry.
- Weary: Physically tired. Exhausted. Fatigued. Sluggish.
- Depressed: Sad. Heavy hearted. Depression is very common in eating disorders.
- Egocentric: Obsessed with their eating disorder; thus, the eating disorder is obsessed with them.
- Selfish: Self-centered.
- Anxious: Anxiety is the most common characteristic. It can begin at the onset of an eating disorder, or inherent anxiety can have existed before the disease. Some typical disorders that coexist with an anxiety component are obsessive-compulsive behavior, social anxiety, and panic attacks.

I find comfort that when my child is "being selfish," I can now understand that the behavior is part of the mental illness process. It is a symptom, not a reflection, of my child.

—Mom of a child suffering from anorexia

Learn the Terms and Definitions of Eating Disorders

Caretakers need to learn and understand the vocabulary of eating disorders so as to recognize the signs and symptoms of the disease and be educated when speaking to professionals. If you are familiar with eating disorders, feel free to skip this section.

There are many categories used to explain the variety of eating disorders; in this chapter, we will address the four most common, with subsets in each area:

- Anorexia nervosa (AN)
- Bulimia nervosa (BN)
- Binge-eating disorder (BED)
- Other specified feeding and eating disorders (OSFED)

For information on less common disorders, such as orthorexia, avoidant restrictive food disorder (ARFID), pica, rumination disorder, unspecified feeding or eating disorder, laxative abuse, or compulsive exercise, please see "Information by Eating Disorder" on the website of the National Eating Disorders Association.[3]

Below, you will find our descriptions of the common disorders in laymen's terms, derived from what we have seen and experienced as caretakers. For the diagnostic criteria described in the fifth edition of the American Psychiatric Association's *Diagnostic and Statistical Manual of Mental Disorders* (DSM-5), visit the website of the American Psychiatric Association, which you can find in the appendix at the back of this book. Please also refer to the appendix for more details on the descriptions in this section.

Please know that educating yourself is worth the effort so that when you communicate with professionals about eating disorders, their advice and medical jargon will make sense. If you're just beginning the process, please approach your education intently, not hastily. The vast amount of information is overwhelming at first.

Anorexia Nervosa (AN)

Anorexia nervosa comes from Latin words that mean "nervous inability to eat."

Individuals with anorexia have a distorted body image and a fear of gaining weight. The fear of weight gain is characterized by self-starvation, restricting/controlling food intake, and overindulging in exercise. Sometimes the "obviously starving body" is not as apparent, but the

---

3   "Information by Eating Disorder," National Eating Disorders Association, 2018, https://www.nationaleatingdisorders.org/information-eating-disorder.

abnormal behaviors based around food topics, weight, body image, and/ or self-esteem are alarming. Typically, a person struggling with anorexia develops a skewed perception of their physical body that causes them to see themselves as abnormally heavy. This is known as body dysmorphia. Anorexia nervosa has the highest death risk of any psychiatric disorder— more than twice that of depression, schizophrenia, or bipolar disorder.

This illness is a mental sickness that aims to fully control the minds of our loved ones. It lies to them, and in turn, they lie to themselves and others.

> I knew my parents were concerned that I wasn't eating enough, so I insisted nothing was wrong—I was fine, and I hid things from them. I would purposefully eat something in front of my mom just so she'd think I was eating, and then I'd punish myself by restricting the rest of the day. I eventually lost interest in things I had been passionate about. Looking back, it was as if I had sold myself to the eating disorder, and it was my master.
>
> —A survivor reflecting back

The mental illness is equally severe physically, as anorexia can cause medical complications such as heart dysfunction, hair loss, bone loss, skin discoloration, amenorrhea, and more. Whether we call it a disease or disorder, anorexia is extremely serious and should be addressed immediately because we know the best results for healing come from early intervention.

Bulimia Nervosa (BN)

Bulimia nervosa is an emotional disorder characterized by an individual's response to their intake of food, which is perceived to be overabundant. We say *perceived* because, when eating, how much is too much is up to the discretion of the individual. A person with bulimia nervosa often "binge eats" by consuming large quantities of food (insatiable overeating) and then, because they have poor body-image issues, vomits what they have eaten to rid their body of the consumed calories in a false hope of losing weight. Sadly, the individual is ashamed of this behavior, so they then sneak food in private, causing more guilt and self-ridicule. Similar to anorexia, there are issues with body dysmorphia, low self-love, poor body image, depression, and anxiety.

There are two common subtypes of bulimia. Purging is when, as a result of what they consider excessive overeating, the individual rids their body of food by inducing vomiting and/or by taking laxatives, diuretics, or self-administered enemas. The second common subtype is called nonpurging. To manage compulsive overeating, the individual compensates with bouts of fasting and/or excessive exercise. This ill-judged behavior toward the self and toward eating is abnormal and dangerous from a mental and medical standpoint.

During one of the first intensive outpatient (IOP) parent meetings I ever attended (and I ended up going to many), I found myself sitting in a room with nine other parents, discussing our children's eating-disorder cases. One mom explained her child's bulimia, and what really hit home were two things: one, she had not known for several years, and two, when she began to suspect something was really wrong, she started looking for clues. What she found shocked me then, but now I realize it is not abnormal. This mom said she found a drawer full of Ziploc baggies with vomit in each one! During the following weeks and months, she found up to twelve Ziploc baggies a day full of vomit that were hidden in various drawers, under the bed, in her car, and in the alley trash can. The discovery opened the family up for a long journey of healing, yet the mom had a tremendous amount of guilt. During these parent meetings, she would often hang her head and say, "How could I have not known this?"

—A surprised mom

All of us—each and every one of the individuals who has been a part of writing this book—have been surprised and even shocked by eating-disorder behavior. But we have also worked hard to move beyond those lightning bolts and—probably most importantly—have learned not to judge our loved one for it. And, to be fair, we've had to learn not to judge our own selves. A person struggling with bulimia does not need to be judged or shamed; they already feel shame. They need to be loved. Loving them means addressing the issue and finding help as they learn to help themselves.

Binge-Eating Disorder (BED)

To binge means to indulge in an activity of excess. Binge-eating disorder is when an individual indulges in repetitive, excessive overeating, often with a feeling of not being able to stop. These episodes can lead to exhibiting odd, ritualistic behavior around food and meals, hiding their overeating habits from loved ones, eating alone, or hoarding food. The ritual of eating to excess is most always followed by disgust with oneself. This loss of control promotes physical discomfort accompanied by shame and disappointment. Weight gain may not be obvious or can cause obesity. Less physically obvious, but equally scary, are the unseen depression, self-hate, and suicidal thoughts.

Why would our loved ones binge eat? One reason is that, chemically, it feels good. Certain foods, such as fats and sugars, trigger the brain to release dopamine, the organic chemical of pleasure and reward. Compulsive eating helps to cover pain, social anxiety, loneliness, and sadness. But when people start binging for comfort, no one plans on it becoming a significant and destructive disorder they lose control over.

Other Specified Feeding and Eating Disorders (OSFED)

Other specified feeding and eating disorders (OSFED) describes an individual who is in distress due to an eating disorder but whose characteristics do not fit within the DSM-5's strict criteria for anorexia, bulimia, or binge-eating disorder. OSFED used to be called eating disorder not otherwise specified (EDNOS). This diagnosis serves as a catchall and encompasses a varied group of individuals. It can be a gateway to more severe behavior, but a diagnosis of OSFED can also be just as clinically severe in itself, causing unwanted medical concerns.

Distorted body image, overvaluation of shape and weight, and/or an intense fear of gaining weight are shared characteristics of OSFED, anorexia, bulimia, and binge eating. OSFED is the most common eating disorder and is a diagnosis for adolescents and adults, affecting all people. In many ways, it is also the most confusing when diagnosed. OSFED can feel vague and too open ended, yet the underlying emotional symptoms are congruent with other well-defined eating disorders. Therefore, seeking immediate help is consequential.

All eating disorders share the unkind qualities of self-ridicule and, often, self-loathing. All eating disorders have obvious and unseen characteristics that are harmful to the point of death. All eating disorders also have a high risk of simultaneous psychiatric disorders.

For more information or for definitions outside of the categories above, please refer to the appropriate resources in the appendix. For suggestions on how to obtain professional help, please refer to chapters 4 and 9.

All Eating Disorders Are Treatable, and There Is Hope for Healing

As caretakers, we often ask ourselves, "How in the world is it possible to over-eat to the point of vomiting? Why don't they just stop? Why and how is it possible that my loved one is starving herself? Why doesn't she just eat?" We wonder about these odd behaviors around food. We feel confused and can't believe it is our loved one or even our child. Getting stuck in the vacuum of denial, confusion, guilt, blame, or ridicule will slow down the healing pro-cess. The answers may or may not be formidable in the beginning, but the most important thing to do is immediately reach out for first-rate help. Your questions may be answered eventually. Honestly, however, from experience, we can tell you that sometimes, even after full and comprehensive healing, there still are unanswered questions. Sometimes in this life, there are no ade-quate answers to the questions we so desperately want explained. Being at peace without always having an answer is part of being human.

Getting educated is a wonderful decision.

Pause and Write

Following the prompts in *Working by Their Side*, take notes regarding terms and definitions, observations about your loved one's behavior, and your thoughts, feelings, and concerns.

Unconditional Love

Commit to loving your child, friend, or relative unconditionally, even when it's difficult—and there will be times it is! Unconditional love is the choice to model a consistent love without judgment, even when you are disappointed with your loved one's behavior or choices. It often requires tough love, but never prideful love, nor love given in return for actions of approval.

> Hug her, touch her, kiss her forehead, and open up the physical boundaries to let her be your child. They try to be so grown up, and sometimes what they need the most is the reassurance of unconditional love and comfort.
>
> —A letter from one friend to another

Realities We Know to Be True with Eating Disorders

There are many misconceptions about eating disorders. Unless you've had experience with them, they can be very difficult to understand. Just like each person's thumbprint is unique, each case has its own personal triggers, traits, and behaviors. Below are twenty truths that we feel are important for you to know.

- **You are not alone.** There are thousands and thousands of other families seeking help for their loved one struggling with an eating disorder. There has been unprecedented growth in the number of eating-disordered individuals in the last two decades. Up to 95 percent of those suffering are between the ages of twelve and twenty-five.[4] These are our children, our loved ones. You are not alone in this battle; reach out for help. Please refer to the appendix for referrals.

- **An eating disorder CANNOT be willed away.**

---

4   "7 Powerful Statistics about Eating Disorders," Avalon Hills Foundation, February 4, 2015, http://www.avalonhillsfoundation.org/blog/2015/02/7-powerful-statistics-about-eating-disorders/.

Healing is a process of returning back to a healthy state of mind, and maybe in some cases, a person can work through their pain alone. However, not in the case of anorexia. It is impossible for the sick individual to find healing from one source and especially just from themselves. They cannot "will away" anorexia. They cannot work through anorexia alone. Strength must be attained in numbers. These numbers can be represented in the form of family, friends, mentors, and any person that provides the sick individual a place of safety and empowerment. In my experience, our family had to learn these coping skills together. (And believe me, it was not easy; actually, it was hard!) We learned to set goals that were attainable, to set goals that were reasonable, and, most of all, to understand that healing takes time. We had to learn that consistency is the gateway for a behavioral change to take place. We had to participate in my sister's healing no matter how difficult. Thing is, we all healed. And with assurance, I can tell you it was worth it.

—A brother

- **Eating disorders are *not* a stereotypical white female problem.** Eating disorders grew exponentially in the 1900s due to the media's depiction of radical thinness in white female actresses; however, they do not only affect white females:

  Radical thinness was so de rigueur that a 1993 People cover story dubbed it the "waif wave." . . . Despite the popularity of the skin-and-bones look, when celebrities admitted to eating disorders, they were censured. . . . But the waif wave coincided with a new social awareness of the connection between extreme thinness and a diagnosis—an eating disorder. Before, skinniness was a marker of a svelte woman's ability to control her body better than her peers. Now it was a symptom of a sickness. . . . Recent research has not only disproved the old ways of thinking about eating disorders that hierarchize white women, it has also revealed that women of color suffer from eating disorders, and perhaps in greater numbers.

Today we know that eating disorders affect girls and women in every demographic but that black teens may be most at risk. They are 50 percent more likely to practice bulimic behavior than white peers. One study found Latinas exhibit bulimia more often than non-Latinas. . . . The truth is that there is not one body, or race or skin color that telegraphs an eating disorder without question.[5]

- **Full and comprehensive healing is possible.** The earlier the disorder is caught and dealt with, the higher the potential for success. Though eating disorders are the most life threatening of all psychiatric illnesses, there is hope for recovery. The essence of full recovery is learning to honestly love oneself, both physically and emotionally, and to find worth in one's own existence.

The bottom line is that positive self-esteem and acceptance of oneself are key to healing.

> She is "back." What a joy it is to witness our healthy, happy grand-daughter, who once had a part of her life stolen by anorexia. Today, she exuded a glow from within that is evident to all around her. She is confident in her relationships, both with others and with her own self—it reminds me of the little girl I use to know. She is proof that an eating disorder can be beaten.
>
> —A relieved grandmother

- **People with eating disorders are not selfish.** People dealing with an eating disorder become hyperfocused on themselves. It's part of the disease. The clinically ill often seem selfish, but it's the disease that is selfish, not the person. No one gets this until they are in the position of taking care of a person with an eating disorder. It's easy to judge from the outside.

---

5   Allison Yarrow, "How Eating Disorders Became a White Women Problem," *HuffPost*, February 27, 2018, https://www.huffingtonpost.com/entry/opinion-yarrow-eating -disorders-white-women_us_5a945db3e4b0699553cb1d00.

It took me a while to understand what an eating disorder was; still not sure I totally get it! When my niece was in the depths of an eating disorder, her behavior seemed selfish and self-centered. At the time, I wondered how in the world such a brilliant, kind kid could do such a selfish thing. But then I came to realize that my precious niece had a real problem. Her intention was not to hurt my sister, or anyone for that matter. She was slave to a complicated disease, and it's a deep and very heavy subject. Grasping the overwhelming emotional toil, I offered for my niece to come live with us and seek day treatment in the city where my family lives. It was in those months that I learned how emotionally crippling the struggle was for my niece. She was not being selfish; she was fighting for her life.

—An aunt and witness

- **People with anorexia are not always strikingly skinny.** Some might visually look sick, but this is not true for everyone who suffers. From the outside, they may look "normal," even if they are dying internally—both physically and emotionally.

- **The core of an eating disorder is driven by underlying issues.** Look for underlying issues like past trauma, bullying, depression, verbal or sexual abuse, low self-esteem, or self-loathing.

- **It is not just about food.**

- **Control is an issue.** Eating is one of the few things a person can control. Thus, they cover the pain through behaviors of not eating, overeating, and/or binge eating.

Though it goes against everything you understand, you have to realize that in most cases, this struggle is not about body image or weight or food. The obsession with exercise or food—be it overeating or undereating—is at its root a coping strategy, a way to cope with something much deeper. For me, it was about control. I've always been more of a type A, anxious, orderly, and disciplined person. From what seemed like out of just boredom, my ED was almost something to be preoccupied with, to work at, to practice, and to feel accomplished with when I saw that number on the scale ten pounds lower or when someone commented on my thin frame.

I had a very healthy home environment where I felt loved and encouraged and beautiful as I was. So, when I told people it was about control, they assume my life was spinning out of control. It wasn't. I believe that nurturing this obsession was a way for my fifteen-year-old self, insecure at my core and seeking worth, to find a sense of identity and meaning.

—A teenager's desire for control

- **Parents do not cause their child's eating disorder.** However, a parent's actions can result in a child developing an eating disorder to cope. We are responsible for helping healthily influence our child's attitudes about eating, body image, weight, and weight management. Positive influences and body image are vitally important in their recovery. If you question your own understanding of body positivity, please see chapter 7 on self-reflection.

- **Anybody can have an eating disorder, no matter their gender, race, sexual preference, socioeconomic status, or religion.** According to the National Association of Anorexia Nervosa and Associated Disorders (ANAD), "In a large national study of college students, 3.5% sexual minority women and 2.1% of sexual minority men reported having an eating disorder. 16% of transgender college students reported having an eating disorder."[6] In reality, no ethnic, gender or socioeconomic group is immune to the dangers of this disease.

---

6   "Eating Disorder Statistics," National Association of Anorexia Nervosa and Associated Disorders, 2019, https://anad.org/education-and-awareness/about-eating-disorders/eating-disorders-statistics/.

Despite the stereotype that eating disorders only occur in women, about one in three people struggling with an eating disorder is male, and subclinical eating disordered behaviors (including binge eating, purging, laxative abuse, and fasting for weight loss) are nearly as common among men as they are among women. In the United States alone, eating disorders will affect ten million males at some point in their lives. But due in large part to cultural bias, they are much less likely to seek treatment for their eating disorder. The good news is that once a man finds help, they show similar responses to treatment as women. Several factors lead to men and boys being under- and undiagnosed for an eating disorder. Men can face a double stigma, for having a disorder characterized as feminine or gay and for seeking psychological help.[7]

- **Primary-care physicians and pediatricians can miss the diagnosis of an eating disorder.** A person's low weight and thin body might fit within medical standards, which is deceiving. Even if they're within the standard range, your loved one could still have an eating disorder. It is critical that you have your loved one assessed by an eating-disorder specialist.

- **Eating disorders are not just a phase in a child's development.** Eating disorders are a serious, potentially fatal brain disorder.

- **A caretaker cannot fix a loved one's eating disorder alone.** Get help and support from loved ones and/or experienced friends. Seek help from a professional in the field of eating disorders. You cannot do this alone. See the appendix for suggestions on where to find help.

After several late-night trips to the emergency room and multiple doctor and specialist visits with my adult friend, who was suffering from a long battle with anorexia, I realized what I was doing. I was

---

7   "Eating Disorders in Men & Boys," National Eating Disorders Association, 2018, https://www.nationaleatingdisorders.org/learn/general-information/research-on-males.

trying to fix her. It had become something I wanted to do, and I wonder if too much of "me" got in the way. No matter how much attention I gave her and how hard I tried, cried, and prayed, she ultimately had to make the decision to get help. She needed to do the work, not me.

I don't regret the love, compassion, and support I gave to my friend, but in the end, I realized this soon-to-be-thirty-year-old had to make a decision to choose healing.

—A friend with good intentions

- **An eating disorder is not contagious.** However, there are predisposed genes that can be inherited from biological family members who have or had an eating disorder, especially parents.

- There is *always* a change in behavior with food.

- **When a person is in the depths of an eating disorder, their brain is deprived of nutrition, and their perception is altered.** But that perception is as true to them as your truths are to you. So here are two thoughts we would like to share: (1) cognitive behavioral therapy is extremely helpful in sorting out thoughts and patterned behavior, and (2) even if you do not agree with the other person's perception, validating their pain and feelings is important. Pain and feelings are different than tangible memories. While they may remember things differently, what's important is how they felt, and addressing their feelings is key.

Memory? Truths? There are things she does not remember. Is that normal with anorexia? She tells me things I have said, things my husband has said, and . . . to my knowledge, they just are not my truths. Does anorexia hear our words and manipulatively twist them into the negative thoughts of the disease? Our child with anorexia has a brilliant mind with an amazing memory. But our memories can be so very different!

Or is it just that I am not privy to some of her truths? Am I wrong in what I remember? As she matures, will she remember differently? Is it a gift not to remember everything so she can let go of the shame? Maybe I am the one who is wrong! Maybe this is where forgiveness begins.

—A confused mom

- **Initially, no one chooses an eating disorder.** However, at some point in recovery, they will have the choice to engage in healing. They have to choose to get well.

- **The ripple effect from an eating disorder is inevitable.** When a loved one is victim to this hideous disease, everyone in their inner circle is affected, most especially the immediate family unit.

A Brother's Thoughts

I am a brother to a big sister who struggled with an eating disorder. The truth is that a "monster" cast itself over my sister and began to take control of how she viewed herself, not only physically but mentally as well. After long years of torment, which I felt and personally watched, I have some things I would love to share.

- Don't judge your sister for any problems; instead, try to remember that the beauty she had before the illness is still within her.

- Understand that there is a time to be a pusher and a time to be a listener.

- Don't be afraid to be in uncomfortable situations with your sibling who is struggling with the problem, because it's damn sure they are uncomfortable all the time.

- Understand that the hurting individual has unmet needs, and focus on how you can help meet those needs.

- Therapy helps.

- There will be a lot of guilt and shame in the individual's heart. Be OK with sitting in that guilt with them, and try to make sure they do not push to extremes to take revenge against their body.

- Know the struggle within yourself is real. The pain you feel is harsh and at times only sharpens. Don't be afraid to be vulnerable with the ones you love. Try to share the burden.

- The battle is real, but in order to fight fairly, you need to be still with yourself and strengthen your own heart.

- Accept the individual for who they really are, because at the end of the day, they have just as much worth as all people.

- Most importantly, love them unconditionally, and let them know you love them no matter what!

Honestly, I could go on for pages, as this has impacted my life greatly. Just know that every moment you see a sign of worth being restored in the sick individual, be joyful, and fight for more times like that. There is no pain like it, and it's a hell of a ride.

—A brother who was just eight years
old when the battle began

- **An eating disorder is not healed by affirming one's outward appearance.** To the contrary, that can be very harmful. Try commenting on your loved one's internal beauty and empowering their purpose, not their looks.

When you comment on how thin she is, even if you mean it negatively (trying to show her she doesn't need to lose any more weight), it feeds the eating disorder. It's backward, and it doesn't make sense, but what she will take from that is, "It's working, and I like this feeling. My attempt to control my weight and food is working, and I'm going to pursue it even further."

—A fifteen-year-old

- **It is not just about the food!** We will say this several times throughout the book and want to be clear about this statement. Restoring weight to a starving body is critical. The mind cannot function properly until the intake of adequate nutrition balances the brain. Once nutrition is balanced, however, the underlying issues have to be addressed, as well as the mental disorder's constant mantra of self-hatred and worthlessness. Comprehensive healing is when an individual's self-worth, purpose, and self-love are restored. Food is just simply something they can control

- **Individuals suffering from an eating disorder have a distorted perception of the self.** They do not view themselves the way others physically see them, nor do they think with a clear and levelheaded mind.

I didn't need people to tell me I was beautiful. I didn't need people to tell me I was the perfect size. I needed people to tell me that I wasn't alone and that I wasn't the only one fighting this. Let's be clear. I'm not talking about the eating disorder. Obviously, I knew lots of others struggled with eating disorders—but not me. I didn't think I had one. What I'm talking about is the war waging within me. I'm talking about the battle with the monster inside my mind that told me he had a way to control the insecurities and anxieties that seemed to weave together in an entanglement of chaos and destruction. Know that my eating disorder had nothing to do with the world around me; rather, it was about my distorted perception of the world. It is for that reason that I want you to know that you are not a failure. You and your loved one can survive this, and when you make it to the other side, there will be life after that survival. Love wins, and in the end, that's all anyone really has to offer. I wanted to believe the idea that the people around me were the problem. The problem was the distorted perception I had of them. I had a distorted reality. I thought everyone was watching me eat and waiting to see what size I would be next.

—A poet and self-love warrior

If you are just learning about eating disorders and concerned about your loved one, this first chapter can feel overwhelming. It is with deep empathy that those of us who have written in this book understand how you feel. It can be scary. No matter who you are, how successful, how important, famous or not, feeling distraught and uneasy about your loved one is a normal human response. For your mental and physical health, you must believe there is hope for full recovery. You must believe you are capable of handling this unwanted situation. You are not alone. Reach out for help, and don't stop inquiring. Our hope is that, by reading this book, you will began seeing and feeling a sense of oneness and commonality, will find a community to help support you, and will understand what positive progress looks like. Ultimately, we hope you experience physical and soulful healing. That day is possible.

Pause and Write

Refer to *Working by Their Side*, and consider the prompts about truths in eating disorders. What do you notice about yourself as you observe changes in your loved one?

Does This Feel Familiar?

An eating disorder? No, not my loved one!

An eating disorder? I didn't even know what an eating disorder was! But what I did know was that something was not right with my child. Actually, something was terribly wrong! Her lips were blue—why was that? The pediatrician said the erratic behavior, crying, defiant reactions, odd immaturity, and withdrawal were just hormonal and that this, too, would pass. She actually commented on Sten's weight loss and how she must have taken good care of herself that summer at camp. "You look good," she told Sten. The pediatrician was wrong. It did not pass.

I have lived a colorful life, seen some of the worst the world has to offer, and experienced the best. Gifted with wisdom, experience, street smarts, and a strong female psyche, I was afraid of little. But this? This confused me. I did get scared. I was afraid. I could not tap into my own wisdom for answers, and my forty-two years of experiences did not offer me any peace. My young daughter, at thirteen years of age, was just as confused as I was. Neither of us had experience with anorexia, and neither of us knew the destructive, self-loathing force we were about to face!

For two years, I lived in a fog of guilt after my child was diagnosed with an eating disorder by a specialist and then hospitalized. I constantly questioned myself, wondering how in the world my child could have this problem: *No, not my child. I know her better than anyone else on the earth. She's complex, but no way could she have a mental disorder! I'm a great mother. What did I do wrong? I have given all of myself to raising children. Our family is good, well respected, and resourceful. We functioned as a perfectly healthy family. I'm a really loving mom, and I have a grounded marriage and great kids. How could this have happened?*

Well, it did happen, and sadly, I lost my confidence those two precious years to self-ridiculing guilt. All those things I'd wondered were from my misguided perspective on how I viewed my healthy life. I was tight lipped about my daughter's illness because I thought it would protect her from others' judgment. I did not want her to be labeled. I was also hesitant to admit to my child's illness, so I did not confide in friends or family. I did not want to put this type of pain on my siblings, mom, or dad, so I pushed them away, acted strong, and thought I could fix my daughter's issues because . . . for God's sake, I was her mom.

I was scared. Scared to death of losing my child to anorexia, scared of losing my own self, and scared of life imploding around me. Internally, I was sad and constantly obsessing. I blamed my husband, I blamed family genetics, I blamed athletics and unprofessional doctors, dietitians, and teachers. I was lonely but wrote the loneliness off to being misunderstood. My marriage was almost destroyed, and the way I handled—or should I say neglected—my other two children had moments of negative dysfunction.

By being secretive about the illness, I was protecting my child's reputation—or so I thought. Really, maybe I was worried about my own! My feelings were real, but it was my perspective that kept the guilt alive. The guilt was about me! There was no need to air all our dirty laundry, but there was a desperate need to ask for help. Then, finally, I realized there was no shame or weakness in asking for help. So I did. It was at that point that the hard work of healing began and I refocused my energy. I asked for help from friends, family, and professionals. Just like my child and my family, I, too, began learning coping skills.

That was twelve years ago. Today, after family counseling and intense honesty, we are comfortable being not a perfect family but an honest, loving family. With hard work, our marriage has made it, and it is more robust and based in truth than before. Yes, we had bruised hearts, and it hurt like hell—really hurt. But with commitment to genuine, unconditional love, we healed. And yes, there is scarring, but we've learned how to address the past blamelessly and honestly. We were forced to dig deep into our psyches and sincerely lean upon our faith. Our love and respect for one another is far greater than it was a decade ago. Today, we are great together. We know more about who each of us really is and accept the differences, all while working to prop up one another's hopes and dreams. Our daughter, who battled a severe eating disorder for eight years, just graduated college and is living in another state, having fun, working full time, being social, interesting, and responsible, and enjoying a healthy life. There was a moment in time when her success was against all odds. But she beat the odds; we beat the odds, and we are better people for it. Are we perfect? Absolutely not! There is no perfect. But we have forgiven each other, and we have forgiven ourselves.

—A once-scared mother

Pause and Write

As you complete this chapter, record your final thoughts about it in *Working by Their Side*. What resonated with you? Do you feel knowledgeable about eating disorders? These recorded details will be good for future reference when you meet with professionals and will also help with your own personal clarity of mind.

2 What Causes an Eating Disorder?

[
There is a space of intangible measure that has all the
answers we seek. Maybe it's a waste of time to ask
why. Maybe we should proceed with the knowledge
and gift of innate human understanding, learn
from what history has taught us, and proceed with
clarity of mind, risk of love, and vulnerable faith.
]

What causes an eating disorder? There is a substantial amount of research, both decades old as well as new, that addresses that question, and though much of the research is acceptable in defining possible "causes," each case is personal to the individual. Among parents, the most common question we ask ourselves is, "Did I cause my child's eating disorder?" We have all pondered this painful question. You are not alone if you feel the disorder is an odd reflection upon yourself as a person or upon your parenting skills and bear the guilt of wondering what you did wrong. You are not alone if you consciously or unconsciously blame yourself for your child's pain. We are not perfect mothers, fathers, siblings, or family members, and yes, we can intensify and contribute to our loved one's problems. (Please refer to chapter 3, "Are Eating Disorders Genetic?") No matter how imperfect you feel, none of us is the cause of a loved one's eating disorder. But we can certainly contribute to it. Intentional or unintentional negative behavior does feed a person's eating disorder.

This disease is heartless and crosses all boundaries; some statistics say .03–5.7 percent of the world population have eating disorders. And yet there are children and adults who have literally experienced hell on earth, losing all hope, and not developed an eating disorder, while successful,

well-resourced, well-educated, loving individuals have fallen prey to this
unforgiving disease.

> Eating disorders are serious but treatable mental and physical
> illnesses that can affect people of every age, sex, gender, race, eth-
> nicity, and socioeconomic group. National surveys estimate that
> 20 million women and 10 million men in America will have an
> eating disorder at some point in their lives.
>
> While no one knows for sure what causes eating disorders, a
> growing consensus suggests that it is a range of biological, psycho-
> logical, and sociocultural factors.[1]

Life variables, innate personality traits, and environmental factors
can contribute to an eating disorder. The onset can be caused by trauma,
especially a sexual assault of any kind. Abuse is horrendous and debilitating
to any victim, and an eating disorder is often an attempt to cope with the
pain. Less obvious factors might be that a person has a relative with an
eating disorder, is unhealthy in regard to weight management, compares
themselves to their peers, is highly sensitive, or decides to start exercising
and dieting and develops an eating disorder. These onsets/causes may be
affected by the desire for a changed appearance or by feelings of mastery,
power, and superiority.

Initially, a person may choose to control food intake or even take
extreme measures to reshape their body. In essence, they enjoy the control.
In the beginning, the motivation could simply be weight loss, a need for
control, or a need to feel loved. Before long, however, no matter the cause,
the eating disorder takes control. It affects the mind, and then, sadly, one's
life belongs to the destructive, insidious disorder. The victim no longer
controls it; the disorder controls them.

Variables such as unhealthy family dynamics, bullying, depression, etc.
can be present as the problem develops and can also keep the eating disorder active, and other variables can predispose individuals for developing
a disorder. To further examine the potential causes, let's discuss different
variables.

---

1   "What Are Eating Disorders?," National Eating Disorders Association, 2018, https://www.
     nationaleatingdisorders.org/what-are-eating-disorders.

Genetics

Interestingly enough, there is research suggesting that our genetic makeup can be a large factor in developing an eating disorder and that some individual's genes make them inherently more susceptible. For more information, please refer to chapter 3, which is dedicated to the relationship between eating disorders and heredity.

Temperament

Temperament is an individual's predisposed nature at birth as relating to behavior, referring to traits such as intensity, sensitivity, perfectionism, and people pleasing. An individual's inherent temperament can set the stage for an eating disorder. For more details, please refer to chapter 3.

> I believe the child we knew at three and four is the true temperament of that individual.
>
> —A mom

Predisposed Brain Chemistry

We all have chemical imbalances in the brain's neural pathways. The perfect, ideal human being does not exist. These very human imbalances can cause anxiety, depression, and mental illness. Imbalanced chemicals in the brain can often be regulated with medication. Sadly, to date, there are no stabilizing drugs to combat an eating disorder. But there are medications for coexisting illnesses that often accompany eating disorders, such as anxiety, compulsion, depression, etc. These can help, but they do not heal the disorder itself. We recommend you see a specialist or psychiatrist of eating disorders to get a valid diagnosis for any type of support drug.

Predisposed Cognitive Vulnerability

Predisposed cognitive vulnerability shapes the way an individual responds to psychological problems and disorders. This vulnerability is believed to be a pattern of thought that is presupposed in that individual's psyche. For example, when an individual encounters extreme stress or trauma, the predisposed vulnerability shapes the person's response to the particular problem. For our loved ones, the response to underlying issues has morphed into an eating disorder. You might be one of six siblings all raised in the same environment with the same family, but one of you might get an eating disorder the others will never fall prey to because they have different predisposed cognitive vulnerabilities.

Biological and Physical Sensation

Ironically, starving oneself feels "good" to someone battling anorexia. Purging (vomiting) is a positive sensation for one struggling with bulimia. These activities cause a release of feel-good chemicals such as dopamine and serotonin.

Environmental Risk Factors

These factors are the characteristics within a person's environment that increase the probability of triggering an eating disorder. Examples include peer pressure, exposure to skewed media depictions of beauty and perfection, a dysfunctional family life, being bullied, abuse, stress from school or athletics, or having to deal with adult issues such as death, illness, disaster, etc. at a young age.

> He kept teasing, her saying, "You're fat"—she was only in first grade. Those words affected her psyche and, by fourth grade, her behavior. He, too, was just a child. Yes, a bully, but just a child.
>
> —A mom

Pause and Write

Reach for *Working by Their Side*, and answer the first set of questions about causes and variables.

People with eating disorders share similar personality traits, some of which put a person at greater risk for developing the disorder. The following is a list of personality traits commonly exhibited by people struggling with an eating disorder.

- Perfectionism
- Overachievement
- People pleasing
- Attention seeking
- Obsessive-compulsive behaviors
- Anxiety
- Identity issues
- Low self-esteem
- Self-criticism
- Unhappiness with physical appearance
- Sensitivity
- Emotionality
- Peacemaking
- High intelligence
- Routine-oriented behavior
- Persistence
- Emotional intelligence

As we grow to adulthood, many of us learn to channel these qualities into happy, productive lifestyles. What might feel impossible today could be your loved one's gift back to the world as they mature! Are there times it actually feels impossible? You may feel that way right now! But these exact personality traits make extraordinary adults.

> Your responsibility is to keep her safe and get her to adulthood. She will be an amazing adult!
>
> —A psychiatrist

No matter how difficult things get and how distant healing feels, restoration is possible.

Remember that precious, joyful little child who melted your heart with just a simple smile? The one who danced in the grocery store, who ran full steam ahead to you in the carpool line, who buried their head in your neck to cry away the day's hurt? The insidious nature of an eating disorder attempts to steal their victims away. Sometimes it wins for a while, and you don't recognize the angry, depressed, tortured soul now standing in front of you. That unrecognizable person is struggling, but have no doubt, the person you knew is still in there. They are not "an anorexic" or "a bulimic"; they are your loved one.

Your loved one's personality traits and temperament make them unique. It might seem far-fetched right now, but what if we empowered those innate attributes and they became your loved one's gift back to the world? How might you see that possibility in your loved one's life?

Pause and Write

Do any of these personality traits feel familiar? Write down what you see and feel. This will help you center your thoughts. The information can also be taken to a therapist when you decide to get help. Please refer to *Working by Their Side* for prompts.

Next Steps to Take Now:
Putting One Foot in Front of the Other

You might not have the answers you want right now, but being proactive is pivotal. Consider the eight suggestions below for the next steps forward.

Stop Obsessing

Because it does get so personal, we can get bogged down and lost in the quest to understand why and how our loved ones got an eating disorder. It is important that we first move forward in getting help for our loved one rather than obsessively trying to dissect the causes of their illness. Still in a quandary about where your loved one's eating disorder comes from? Know that you are experiencing a normal process. But initially, it is important to let go of aching over the whys and causes. Your questions will potentially be answered in time, especially if and when you engage in therapy, which we highly recommend. It takes time and patience to unravel the complexities of this disease, and hopefully the causes and effects will make more sense in the end.

Stop Blaming

Without a doubt, there are times blame is justified, such as cases of abuse, be it physical, verbal, or emotional and especially as it relates to children.

But there are other times we use blame to release our own pain. When we put the blame on others, it relieves a burden so that we do not have to look at our own selves. Are you using blame to ease your pain? If so, stop unfairly blaming others, and take on the responsibility of learning how to help your loved one recover. You are wasting your time pointing fingers. We can say this only because some of us did just that, and it was destructive.

> I blamed my husband, but why would I not? It helped to ease my pain! It also was not fair. It tore down the trust in our marriage, caused tension in the home, and was reflected in the children's behavior. It was not until I saw a therapist that I learned blaming him was an unconscious way of blaming myself and was a mistake that I wish I could take back. We wasted time that could have been used navigating the depths of my guilt!
>
> —A wife who knows that the "blame game" causes destructive behavior

Let Go of the Guilt

Guilt has a paralyzing effect, especially for moms, who seem to have an innate issue with guilt. An eating disorder is our sick loved one's method of coping with their emotional frustrations. The disorder can also be accompanied by drug use, alcoholism, sex, cutting, radical behavior, or other physical and emotional outcries. Try your best to move out of a feeling of guilt—"This is my fault"—and keep focused on the other aspects of your loved one's life that may be keeping the eating disorder alive. Channel your guilt into action, and seek out help.

By owning our guilt, we can conquer our feelings of inadequacy and reconstruct our motivation for restoring health to ourselves and our families. If there is a need to apologize, then do so. Guilt disrupts and blocks the potential for a healthy, honest relationship with our loved one. We can implode upon ourselves. Go internal; spend time with God, and tap into a spiritual place of forgiveness. We teach our kids to love themselves, so we must love ourselves too.

Keep reading, and believe there is hope. You will get beyond this state of self-interrogation.

Humbled, broken, and weeping, I begged for my child's forgiveness. "Can you possibly forgive me? Honey, can you please forgive me?" Then my own child, the precious baby I had held and loved for her eighteen years of life, took me in her arms and, for the first time, held me. I remember the strength of her physical embrace as she held on so tight. Very maturely and calmly, she said, "Mom, I forgave you a long time ago." Then she took my face and looked me in the eyes . . . My little girl, with such certainty and clarity, said, "Mom, you have to forgive yourself!" She repeated it over and over. It was the first time I'd heard the words. It did not matter how many times I had been granted the out of these same words; I'd obviously needed it from her. So comfortable with her mother in her arms, she reinforced the truth. "You are the only one who can forgive yourself, Mom."

—A mom who finally forgave herself

Keep Focused

Your loved one needs you. To focus on the issues at hand, you will have to prioritize your needs, because healing from an eating disorder takes time and effort.

Let go of the guilt, blame, and obsession, and focus on seeking help and learning how to help your loved one identify their feelings so that, together, you can deal with them in a productive way. This means you will have to listen, be patient, and be supportive.

None of us can do it right all the time, but with a committed focus on solutions, hopefully you will feel less burdened. Ask your loved one what the two of you can focus on together in order to enhance your relationship and their healing. When you ask your loved one's opinion, however, you must be ready to handle their answer.

Get off the Roller Coaster

Are you riding alongside your loved one's emotions, falling prey to their temper, mood, or state of mind? It is almost impossible not to feel the fervent, intense emotions of a loved one, and yet, how do we maintain our own stability and rationality? We first begin by getting off their ride.

> One of the simplest and best pieces of advice was given to me by my child's psychiatrist, Dr. Tyler Wooten. He said, "Get off her roller coaster!" I realized I was sitting in the front car with her, taking every turn, climbing every hill, and plunging down every incline. I had to get off and stand firmly on the platform to the side.
>
> —A mom

Codependency and Boundaries

Is your loved one codependent on you? What does that really mean? Codependency is when someone relies on support from another in emotionally overindulgent and disproportionate ways. This is very common behavior with eating disorders, and many of us contributing writers have experienced this firsthand, especially in mother-child relationships. Codependency is often a difficult issue to identify up front. We must all look at ourselves and determine whether we are enabling our codependent loved one. Ironically, as caretakers, we can also become codependent on our loved one's struggle. Setting boundaries and discussing them with your loved one is a good idea and may help unwind habitual codependent behavior. Consider speaking with a professional who specializes in eating disorders for suggestions pertinent to your situation. Dr. Angela Picot Derrick, a clinical psychologist and senior clinical advisor at the Eating Recovery Center of Chicago and Insight Behavioral Health Centers, shares suggestions on how to set boundaries and on how setting boundaries is actually an act of love:

> Instead of ruining relationships, boundaries help us preserve and maintain connections. This is because, with the right boundaries,

both parties understand what the other needs. Both parties know how to keep the relationship healthy and harmonious. Instead of heading towards a rupture, with the right boundaries, relationships can strengthen and endure.

Let your child know you have thought about ways to support their recovery and want to be clear about what they can expect from you. Tell them your job is not to be their friend, but to be a resource and advocate in their recovery . . . Then, lay out the parameters decided upon with the treatment team and help your child identify what he/she needs in order to be able to meet those standards.[2]

Other relevant resources include *Boundaries* by Henry Cloud and John Townsend[3] and Pia Mellody's work on codependency and boundaries.[4]

Pause and Write

Consider whether you're riding the roller coaster alongside your loved one. Use *Working by Their Side* to journal about ways you might be enmeshed with your loved one that are unhelpful to healing.

Research Professional Help

If you have concluded that your child has a problem, it is time to address professional help. You may be wondering: With whom should you consult? A pediatrician? A psychologist? An eating-disorder specialist? A

---

2   Angela Derrick, "Boundaries in Eating Disorder Recovery: An Act of Love," *Eating Recovery Center Blog*, Eating Recovery Center, July 19, 2018, https://www.eatingrecoverycenter.com/blog/july-2018/boundaries-in-eating-disorder-recovery-an-act-of-love-dr-angela-derrick.

3   Henry Cloud and John Townsend, *Boundaries: When to Say Yes, How to Say No to Take Control of Your Life*, rev. ed. (Grand Rapids, MI: Zondervan, 2017).

4   Pia Mellody is a recognized authority in the field of addictions and relationships whose books include *Facing Codependence*, *Facing Love Addiction*, and *The Intimacy Factor*. Visit her website at PiaMellody.com.

psychiatrist? We recommend diagnosis by an eating-disorder specialist rather than a pediatrician. Professional help is critical to your child's diagnosis and healing. It's critical to your healing as well!

Although we may influence environmental risk factors and psychological vulnerabilities, we have little control over many of the variables in other's lives. We can deliberately tweak, purposefully suggest, and vigorously work to eliminate negative environmental influences, but we often find ourselves at a crossroads while trying to deliver appropriate reactions to environmental variables. Please refer to chapter 4, chapter 9, and the appendix to help you find the professional help you, your loved one, and your family need.

Define Your Loved One with Positives First

To the best of your ability, do not let the disease get a leg up on anything. Do not let it define your loved one. Do not let it define you or your family. You do not have an "anorexic child"; you have a child battling anorexia. You would not say I have a "cancer best friend"; rather, you have a best friend fighting cancer!

Believe, and prove to yourself, that you are stronger and far better than this hideous, selfish, life-gripping disease.

And finally, when you get angry (and you will), be angry at the disease, not your loved one. And be angry enough to do something about the situation. Get help from licensed professionals, and rediscover that person you love—the one you miss and desire a real relationship with. In doing so, you just might rediscover yourself.

Pause and Write

In *Working by Their Side*, take notes about reaching out for support, and start making lists of potential contacts from whom to seek personal or professional help.

Does This Feel Familiar?

My story is complicated. Families are complicated.
Eating disorders are complicated.

Of the six family members living under our roof, here's what I was dealing with in the spring of 2009. Husband: active anorexic. Oldest daughter: obsessive-compulsive eater. Second daughter: active anorexic. Son: thin and in need of gaining weight. Third daughter: confused. And me: scared, lonely, pissed off, and frustrated. Meals at our house were impossible to prepare, serve, or sit through. The stares, comments, and emotions . . . You could cut those with a knife.

I watched cautiously as my second daughter became healthier and unhealthier at the same time. She was very cautious about everything that she ate, eating only "healthy" foods. At the same time, however, she was becoming more and more withdrawn from her peers and me. She didn't want the world to see that everything was not perfect, so she tried extra hard to make it look perfect. It was terrifying to watch a beautiful and brilliant young girl starve herself in order to be *more* than she already was. This child could achieve anything she put her mind to, and being thin was what she focused on.

At the same time, my first daughter was struggling academically, socially, and emotionally, and she soothed herself with food. Food was her friend, her boyfriend, her medication, and her entertainment. She was becoming, and would become, morbidly obese. She was always hungry and completely insatiable. She could not fill the void in her belly, which was loneliness and shame, with enough food. This was also terrifying.

Some of the disordered eating issues in our family are still works in progress, but this story is about the journey—particularly mine. Along my journey to "help my children"—because I thought I could—I delved into my own relationship with my food and my body.

During and after this experience, I realized that I was part of the problem. I still cared about my external appearance and believed that it was relative to my worthiness. I contributed to the complete dysfunction going on in my very own home! Spending time and energy focusing on what I looked like was a giant waste of time and was detrimental to my family members. I was already beautiful, already an amazing human being and mother. I shifted my perspective completely. I moved on.

Do I have regrets? No. We live in a culture in which thinness and dieting are celebrated. Perspective is skewed, and body shaming is acceptable and ingrained in our language—verbally and nonverbally. I was doing my best. My heart was in the right place, but my mind got distracted.

During the healing process, several members of my family and I tried to realign our lives and have integrity with regard to food, exercise, purpose, and each other. In reflection, I have a few recommendations for women who are committed to the healing process, even if it means having to look deeply and courageously in the mirror at themselves.

- *Act!* Do not react. Confront your daughter with your truth. What you see and think is dangerous for your daughter is dangerous. Do not be afraid of her reaction when she gets angry. You are saving her life. Even if you think she is just "dabbling" in weight loss, have your daughter explore why she thinks it's important to change her weight. What is below the insecurity?

- *Network* to get the help you need! Talk to friends and family, and seek the best help possible for your child. Friends and family are your best resource and support system. Once you have a support system in place for your child, set one up for yourself! You cannot do this alone.

- *Stay vigilant!* Anorexia and bulimia mirror addictions, and addicts are master manipulators. They work very hard to get where they are in their disease and will not easily let go of it. Stick with the plan and the boundaries you have set up with your support system.

  My second daughter talked me into a treatment that was the least invasive into her life and the most private. I deeply regret this decision. She manipulated me—again. We were both motivated by fear—afraid that the "interruption" would be harmful to her GPA and college application process. Treat the disorder! Life cannot and will not go on until you do. Intensive treatment is imperative. Patients need 100 percent accountability. An eating disorder is a disease and needs to be treated as such.

I finally got my first daughter into a treatment center in 2015, and I wish I had done so sooner. These disorders become embedded in the psyche. Don't wait to seek help!

- *Surrender!* This does *not* mean give up! Ultimately, you are powerless to help your child. Let them work within the parameters you have set up to find what works for *them*. They will have to figure this out, and the coping skills they learn will be theirs for life. You must surrender and trust God and the process. When we obsess over their well-being, we forget about our own. We matter. We have families that are counting on us. We must be clear about what is healthy for us so we can set good boundaries and examples for our children and the world. Be kind, patient, and compassionate with yourself during this process and forever.

Finally, if we believe in God—and I do—then we believe that we are all born beautiful, imperfect, and with a purpose that only we can fulfill. Help your children see their inner beauty—their characteristics, talents, and passions—by seeing yours first. Self-care is loving and helpful to the entire family. Choose self-love so your children can too.

—A mom who believes everyone is born worthy

3

Are Eating Disorders Genetic?

Genetics + Temperament + Intense Emotional Intelligence
+ Risk Factors = Manifestation of an Eating Disorder

To determine whether eating disorders are genetic, let us examine the combination of genetics, temperament, intense emotional intelligence, and risk factors.

Genetics

Though the exact origin of eating disorders is still a mystery and there currently is no medical cure, research suggests that our inherent genetic makeup can contribute significantly to the cause. But what does that really mean? We have found similarities among our loved ones and friends with eating disorders, and thus a predisposed genetic makeup is obvious. There's no doubt that eating disorders are more common when a first-degree family member has a history of them. The case for genetic predisposition is heavily favored, so much so that the Mayo Clinic recommends researchers, medical providers, therapists, and treatment teams regard eating disorders as a biological illness; research on the subject is on the forefront of the medical frontier, and as you read this book, new discoveries may become feasible.

An international study led by the University of North Carolina researching the DNA of individuals with anorexia has discovered via whole-genome analysis that participants had a significant locus on chromosome 12 that contributed toward an increased risk of anorexia.[1] The fact that this study

---

1   Medical University of Vienna, "Anorexia Nervosa Has a Genetic Basis," news release, Science Daily, June 12, 2017, https://www.sciencedaily.com/releases/2017/06/170612094212.htm.

was able to identify a specific genetic anomaly associated with this disease gives further validity to the idea that biological factors are involved in the development of eating disorders. Similarly, scientists from the University of Iowa and University of Texas Southwestern Medical Center have found that individuals with mutations in two genes, the ESRRA and HDAC4, had, respectively, a 90 percent and an 85 percent chance of developing an eating disorder.[2] Research teams funded by the Price Foundation have evaluated up to seven hundred families with two or three members who have suffered from anorexia and bulimia, and their results suggest chromosomes 1 and 10 have a significant link to eating disorders as well.[3]

One of the most fascinating aspects of the link between biology and eating disorders is the neuroplasticity of the brain. Neuroplasticity is the brain's ability to change—to rewire itself, allowing the creation of new behaviors or the rewiring of old behaviors.[4] Scientists no longer believe our brains are hardwired from childhood to death; to the contrary, the brain can changes via repetitive mental experiences. Experiences and behavior actually create neuroplasticity and change brain structure. Change the behavior repetitively, and the brain will change. Thus, behavioral therapy has a positive probability of rewiring behavior. There are no psychiatric drugs that cure eating disorders, but rewiring negative thoughts is possible.

For detailed information on the biological aspect of these disorders, see Carrie Arnold's *Decoding Anorexia: How Breakthroughs in Science Offer Hope for Eating Disorders.*[5] Written by a scientist, science writer, blogger,

---

2   Huxing Cui et al., "Eating Disorder Predisposition is associated with *ESRRA* and *HDAC4* Mutations," *Journal of Clinical Investigation* 123, no. 11 (November 1, 2013): 4706–4713, https://doi.org/10.1172/JCI71400; Jennifer Brown, "Two Genes Linked to Increased Risk for Eating Disorders," *Iowa Now*, October 8, 2013, https://now. uiowa.edu/2013/10/two-genes-linked-increased-risk-eating-disorders; Allie Bidwell, "Researchers Find Genes Linked to High Risk of Eating Disorders," *US News & World Report*, October 8, 2013, https://www.usnews.com/news/articles/2013/10/08/ researchers-find-genes-linked-to-high-risk-of-eating-disorders.

3   "Genetic Factors Beyond Eating Disorders," Eating Disorder Hope, March 20, 2017, https://www.eatingdisorderhope.com/blog/genetic-factors-eating-disorders.

4   "The Neuroplasticity of the Brain," Emily Program, October 28, 2015, https:// emilyprogram.com/blog/the-neuroplasticity-of-the-brain/.

5   Carrie Arnold, *Decoding Anorexia: How Breakthroughs in Science Offer Hope for Eating*

advisor to FEAST (Families Empowered and Supporting the Treatment of Eating Disorders), and past sufferer of anorexia, this book delves into the disorder from a biological point of view.

Temperament

We are each born with an inherent nature that affects our way of living life, a nature that is different for every single human being. Temperament is wildly complex and absolutely unique. This inherent individual temperament can set the stage for an eating disorder to manifest. To be clear, temperament and personality are related; however, temperament is inborn, not learned. Personality is what arises within a person's lifetime through patterns of behavior, feelings, education, and socialization. Think of it like this: personality is acquired on top of temperament. Both can be nurtured throughout a lifetime, but studying one's temperament is a window into that person's innate strengths and weaknesses.[6]

For decades, scientists have been trying to identify the different aspects of personality and temperament that help make us tick. Over the years, they have found distinct traits in individuals with eating disorders. They can be specific to each disorder and distinguish sufferers from healthy people. Studies have associated aspects of these traits with alterations in the transmission of serotonin and dopamine.[7] Characters often seen in those struggling with eating disorders include:

- Anxiety
- Intensity
- Sensitivity
- Perfectionism
- People pleasing
- High intelligence (IQ)
- High emotions
- Tenderheartedness
- Social dependency
- Ambition/overachievement
- Routine-oriented behavior
- Persistence
- High emotional intelligence (EQ)
- Harm avoidance
- Impulsiveness

Disorders (New York: Taylor & Francis, 2013).

6   Prabhat S., "Difference between Temperament and Personality," Difference Between, June 13, 2011, http://www.differencebetween.net/language/words-language/difference -between-temperament-and-personality/.

7   "Temperament and Personality," National Eating Disorders Association, 2018, https:// www.nationaleatingdisorders.org/toolkit/parent-toolkit/temperament-and-personality.

Intense Emotional Intelligence (EI/EQ)

EI, also referred to as emotional quotient (EQ), is about awareness of oneself and of those around you. Emotionally intelligent people have the capacity to recognize their own emotions, with an understanding of their own self, and also perceive the emotions of others. They are able to discriminate between different emotions and recognize how they affect others. EI also involves your perception of other people and how you think they perceive you. This information is then used to guide behavior and thinking.

High emotional intelligence is often seen in individuals struggling with an eating disorder. Before the brain is fully developed, EI can wreak havoc on one's ability to identify, use, understand, and manage emotions within oneself, as well as on the ability to read and react to emotions in others. Everything feels dramatic, like it is in overdrive. EI can be seen as a problem, but when channeled positively and with maturity, it can be beneficial. Once high emotional intelligence is identified, it would be constructive to support the individual's ability to manage emotions in positive ways, such as relieving stress, communicating effectively, empathizing with others, defusing conflict, solving problems, and learning to adapt these characteristics when dealing with others. Most of us involved in writing this book have noticed these characteristics in our children since childhood. An emotionally intelligent child is often more challenging to raise, but when mature, they make the most awesome, sound, and well-rounded adults. Is your loved one emotionally intelligent?

For more information on emotional intelligence, please refer to chapter 14, "Therapies, Practices, and Innovative Treatments."

Risk Factors

Risk factors vary but can be attributed to the structure of the culture one lives within as well as one's personal history, including childhood, family history, traumas encountered, transitions and change, low self-esteem (learned or innate), involvement in competitive sports, work, artistic activities, gender, sexuality, or a combination of humanity's influences. Along with biological influences, exposure to Western culture's obsession with beauty, society's depictions of thinness, distorted media, false success, situational stress, mishaps, and copious lifestyles make individuals more susceptible to developing an eating disorder. Review chapter 2 for more information.

Comparison can be an ugly thing. As an identical twin, the world always compares you. Even as a sibling, the world compares you. Your identity can easily be either enmeshed with your twin or based off a scale of comparison measured against your twin. You have to truly develop a new mantra in terms of who you are. Rather than "the more athletic one," "the more artistic one," "the thinner one," "the one with the cowlick," you must train yourself to turn off that voice and look inside to who you really are. One can easily take this challenge as a slight or as cause for feelings of unworthiness.

—A twin who lost her sister to anorexia

Pause and Write

Please refer to the first set of questions in *Working by Their Side*, and take notes about temperament characteristics, EI, and risk factors.

Next Steps to Take Now: Putting One Foot in Front of the Other

The origin of our genes extends beyond just our mother and father. Genetics are developed from generations past—both the paternal and maternal sides. That's a bundle of genetics! Below are five ideas to consider.

Recognize That This Is Not Your Loved One's Choice

They did not choose this disease, even if it began by dieting or desiring weight loss. Some people diet and never fall into the trap of an eating disorder; others fall victim quickly. This has to do with the innate characteristics and environmental factors making up each individual. Even in the most frustrating of times, step back, and remember that this is not the choice your loved one would prefer. Remember to fight the disease, not the person. In order to fight effectively, we have to know the enemy and also, to the best of our ability, understand the temperament and personality of the suffering individual. Educating yourself with the information in this book is a great start. Your loved one will not remember all the details from the depths of the illness, but they will remember feelings like affection, love, and abhorrence. No one would choose the type of pain an eating disorder causes.

> I remember specifically that when I would cry and get overwhelmed, my parents didn't condemn me for struggling; they hugged me, and they told me it was OK to feel what I was feeling and that they believed in me. My mom became a very safe place for me, where I could confess if I had been deceptive, if I had lied about my food, where I could just cry and be held. Now, ten years later, that season of my life remains very blurry. Whether the fogginess is a side effect of my actual brain and body being so unhealthy or whether it's protection from difficult memories, it's pretty blurry.
>
> —Now a healthy and happily married woman

Work Preventatively

In the second edition of the book *The Parent's Guide to Eating Disorders: Supporting Self-Esteem, Healthy Eating, and Positive Body Image at Home*, you will find deliberate and detailed discussion on prevention, what families can do to help their child, and a focus on the Maudsley Approach to eating disorders.[8] The Maudsley Approach is a family-based intensive outpatient treatment for anorexia and bulimia in which parents play an active role.[9]

All parents want a meaningful relationship with their children. Learning how to provide warmth, attention, affection, and empathy sounds like

---

8   Marcia Herrin and Nancy Matsumoto, *The Parent's Guide to Eating Disorders*, 2nd ed. (Carlsbad, CA: Gürze Books, 2007).

9   "The New Maudsley Approach," New Maudsley Approach, http://thenewmaudsley approach.co.uk/index.php/main/the-new-maudsley-approach/.

natural behavior, but for some parents and other caretakers, it must be learned. It is important to take the time necessary to learn both verbal and physical communication skills. We can work preventatively by nurturing our children's self-esteem and helping them develop a secure and healthy outlook on body image. Our child's ability to have a healthy body image despite culture's toxic attitudes of unrealistic beauty standards and body shapes begins with us.

> My anorexia started the summer between my sophomore and junior years of high school. I was at a vulnerable position that summer, having broken up with my boyfriend of two and a half years and taken on a very stressful academic and extracurricular load. In truth, the roots of it were there much earlier. As a child, I watched my mom struggle with diet after diet. When I was ten, I can remember drinking diet shakes to be like her. Of course, at that age, I also chased that with a cheeseburger. But the message was there: women struggle with food, with weight, with body image, and somehow this is all tied up in the core of who we are, how we perceive ourselves, how others perceive us.
>
> —Now a mother of two, redefining body image

Do Not Enable

Back to intuition! The question of how to truly help, not enable, your loved one might just be the most difficult one. It is important to focus on what you can do to help empower your loved one and yourself with true, comprehensive healing. It is also important to recognize that there are times you cannot help your loved one in the healing process if they are not willing to help themselves, especially with older teens and adults. There is a fine line between enabling and empowering. There will be decisions you cannot make for them, and in the end, it is up to the person battling the eating disorder to make a choice toward healing. As stated throughout this book, none of us caretakers can fix our loved one's disorder alone. This recognition of our limitations takes time and patience because, naturally, we want to fix the problem. Learning empowering words, how to perceive your own body language, when to say no, and how to stick within the boundaries is very important—but not easy! How do we help them help themselves?

Do Not Shame

There is no shame in mental illness; there is no shame in emotional disorders. These things are part of who we are, and greatness often comes from those minds. There is no shame. Discernment? Yes, but not shame. We should all remember never to use words that shame our loved ones in a crisis.

Brené Brown, PhD, LMSW, is a research professor at the University of Houston Graduate College of Social Work, an author, a speaker, and a philanthropist who has spent the past decade studying shame.[10] According to Brown, "Shame is the intensely painful feeling that we are unworthy of love and belonging."[11] This is so very true with an eating disorder. It is critical to mindfully and intentionally *not* shame our loved one.

In her meaningful TED Talk on shame, Brown makes several key points, including:

- Shame is the most powerful master emotion. It's the fear that we're not good enough. Shame, blame, disrespect, betrayal, and the withholding of affection damage the roots from which love grows. Love can only survive these injuries if they are acknowledged, healed, and rare.

- If we can share our story with someone who responds with empathy and understanding, shame can't survive.

- Shame corrodes the very part of us that believes we are capable of change.

- If we share our story of shame with the wrong person, they can easily become one more piece of flying debris in an already dangerous storm.[12]

---

10   For more information on Brené Brown, visit BreneBrown.com.

11   Cathy Taughinbaugh, "Guilt, Shame, and Vulnerability: 25 Quotes from Dr. Brené Brown," CathyTaughinbaugh.com, October 2017, https://cathytaughinbaugh.com/guilt-shame-and-vulnerability-25-quotes-from-dr-brene-brown/.

12   Brené Brown, "Brené Brown: Listening to Shame," TED video, March 2012, 20:31, https://www.ted.com/talks/brene_brown_listening_to_shame#t-1219024.

Pause and Write

Take a minute to write in *Working by Their Side* for this chapter and list the ways you see yourself helping your loved one. List your strengths, your weaknesses, and the gray areas in which you feel you are not being helpful. It's a great idea to review this list with a therapist or counselor who specializes in eating disorders.

Self-Reflect

When looking at genetics and environmental factors, we must also look at our own behavior. All of us should take a good look at the inventory of our strengths and shortcomings regarding the ways in which we model self-love and acceptance. This is especially necessary for parents, as our children watch us closely and model our behavior.

> Be it subconscious or with full awareness, I want you to know, Mom, that I am affected by the example you set for me. I think it started from the moment I first opened my eyes.
>
> —A twenty-year-old daughter in recovery

On several occasions over the years, the adults writing this book have all had to look into our own mirrors and, at times, make changes. We've had to seek personal help from therapists and counselors. Sometimes it was difficult to see our own fallibility, yet we are grateful and better for the work. No one is perfect. Our own genetic makeup is not perfect. Not yours, not mine—not one of us is or will be perfect! That's the beauty of being human, and that imperfection is perfectly exquisite! Below are some personal questions to ask yourself in private. Answer honestly, being true to yourself.

- Do I portray body image positively?

- How do I portray body image in relation to gender? Do I portray a positive female body image? A positive male body image?

- What is the relationship between my body image and the culture I grew up in?

- What did my culture teach me about my body? What do I teach my children about that culture and that messaging?

- How do my children define me as a parent?

- How do my loved ones perceive our relationship?

- Am I overbearing, controlling, critical, fault finding, judgmental, or negative? If so, how can I adjust these parenting traits? If not, how can I continue the cadence of positivity during this difficult time?

- Am I trying to be the "perfect" parent, or do I accept my mistakes while also loving my child and admitting my human shortcomings?

- Are my expectations reasonable, both for my child and for myself?

- When I discuss issues with my loved one, do I handle their perspectives firmly but thoughtfully? Am I truly listening to hear what they are saying?

- Am I asking my loved one to be a part of my plan, or am I trying to understand their own?

- Do I nurture my loved one's self-esteem? If so, how?

- Do I help my loved one see their strengths? Do I discuss those strengths in positive ways?

- How do I cultivate self-worth and self-respect in my loved one and in myself?

- If I have had or do have my own eating disorder, am I working toward my own recovery?

- Am I choosing to rejoice in the positives of life or dwell in the negatives?

- What is my relationship with the way the media depicts bodies and appearance?

- Am I mindful of my words? Do I:
  - » Call my loved one fat or pudgy?
  - » Comment on other people's bodies?
  - » Compare my loved one to others?

- Do I allow for vulnerability in others and within myself?

- Do I shame my own body or looks, or those of others, even in jest?

Honest exchange can be worthwhile, but hateful arguments are harmful. You must be steady and ready. We have learned that staying grounded is essential.

Power struggles and control-freak issues between a parent and a child struggling with an eating disorder are destructive. Nurturing a child's self-worth is imperative. Fighting the disease rather than the child is critical.

This conversation about self-reflection is important and personal. Take a step back, and look at yourself objectively. What are your motives? Why do you (or don't you) respond in a particular way?

How will you know, if you are not brutally honest with yourself?

For more detail, please refer to chapter 7, "Self-Reflection," and chapter 9, "Get Professional Help for Yourself."

Pause and Write

In *Working by Their Side*, reflect on the list of personal questions, and answer with raw honesty.

Does This Feel Familiar?

My wish is that you grow up loving yourself.

Dear darling daughter,

That's what my mom called me—her darling daughter. I have different pet names for you, my sweet three-year-old, but the one my mom had for me is still close to my heart. I am writing this to you today, but I will not ask you to read it until you are much older. This is a story about me and my mother, about you and me, and about all women who need to learn the valuable lesson of valuing themselves.

My mom loved me more than anything, just as I love you more than anything. Sadly, my mom did not always love herself. She did not have very high self-esteem. She struggled with her body image and her weight. She was overweight, even as a very young child, and never outgrew it. She was on diets as long as I knew her. Even though she was one of the sweetest, most beautiful people you could ever imagine, she did not always think highly of herself. She put everyone else first. More often than not, she did not meet her own needs. She was an amazing caretaker, mother, wife, friend, and teacher. Everyone who knew her was lucky to have her as part of her life. I just wish she had realized more clearly how incredible she was and had been a little more selfish with her own self-care.

I never doubted how much my mom loved me. She was my best friend. I hurt her very deeply when, during high school, I decided to stop eating. I had always been a very thin and active child; I played lots of sports and never had trouble with my weight. Then, at the beginning of high school, I began to get "rounder"—but wanted to stay very thin. I started to restrict what I ate and exercised more and more. Eventually, I was hardly eating anything and was exercising twice a day. I looked like a skeleton. Finally, one day, my mom confronted me and said, "I know you are doing this because you don't want to look like me."

"That's not true," I said. But it was partially true. Even truer was that I didn't want to lose control of my body and felt a need to have greater control in my life. In an effort to maintain control, I completely lost myself.

I lost my self-esteem. I lost my personality. I withdrew from my friends and family. My plan to be perfect and look perfect backfired. I lost sight of what was important in life—my own self-worth. I was worth more than skin and bones. If I had loved myself, I would not have starved myself. If I could have seen my own value and beauty, I wouldn't have tried so hard to give myself more value and beauty by seeking an unattainable "thin and attractive" body.

For you, my dear, my wish is that you grow up loving yourself. I hope you will take the time and energy to meet your own needs. Feed yourself nourishing food. Get healthy amounts of exercise. But even more importantly, speak words of kindness and support to yourself. In the end, as much as mothers try to help and love and support their daughters, you will need to be your own best friend, your own support, and your own cheerleader. When the stresses of school, work, relationships, marriage, babies, and friendships get you down, you will need to call on your own inner reserves to sustain yourself and tell yourself that *you are worth it*. You are worth spending the time to care for yourself. Find things you enjoy, and practice them. Realize that you are beautiful inside and out, no matter what shape or size you are. I hope I live a long, long time and can tell you these things myself. My mother told me these things all the time. But I think if she had told them to herself, that would have been much more powerful.

For you, my girl, I am going to love myself every day. I'm going to tell myself that I am beautiful and strong. I'm going to exercise and eat and grow and learn. I'm going to take time for myself when I need it because I deserve it. I'm going to enjoy dressing up in clothes to go on dates with your father, no matter what size I am. I'm going to have fun swimming and playing with you even if I'm not the thinnest mom at the pool or on the beach. I'm going to keep up my own hobbies and try to do things that bring me joy so I can show you what that looks like. I'm going to work hard and use my gifts and talents in my craft. I'm going to tell you very clearly that I love myself and that *I am worth it*. That will be my greatest lesson for you.

All my love, from the very bottom of my heart,
Mom

4 Getting Professional Help For Your Child

$$\Bigg[\quad \text{Getting professional advice for your child is potentially your most consequential responsibility as the parent.} \quad\Bigg]$$

No matter your efforts, positive intentions, and unconditional love, you cannot fix your child's eating disorder alone. You, your child, and your family members need to learn the coping tools necessary to aid in your child's recovery as well as the recovery of the family. We believe it is imperative that you and your family are involved in your child's therapy in a healthy, productive way. Healthy, productive ways may include individual therapy, therapy with both the caretakers and the struggling individual, or family therapy. Educating yourself by reading this book is a great start.

If your child is over eighteen years old, and if they are willing, we recommend they sign a waiver to allow interaction between you and their doctors and therapist. Adult children are just that—adults who need to be accountable for themselves—but if your adult child's life is in danger, you need to intervene. Most of us participating in this book understand that there are times our adult children are incapable of making logical decisions due to the grip of the disease.

So where do we began? If your child is old enough to understand, ask them what they need and how they feel about therapy, and open up a discussion on those possibilities. Your delivery, body language, and mood matter as you discuss the feasibility of introducing therapy into their life, your life, and the life of the family. You can be inflexible in your decision and demand therapy, but mindfully walking them through the gate of understanding as to why you feel so strongly seems to be most effective approach.

It's not just about food. Recovery is about developing into the person you want to be. Worthy. Purposeful. Validated. Knowledgeable. Connected. Loved and loving.

Next Steps to Take Now: Putting One Foot in Front of the Other

You probably know your child better than anyone. If you are concerned, do not procrastinate. There is every reason in the world why therapy might not fit into our busily scheduled lives, but find the time and space. It is worth the effort. If your child had a broken leg, would you hesitate to take them to a doctor? Mental health is equally as important, if not more. It can be complicated, but this is your child's life we are talking about. Below are suggestions on how to be proactive in securing professional help for your child.

React to a Medical Emergency

If you believe your child is in medical danger, take them to the nearest emergency room immediately. The team of ER doctors will evaluate your child and, depending upon the severity of the condition, will admit your child into the hospital or give you reasonable referrals. If they do not give you sound advice you are comfortable with, ask until you get the help you believe your child needs.

Intervene Early

If you recognize (or think you recognize) the signs of an eating disorder in your child, take it seriously from the beginning and move forward in an active, productive way. Statistics prove that the earlier the intervention, the higher potential for healing.

Understand the Types of Therapists and Eating-Disorder Professionals Available

There are thousands of therapists, and the task of hiring one can be tiresome. Be relentless but speedy until you find the right fit. We recommend you stay within the eating-disorder community of health-care providers in your area. Here are some categories we can recommend:

- Eating-disorder psychiatrists. These are medical doctors (MDs) who are licensed to prescribe medications and manage drug therapy. Psychiatrists are trained extensively and knowledgeably in the unbelievable complexities of psychiatric drugs. Psychiatrists are able to treat coexisting disorders with medication, but to date, there is no medication that cures an eating disorder. Some psychiatrists also conduct regular therapy sessions.

- Licensed therapists specializing in eating disorders. This includes eating-disorder psychologists, PhDs, eating-disorder counselors, social workers, faith-based therapists, and family therapists. We recommend you engage a licensed professional. These therapists provide regular therapy sessions, group therapy, and family therapy and may also treat co-occurring disorders in their practice.

- Physicians who specialize in treating eating disorders. We recommend these MDs work in conjunction with your child or family therapist. They oversee medical complications that might arise from eating disorders, such as heart problems, muscle atrophy, migraines, osteoporosis, etc.

- Registered dietitians and nutritionists. For details outlining the role of dietitians and nutritionists, please refer to chapter 9.

We felt most successful when working with a "treatment team"—a psychiatrist, dietitian, medical doctor, and therapist who collaborated on behalf of our children and family. The therapist, working with the person healing from an eating disorder, is usually the team leader and point person. The team will vary depending on the type of treatment required, the severity of the illness, your family's structure, etc. Find what works best for your child and family.

Have a Professional Assess Your Child's Health

If you suspect or know that your child has an eating disorder, have your child assessed by a licensed professional who can officially diagnose them. We recommend that you do not diagnose your child. Keep in mind, some pediatricians and primary-care physicians are not well versed in eating disorders; however, they can give you a solid referral.

- Ask your child's pediatrician for a referral to a licensed professional who specializes in eating disorders.

- Ask for referrals from anyone you know who is familiar with eating disorders, has experience with them, or is currently dealing with such an issue.

- Use your village of support, and ask for help.

- Call the National Eating Disorders Association Helpline at 1-800-931-2237.

- For a free crisis counselor, contact the National Eating Disorders Association at NationalEatingDisorders.org.

- Contact the Crisis Text Line. Please refer to CrisisTextLine.org for details.

- Search for treatment in your area of the country at EDReferral.com.

- Visit the website of the National Association of Anorexia Nervosa and Associated Disorders at ANAD.org.

- If all else fails, go to the nearest emergency room, and ask for help.

Understand the Intentions of Therapy

It's a plus if you are already well versed in therapy. You are well on your way. If you are unfamiliar with therapy, we think it's important to try to educate yourself before you hire a therapist. If you have a professional contact, friend, or acquaintance you can learn from, ask them for help. Do not procrastinate! Take action intelligently and intentionally for the highest probability of full and comprehensive healing. If time allows, and if you are not in a crisis situation, read the section on therapy in the American Psychological Association's Ethical Principles of Psychologists and Code of Conduct.[1] This will help you to better understand what to expect as you begin your search for a therapist. It is cumbersome information, but if you are a researching personality, the APA is a good resource.

---

1   "Section 10: Therapy," Ethical Principles of Psychologists and Code of Conduct, American Psychological Association, 2017, apa.org/ethics/code/index.aspx.

Be Patient, but Persistent

Finding the correct fit can be frustrating, and it can take time. Be persistent! If your child is in danger, however, go to the nearest emergency room and ask for help.

As you learn your role in your child's therapy, surround yourself with positive support from the professionals you hire. You need to genuinely support and immensely trust your professional team, including your child's doctors, therapists, psychiatrists, etc. And, to the best of their ability, the professionals need to become advocates for your child as well as for you.

Seek a Therapist for Your Child

We recommend you pick up the phone and, on behalf of your child and family, find a licensed eating-disorder professional.

Finding a therapist who is a good fit for the person struggling is vital. In order to heal, one must feel that they can be vulnerable with their therapist, and they must feel that they can trust their therapist. There are all kinds of therapists, and they operate from all kinds of philosophies and under a vast array of training. Sorting out who believes what can be daunting. As a therapist who specializes in eating-disorder recovery, I'd like to offer some suggestions.

- We all have different areas of expertise and training. Eating-disorder treatment is difficult. It requires specific supervision and experience. Many ethical therapists who do not have the skills to treat an eating disorder will refer you to someone who specializes in this field. Others may decide to take on a client without necessarily having the capacity to do so skillfully. Please make sure your therapist has significant experience in treating eating disorders.

- It is unethical for therapists to ask for testimonials from clients. If you are able to get a word-of-mouth referral from a friend, take it. Do not be alarmed if a therapist does not have a website or marketing materials, as it may indicate that their practice is fully based on word-of-mouth referrals.

• Therapists are human beings. Some of us have done a significant amount of work on our own therapy, digging deeply into our own psyche and attempting to get an understanding of what we are bringing into the room as we work with clients. Others are less invested in working on themselves and more likely to have blind spots about what they are bringing into the therapeutic space. You should feel comfortable asking your therapist about their relationship to their own body and to food. Some therapists are in recovery from eating disorders, and that is wonderful. Who better to help someone in the struggle than someone who has been through it and has come out the other side successfully? However, other therapists may be avoidant of their own struggles and could therefore become an obstacle to the recovery of clients. If you ask your therapist about their interest in working in this field and with this population, you should get a straightforward and direct answer.

• A good fit means just that: it's a fit. One therapist does not fit all. You may have to shop around to find a therapist who feels safe, present, engaging, and trustworthy to you and the client. If this takes time, the time is well spent. This will become a vital relationship and one of the key aspects of long-term recovery. Make sure that you find a therapist who creates an environment in which the conditions of safety can be met.

—Melody Moore, PhD, E-RYT, licensed clinical psychologist and experienced registered yoga teacher; founder of the Embody Love Movement Foundation

If you do not know a therapist in your area, ask a friend or acquaintance for a recommendation. Ask your child's pediatrician for a referral. You can always tap into resources at your child's school. Talk with the school's counselors, coaches, teachers, or nurse. If you have a primary-care physician, ask them for a referral. If you are truly stumped and cannot find a therapist, search online.

Consider the following resources:

- "Help & Support," National Eating Disorders Association: NationalEatingDisorders.org/help-support

- National Eating Disorders Association Helpline: 1-800-931-2237

- "Eating Disorder Therapists, Nutritionists & Specialists Directory," Eating Disorder Hope: EatingDisorderHope.com/treatment-for-eating-disorders/therapists-specialists

- "Top Rated Help for Eating Disorders," EDReferral: EDReferral.com

- "Find an Eating Disorders Therapist," *Psychology Today*: PsychologyToday.com/us/therapists/eating-disorders

- "Find an Eating Disorder Therapist Near Me," Welldoing: Welldoing. org/therapy/eating-disorders

I'll tell you what: I got to my goal weight, and I still wasn't satisfied. I had actually just internally sworn off bread as a "bad food" I was no longer "allowed to eat"! When my parents realized the extent of my struggle, they got me help. Without treatment, I would have continued to push my goal weight lower and lower, because it was "never good enough." In my disordered mind, there was always more weight to lose, more food groups to outlaw.

—One who is grateful their parents stepped in

Consultation

If time allows, before hiring a therapist, set up an in-person consultation. Ask the therapist to meet with you (or you and your spouse/partner) first before meeting with your child. You may need to interview several professionals before you find your optimal match of therapist, licensed professional, or psychiatrist. You want one who is well versed in the field of eating disorders. Pick the one you feel is fundamentally best suited for you, your child, and your family. Use your intuition. Your child needs to be invested in the therapist. If it is not a match, move on. All good therapists understand that action.

If you have an adult child, you can be the catalyst, but they must choose their own therapist. Most likely, you will not be granted an in-person consultation unless your adult child agrees.

Questions We Suggest You Ask a Therapist

During the consultation, ask the potential therapist questions to better understand the reasons for therapy and the relationships to be developed between all parties. There are no wrong questions, and you should feel free to ask whatever you deem necessary. For suggestions, please refer to NEDA's Parent Toolkit, which is a great reference for questions.[2]

Here are some specific questions we have found helpful when securing a therapist:

- How long have you been treating eating disorders? Are you licensed, and if so, how?

- How long are your sessions? What is your fee? What is your availability?

- What preferred form of therapy do you use with your patients? (Some types of therapy commonly used for eating disorders include cognitive behavioral therapy, dialectical behavioral therapy, and acceptance and commitment therapy. See the National Eating Disorders Association[3] or Eating Disorder Hope[4] for more information.)

- Will you work in tandem with my child's school, coaches, etc.?

- How do you handle insurance? If I don't have insurance coverage, do you offer scholarships? Do you have a sliding scale for fees?

---

2   "Parent Toolkit," National Eating Disorders Association, 2018, https://www.nationaleatingdisorders.org/parent-toolkit.
3   "Types of Treatment," National Eating Disorders Association, 2018, https://www.nationaleatingdisorders.org/types-treatment.
4   "Types of Eating Disorder Treatment & Therapy," Eating Disorder Hope, 2019, https://www.eatingdisorderhope.com/treatment-for-eating-disorders/types-of-treatments.

- What are your fixed boundaries between the parents and you as a therapist? Will you communicate with us, and if so, what is your style and preference?

- If my child is over the age of eighteen, will you allow them to give written consent for me to communicate with you about their therapy?

- Do you offer family therapy? If not, whom do you recommend? What is your professional relationship with them?

- What do you need from us? Medical records? Medical history?

- Do you prescribe medication? If so, we want to discuss this before giving our child a prescription.

- Will you communicate regularly with other doctors on my child's treatment team?

Questions to Ask after You Have Hired a Therapist

After you have chosen the therapist who is the best fit for your child and family, continue to ask questions so that you fully understand the boundaries of that therapist's practice. Some therapists have conventional boundaries; others have unconventional boundaries. Ask questions like:

- What roles do I play and not play as a parent within your practice?

- What do you expect from me as the parent/guardian?

- Can I expect a call if my child is in danger or needs extra support?

- Can I call, text, or email you my concerns? Will the call be kept confidential, or will you tell my child about our conversation?

- What are the "big picture" goals?

Parent-Therapist Conferences

If your child is under the age of eighteen, we recommend you commit to partaking in parent-therapist conferences. (If your child is an adult, they must sign a waiver to allow you to communicate with their therapist.)

Sample questions to ask the therapist:

- Will my child be involved?

- Will the information shared in the conference be confidential, or do you feel it's important to tell our child about the conversation?

- Will you inform us if our child is in danger? Will you aid us in helping to prevent a potentially irrevocable decision?

Do Parents Partake in Regular Sessions with Their Child?

This question can be answered only by the therapist. Sometimes we get confused about what our parental role is in regard to our child's therapy. We recommend you ask the therapist up front so you understand the connection or lack thereof. Each therapist/counselor has their own principals about parental involvement and communication, which are often set according to the age of the patient, the diagnosis, and the reasons for therapy. It can be comforting for a child to have a parent present during a session, or it can feel awkward, especially for teenagers. Find a therapist whose approach is accommodating, and remember to ask about their level of disclosure.

Trust is a critical component in the confidential space of a therapist's office. If a therapist does choose to confide in you—and we recommend this open line of communication—you are responsible for respecting and never abusing the information shared. It is to never be used against a child in any way. If you want to be involved in your child's therapy, ask the therapist's opinion. Ask the therapist any questions you deem important, and be open to the answers.

Pause and Write

Follow the prompts in *Working by Their Side* to answer the questions and write down your ideas. For example: Where can you find a therapist, and what questions should you consider before and after you hire them?

Share Important Information with the Therapist

Never hesitate to share information with your child's therapist that you deem critical or important to the well-being of your child. A therapist is better when they have knowledge of their client. Also, recognize and be respectful of the therapist's time. A text or email from you might be more appropriate than expecting regular phone conversations. Your child's therapist will read your text or email, and they may or may not reply depending on their philosophy of parent-therapist boundaries.

There is absolutely no shame in asking for help. We keep saying this over and over in this book because some of us wish we had trusted a therapist earlier. We cannot go back and change our course of action, but we can recommend you take your child for help now. Hiring a therapist just might be the beginning of the new relationship with your child you desire. Deciding to take a child to a professional is not an easy commitment; therapeutic work is often difficult and time consuming. But it is worth the time and effort. Every single person who has written in this book has asked for help and seen a professional.

The struggle to find effective treatment for a child suffering from an emotional disorder is a journey unto itself. There is not a "one size fits all" solution, and typically, there is not a defined and smooth pathway that assures any of us will have a successful therapy road. What I have learned, as the mother of a child who suffers from disorders that affect the presumed "normal" teenage life, is that you have to empower yourself to become an educated advocate for your child, put one foot in front of the other, and get to it. We all have our own methodology when approaching the unknown. But I believe that the more we learn and educate ourselves as parents, then the more we can filter through for our child in advance so they may utilize their energies and emotions to get better. No one wants to sit back and watch their child suffer . . . But sometimes the path to therapy can be so overwhelming as to who, what, and when that the winner is indecision. Then no one gets better.

I highly recommend that parents first interview a therapist whom they might be considering for their child, without having their child at the first consultation. This worked well for me, as I wanted to ask the hard questions, and it gave me a chance to get a feel for whether the therapist felt like a good fit for my child. Secondly, never feel that you cannot make a change if it's not clicking for your child. Developing a good relationship takes time, and everyone will need to be extremely patient; but sometimes your intuition is the best guide, and you must empower yourself to be the leader of your child's care. It's important to respect your child's opinions and feedback, but it's also important for them to experience progress. Above all, keep growing your heart bigger as you advocate for your child, and although they might not express to you in words how much your unconditional love means to them, just know that they feel it and need it every step of the way.

—A mom in the fight on behalf of her child

When Is Enough, Enough?

The intention of therapy is to set the individual's needs in motion, helping them to learn coping skills, solve issues, and deal with problems that are blocking them from a full and healthy life. Eating disorders often require long-term therapy, but there should be goals set from one milestone to the next. This takes time; however, if, after three to six months, you have not witnessed any change, consider hiring a new therapist. Progress in your loved one's therapy sessions is vital to their emotional health. Hopefully, after six to ten sessions, you will witness behavioral changes or better communication skills. If you feel like they are "stuck in reverse," consider a change. Ask your loved one if they feel like they are getting what they need out of therapy. If they say no, consider a change.

Remember that if your loved one is undernourished, they are incapable of thinking with a clear mind. Therapy is extremely helpful, but you have to be honest about the state of health your child is in. If they need hospitalization or full-time residential care, therapy is a waste of time and money.

An experienced, reputable therapist will "graduate" their clients and even refer them elsewhere if the relationship is not a good fit.

> My niece is one of the most capable individuals I have ever met. She is very smart, driven, and well spoken. This is often the same description given of girls with eating disorders. Well, aren't these the same girls who can change this world? Aren't these the people we want to run our companies and educate our kids? Well, let's put them out there to do just that. Let them use therapy when necessary, but don't leave them in therapy to talk about their problems forever. Let them use therapy, then put them out there as a gift to others!
>
> —An aunt

So what is the purpose of therapy? Over time, the work should help relieve pain, shame, and hurt and should ultimately help in your child's efforts to help themselves. A good therapist guides their client in learning important behavioral changes, developing effective habits, and finding comfort in coping with feelings, all with the goal of living a more authentic life of purpose. Once honesty is established between your child and the therapist, the hard work of discovery and recovery begins. Our hope for you is that with time, you will notice a happier child who is more insightful, less fearful, and more empowered, understanding that they were created unique and beautiful. This discovery takes time. It is our deepest hope that you will once again feel a connection with your child and that they will open up to you and share their life with you and the family.

Seek a Mentor for Your Child

When seeking out a mentor, you may have a particular individual in mind, or you might want to ask your child whom they want as a mentor. If your child is in therapy, ask the therapist's advice. If you have an adult child, they get to seek out their own mentor, but you can be suggestive and helpful.

Possible mentors include a family member (outside of the ones living in your home), a friend, a teacher, a coach, or a member of your village. Explain your intention to the potential mentor, and be honest. Tell them why you feel your child needs a mentor and that you hope your child and the mentor will cultivate a relationship outside of you or your spouse. It is crucial that the mentor relationship is positive, confidential, safe, and loving. Be wise about whom you ask to mentor your child. The mentor should know the child well enough to have an idea of what is supportive rather than destructive. For the relationship to be successful, it is important that you allow the relationship to grow between them without constantly involving yourself. For example, the mentor can ask the child to join them for coffee or hot chocolate, a fun activity, a cultural event, a movie, a meal, a walk, etc., and you cannot go with them. A shopping date is not recommended!

Confidentiality between the mentor and child is important. The mentorship is not to be seen as a means of gathering information for the mom, unless, of course, the information deals with consequential harm or the potential death of your child.

My Yoga Teacher

I came to her a broken and entangled mess of a human. My soul was waging war against itself, riddled with anxiety and self-loathing. My perception of myself was drenched in hatred, disrespect, and frustration. I wanted to be different. I craved alteration and bathed in the concept that I would never be enough. I was sixteen.

I left her a new creation. I was strong. Clothed in worthiness and seeping with gratitude, I loved myself. I loved my body. My capabilities were now known to me; just as the body knows to breathe, they were obvious to me. The intricacy of my soul fascinated me, and I had so much more room in my head to practice compassion for others. I stopped apologizing for being magnificent.

What happened in between the time we met and the time I left is beyond linguistic explanation. It was how I grew to love yoga practice through the acceptance I felt on my mat. It was the way she taught me to give myself the praise I had been looking to gain from others. It was how she had an uncanny ability to ooze wisdom and perspective into every conversation. It was the space she so gently held for me to unapologetically feel whatever was buried in that broken heart of mine. It was the belief she taught me to instill within myself. It was the way yoga infiltrated and applied to every aspect of my life. It was the strength I found within my own body and the appreciation of ability discovered through movement. It was growth in the purest and most loving form. It was nourishment. It was healing. So when people ask me how I recovered from all of that wicked pain that used to lay dormant in my soul, I say my yoga teacher. I say yoga.

—A mentee who is grateful for her mentor

Pause and Write

Follow the prompts in *Working by Their Side* to answer the questions and write down your ideas. For example: What is the most important information you want to share with your potential therapist? Use *Working by Their Side* to keep track of resources, referrals, and contact information for therapists, professionals, and those you want to add to your village of support.

Does This Feel Familiar?

Please help me out of this hell!

If you had told me when I first started out on this journey that, by the end of it, I would've been in therapy for seven years, seen over fifteen different doctors, and been to two different treatment centers . . . I would have called you crazy. You see, I didn't think that I had a problem—at least not one that I couldn't fix myself. I was a self-helper, a perfectionist, a grade A student. I didn't need some treatment that was going to be a useless waste of money. I didn't need someone to tell me what I already knew. I was fine. Everything was fine. These are the lies that I lived in and went to bed with. They became so normal that I actually started to believe them. I convinced myself that my eating habits weren't "that weird." That my weight loss was "not that bad." That my addiction to exercise was simply being "healthy."

Let me be clear here: if you want your loved one to have a chance at beating this thing we call an eating disorder, get them professional help now! It is the most powerful way you can love them; it is their best shot at full recovery; it is their hope. Do not overlook the struggle they are facing simply due to their ability to convince themselves that they are "fine." They are not. They need help. They need the help of a professional. This beast of a disorder cannot be fought alone. Your loved one is going to need the absolute *best* team of warriors possible, and trust me, you want the warriors to be ones with experience in the field. Help them build that team of warriors—by doing that, you are actually fighting alongside them as well.

I needed my team. I needed them to fight with me for years. It took me a long time to unravel the causes, triggers, and nuances of what fueled my disorder. It required really painful, really hard work and the willingness of my professional team to help guide me toward the healthy and happy life that I wanted to be living. My doctors and therapists saved my life. Without the treatment, without the professional help, I would likely be dead. Thank God my parents knew the crucial need for this type of care and were able to get me into the right hands at the right time.

My plea is that you not wait for your loved one to get any further into the depths of their struggle. Help them begin the climb out of their hell into recovery now by getting them to the warriors who can help them to fight with all their might for the life that your loved one deserves!

—An advocate and healthy, recovered woman

Getting Grounded and Preparing Yourself for the Journey Ahead

Will I be enough to love, to want back? Am I worthy of affection? Because I can't find anywhere that says I am. All I want is to belong, to be validated . . . I'm not simply damned. Because here is my struggle, day in and day out. One way or another, I will not be enough for someone else. Because I am lost in the self-obsession of my own mind. Getting high off of self-abuse, hatred, and crime. But it is an issue, you see, because the intoxication begins and ends with me. I am not enough. I am unworthy. I am not loveable. I am not beautiful. I am too much to handle . . . too sensitive, too emotional, too dramatic.

—Diary of a teen fighting an eating disorder

5 Finding Your Strength

[
Preparing your mind in advance of the potential
storms seems critical to one's sanity.
]

Now that we've discussed what an eating disorder is, the potential causes, the impact of genetics, and the debilitating effects this illness has on the brain, it is time to prepare yourself mentally for what is to come.

You Are Stronger Than This Disease

You, your loved one, and your family are more than this disease. Believe that you are stronger, wiser, and considerably more significant than an eating disorder. You *do* have the ability to discuss topics other than eating disorders. Go do something with your loved one other than therapy; find areas of commonality outside of constant conversation about the disorder; and recognize that there is more to life than constantly obsessing over the illness. Obsessing gives it power!

Seasons change, and so do we. Just as some of us prefer the sunshine, others love a rainy day. This analogy seemed to fit my emotions as I faced the ups and downs of living with a child with a disorder. Part of living through the experience and coming out a stronger person is respecting the basket of emotions you will go through in any given day. And it's OK. You will be sad. You will be happy. You will think it's better, and it will not be. You will think it's worse, and it will not be. Will your heart grow bigger? Yes . . . because it must. Everyone affected will come through the darkness a changed person. You will keep moving forward with an internal badge of resiliency and courage that sometimes only you can see. Just as a scar is always there, so is your experience . . . and your ability to accept that the disorder can raise its ugly head again. There are no guarantees, but now there is a new light ahead, and you move forward. Now you have a story to tell if, when, and how you want to share it. I hope you do because that is how we help one another. Share the good, the bad, and the ugly . . . and always remember that the sun always shows up again.

—A mom weathering the storms

Parents and Guardians

If you are the parent or guardian of someone fighting an eating disorder, you may become paralyzed by the fear of losing them to this unforgiving disease. You will experience loneliness and isolation at times. It can feel overwhelming, and there are moments you'll feel your world crashing in. It's imperative that you do your best to stay strong in mind, soul, and body.

Parents are potentially the most influential force in their child's life. A parent plus their child or children equals a family; whatever family looks in your life, it is impactful. All family units have effects and consequences, for interaction within the family helps us develop our identities. Family members feel the effects and consequences of each other's actions. Each member has a role within the family, and if one struggles, the rest of the family feels that pain. Similar to wind chimes, when one is broken, the melody is no longer rhythmic; the harmony declines. These diseases affect the whole family.

Recognizing your pivotal role as a supportive guardian to your child is extremely important. Consider yourself a resource and an advocate for your child. And remember: to be that pillar of support, it is imperative you take care of your physical and mental health.

Mothers

If you are a mother, you must believe your role is important in your child's recovery and then own the responsibility as the most influential person in their life.

By birthright or choice, your child is exactly that: your child. You are the mother—not your child's friend, not one of your child's peers. But neither are you a god or superwoman. No matter how loving and strong you are, you are perfectly imperfect and cannot do this on your own! Mothers, we are bound by the gift of motherhood. You are not alone. Ask for help!

> The bond and unconditional love between mother and child is as ancient as history itself. Perhaps maternal love is the most intoxicating, powerful emotion on earth. It can destroy you, or it can make you stronger. We do have the choice.
>
> —A mom, aunt, and guardian to many

Below, we have listed proactive suggestions to help you build your pillars of strength. How can you keep yourself grounded, stable, and able? Who is in your support network? Of course, you cannot implement all these suggestions immediately; also, you may not fit within every category, and you will have additional ideas, thoughts, and opinions that pertain to your life.

Next Steps to Take Now:
Putting One Foot in Front of the Other

Listen to Your Gut

There is something to be said for the power of intuition. It acts as an internal guide, urging you to do, to sense, and to react. It is always present, yet we sometimes ignore this innate gift.

Intuition is not always the easiest way, but it is the right way. It scares me because even when I know what is the right and most wise thing to do, I hesitate. I hesitate because sometimes it's the most difficult choice!

—A dad to two young adults

We may not always read our gut correctly, and sometimes, we second-guess ourselves. Remember that the gift of intuition is ever present, no matter how deeply buried within your soul.

Listen to your intuition, and motivate yourself to react when you know something is just not right with your loved one. No doubt, a mother knows when her child is in distress. As said before, intuition knows right from wrong and often means having to do the hard thing for the sake of your loved one's health.

Pause and Write

Find the words to explain what your gut is telling you. Share your feelings, and seek proactive advice from a doctor, a friend, a family member, or a trusted kindred spirit. Follow the prompts in *Working by Their Side* and write down your thoughts. Remember, the mind can lie, but the gut cannot!

Build Your Village of Support

Do any of your friends or family members have experience with eating disorders? Go talk to them, and get educated on how they chose to deal with the issue. You may choose a different method, but the education is worth it. Be bold, and ask them for advice, referrals, and knowledge. In the early stages, it is easy to doubt yourself and your choices. "Are they right? Am I wrong?" However, this is not about who is right or wrong;

it's about getting the necessary support from others to help strengthen your foundation. Ask for help, accept help, be thankful for help, and believe that there will be a day when you will give that help back to others.

I heard the fear in your voice, the torment of wondering what the future had to bear. I can only speak from experience as a mother, but I want you to know that I, and millions of other mothers, know that feeling of being overcome with fear. Not fear for our own selves but distress and angst on behalf of our child. No matter how strong we are perceived to be, the skillful roles we perform in life, our accomplishments, and our significance as women, when we see our own children in pain, we can become momentarily incapacitated and paralyzed by the fear. We have immense fear of losing them and of what they have to personally face. I am so grateful you reached out; you know I have been there. We will do this together. You are not alone.

—One mom to another

We have found that supportive spouses, friends, and family members can and will come to your rescue. You have to ask for help. This is critical: ask for help. You cannot do it all, and others are capable of helping. If you have a spouse or partner, lean on them for help with the children, who belong to them as well. Good family counseling will benefit everyone.

You will be angry, and if you are not educated to understand this disease, your anger will mistakenly be directed at your loved one. Anger, impatience, and frustration are normal reactions.

My first reaction was to be mad at her, and I was for a long time. After all, her behavior reoriented the dynamic of her family, propelling them down an exhausting path of anguish and frustration. It was hard to understand how a teenager with an eating disorder could seemingly become the self-centered, disruptive gravity point of the family . . . It was hard to understand until years later, after she'd (with the irreplaceable help of faith, family, and professionals) fought her way out of the disease. It was hard to understand until I realized she'd battled a disease, not a choice. It was hard to understand until I saw my sister advocating for her daughter and fighting alongside her every day. It was hard to understand until I saw the aftermath of the struggle—a healthier family than it would have been without the pain. A family that is now more deeply anchored by abiding and loving relationship. Now in her midtwenties and fully adjusted, she is thriving in her workplace and enjoying life. As I recall the difficult days, my thoughts quickly pivot to the reality of a happy and inspiring young lady whose life illuminates a path of hope for others to follow.

—An uncle who finally understood

You do not need to reinvent the wheel; most likely, there are others who have been where you are or who are currently in the same position as you. Surround yourself with a community of caring individuals who will encourage you, not interrogate you, judge you, and deepen your wounds. A true friend, loving spouse, or reliable family member who is honest with you can be very helpful. Listen to their constructive criticism! It all depends on the person's motive. Find the people whose motive is to include, understand, support, and love you through this trying time. Make phone calls to *those* people, and do not procrastinate. A lonely, idle mind does not serve you well! You need your friends, and you need to talk! Human beings were not created to live alone. We thrive most successfully together. We have always lived, worked, and played in "villages"—it is up to you to reach out and find that community.

I lived three very lonely years because I was afraid to ask for help. I lost productive time as my child continued to get sicker and sicker.

I know now it was a mistake to keep the pain to myself. It actually caused my child more pain.

—A mom who was lonely

Pause and Write

List your support team in *Working by Their Side.*

Get Centered in Your Faith

We live in both the physical and spiritual realms. As humans, we have a tangible, physical body as well as the mysterious soul within it—soul, spirit, call it what you may. Recovering from an eating disorder is most successful when we nurture both realms of life, as is caring for a loved one battling a disorder. Ultimately, love is the answer. For more on this subject, please refer to chapter 16, "Faith Practices."

If we are not able to love ourselves well, we will have a hard time loving God and others. Loving ourselves is the beginning of reconciliation. Loving God, others, and oneself is the beginning of a new chapter in faith. After all, we are created in a divine image.

—A nineteen-year-old boy

If you currently practice a faith that works for you, we recommend you continue. If not, perhaps it's time to seek out your belief system. This connection can help alleviate stress and manage uncertainties.

Get Healthy Physical Exercise

If you are involved in a healthy exercise program, continue. Exercise helps with stress management, boosts brainpower, clarity of mind, and cognitive functions, and can aid in revoking depression. Moving the body also inhibits an idle mind and obsessive thoughts! But be aware—when you exercise, your loved one will watch your every move! Your physical activities can be triggering for a loved one whose exercise has been reduced or stopped by their doctor or treatment team. This is true for family members as well as for friends. If that's the case, do not exercise in front of them. Also, be aware that your loved one hears your words, so stop constantly talking about your exercise programs, your weight, your body, or the latest diet craze. Responsibly evaluate your exercise habits. Do they impair your family time or personal relationships? Is your exercise healthy or compulsive? Are you teaching your loved one a positive attitude toward exercise?

Be accountable with your exercise regimen, and be respectful of your loved one's perspective regarding your regimen.

We recommend yoga for overall health of body, heart, and mind.

Practice Ten-Minute Meditation

Taking the first ten minutes of the morning for self-care just might change your day! Use these first ten minutes to set an intention. For guided meditation, consider the app Calm (Calm.com) or Sam Harris's Waking Up (WakingUp.com).

Meditation has been found to increase happiness, lower stress and anxiety, aid in the treatment of depression, develop perspective, increase compassion, and lead to an overall higher sense of personal well-being. The practice has been utilized as a healing tool for over five thousand years, originating in ancient Vedic traditions in what is now India. The practice has no religious affiliation and can be accessed by anyone, regardless of belief system or lack thereof.

Engage in Life

During this challenging time, try your best not to lose yourself to despair and worry. This is a common problem and easier said than done. Lighten up when appropriate. Engage your village, and go do something fun outside of the world of the disorder. Go see a movie, have a picnic, take a long walk, listen to live music, enjoy a date night, go to an event, spend time with adult friends, visit a museum, get outside of the home environment, travel if appropriate, practice your art form, join a book club, go to your place of worship, share a meal with friends, and partake in activities that stimulate you mentally. You need to seek out joy and feel like a whole being, not just a caretaker. Don't just exist. Find that connection to your soul, and attempt to experience life fully. The way you choose to live your life is an example to your family, friends, and your struggling loved one.

> Each one of us, and every action we make, has a quality of aliveness to it, a fragrance or vibrancy uniquely its own. If the outer form of who we are in this life is conveyed by our physical bodies, the inner form—our real beauty and authenticity—is conveyed in the quality of our aliveness. This is where the secret of our being lies.[1]

Visualize

Visualization is an easy and healing practice. Close your eyes, go internal, and picture your loved one healthy and happy. Parents, see your child healthy. Visualize them healthy in your mind's eye. Your brain simulates visualization, and a reality of that vision can be manifested. For example, we often ask, "Do you see what I mean?" Imagery is habitual. Practice visualization, and then teach visualization to your loved one so they may see what you see: your loved one untroubled, happy, and relaxed.

Turn on the Music

Literally, turn on your music. If you play an instrument, pick it up, and play it. It is a known fact that music taps sensation in the human brain. This international language has the power to create a shift in mood. Lift yourself up with music. Play your favorite cheerful and pleasant music in your home.

Music, Kitchen, Dance!

Still, to this day, I can hear the music when I walk through the side door of my home. Life seemed brighter when the music blared through that kitchen window. Mom smiled more than normal,

---

1   Cynthia Bourgeault, *The Wisdom Way of Knowing: Reclaiming an Ancient Tradition to Awaken the Heart* (San Francisco: Jossey-Bass, 2003).

Dad danced more often, and the rest of us loved life just that much more. When the music was turned up, the air smelled better, the colors in the room were brighter . . . Indeed, it changed the entire aura of that house for the better. Not only did the music change the aura of our home, it changed the rhythm of our souls. That music-filled kitchen became a happy place—a place to dance and a place to feel united as a family who shared a home and a tune. The music allowed us to dance our butts off, to jump up and down hand in hand, reminding us that we had commonality. It taught us how to love each other, how to laugh at each other again; the music brought us all back to how our family had been created to be. So turn up the music, and get your groove on!

—Written by an adult child who still hears the music

Sleep

Literally. Sleep. Be wary of exhausting yourself and becoming fatigued. You will need your sleep to help you think straight and maintain control over your emotions, whether at home, at work, or socially. Whenever and however you can prioritize sleep, please do.

Have a Sense of Joy and a Sense of Humor

In *The Happiness Project*,[2] author Gretchen Rubin describes an approach to changing your life. Now, it is no longer just a book; it is a movement toward a happier life! "Your Project would look different from mine," she writes, "but it's a rare occasion a person can't benefit from a happiness project." What makes you happy? What makes you laugh? What brings joy to your life? Do you deliver the joy to others? No doubt, taking care of a loved one battling an eating disorder is extremely difficult—all the more reason you will benefit from rediscovering your joys and your sense of humor. Your happiness will rub off on those around you!

---

2   Gretchen Rubin, *The Happiness Project: Or, Why I Spent a Year Trying to Sing in the Morning, Clean My Closets, Fight Right, Read Aristotle*, and Generally Have More Fun, rev. ed. (New York: HarperCollins, 2009).

Laughter makes the heart beat stronger. It gives your day purpose and your rest reason. Laugher gets your body moving, vibrating, sending out sensations that bring the light into the world. To laugh every day is to live every day. It's to heal, it's to cope . . . It's how we made it through. In our family, we tried to remember the good: the blessings and the joy. Our laughter gave us presence, a hope to exist in a world that felt so sad at times. My grandmother once told me, "Never let your head hit the pillow without having laughed so hard your tummy hurts." Finding that joy again became the anthem of our story.

—An adult child who loves to laugh

Engage Your Passion

We must learn to allow ourselves to have experiences that make us passionate and to embrace them. This is not being selfish; passion is self-preservation! Is your passion art, gardening, worship, music, writing, sharing time with friends, being outdoors, time with family, puzzles or crafts, travel, visiting museums, mission work or humanitarian care, volunteering, or time alone?

We all struggle with the balance of caretaking. My guess is that you are reading this book because you are currently caretaking a loved one who is battling an eating disorder or some other coexisting illness, such as depression or anxiety. Rest assured, you more than anyone need to find your passions and believe you will get beyond your current state of difficulty.

Fulfillment comes in many forms, so continue to search out what makes you smile and feel purposeful. Try not to get stuck in the trap of obsessive caretaking! If we're lucky, we can identify a passion or two before our children grow up and leave the nest. What's important is making sure we find something that brings us joy. We all need and deserve joy in our lives.

For me, assisting the nursing staff with critically ill new-borns and interacting with frightened new parents in a neonatal intensive care unit has become my passion. Allowing myself to explore this opportunity and learn new skills has not only given me a tremendous sense of fulfillment but helped me discover a new level of self-confidence and compassion that I did not know I was lacking. And it felt good to think, *This is something I really want to do for myself.* Stretching and growing as an adult can almost be harder than when we were maturing as children. Finding a balance of "me time" with something that really motivates us to get up, get out, and flex our minds and heart muscles is critical to our continued growth. And continuing to model behavior for our children is equally as important when they are adults as when they were young. We want for them what we want for ourselves, for the remainder of our lives as well as theirs.

—A mom who stepped out and found a passion

As adults, it is our responsibility to find and continue our passions. Do you need to create? Are you relational? Do you love to cook? Do you need to lie quietly under a tree? Enthusiasm, purpose, and positive energy do trickle down to everyone around you.

So how does a person acquire passion? Well, honestly, I have come to find that a person cannot just buy it off a shelf or get it from someone else. Passion comes from within oneself, but it can be found in all things. Hidden in places no one would dare to look, passion is found in simplicity but at the same time in intensity. See, passion is all in one's perspective. To be passionate about something does not mean that one has to do it all of the time or let it become their obsession. Actually, it can be in something as simple as the sound of ballet shoes on the dance floor, as seeing God's presence in someone else, as the colors of the sunset, or as the sound of a familiar voice that makes one smile. It is not only influenced by extremes; passion is ambiguous.

—*A fifteen-year-old girl*

Become a Kinder Human Being

Practice kindness, and the action of kindness will become habitual! Acts of kindness are actually a benefit to your health; they reduce stress, boost serotonin, and help one feel less depressed or anxious. You first have to take care of yourself. Be kind to yourself. When you are depleted, it is far easier to be angry, resentful, impatient, short-tempered, and frustrated, and then it is almost impossible to be kind to others. Treat yourself with the same tenderness you would show another; be gentle with yourself during this trying time.

Teach your child kindness by example. At first, it takes intention and a conscious mind to remember to be kind. But in time, it becomes a natural habit.

Pause and Write

In *Working by Their Side*, answer the second set of questions in this chapter.

Does This Feel Familiar?

I was the wingman.

A decade later, I am still here. Always will be. The precious child who once suffered from anorexia has grown into a beautiful and productive young woman. I understand her, and she understands me . . . We are kindred spirits. Her mother has often laughed and said her daughter came out of the wrong uterus. But in reality, I think God knew best when he gave her the mother he did. Anorexia takes patience, perseverance, stamina, lots of courage, and the ability to communicate your own needs as well as the needs of your child. My sister-in-law is a master at getting to the bottom line.

I love my sweet niece, scars and all. She certainly doesn't need or want constant contact . . . We tag up, touch base; she knows I would drop everything for her at a moment's notice. The beauty is that, a decade later, she and her parents don't need a wingman anymore.

One learns an awful lot about people's character and integrity when trudging through life. Do they give up and walk away, or do they dig in deep? Educate themselves and those around them, or bury their heads in the sand?

Fathers play such an important role in the healing of the anorexic. No one is prepared for this role, least of all the daddy. My brother dug deep. Deeper than he ever dreamed, I can assure you that. He was always there. Present, listening intently. Loving unconditionally. He now has a relationship with his daughter, wife, and two younger children that he probably wouldn't have otherwise. Certainly, he would give it all up to erase the pain, the tears, the self-loathing. Did the entire family suffer at the hands of the anorexia? You bet. Big time. But it has made each member the person they are now. Compassionate, empathetic, and understanding of others, with a far deeper capacity for love than most of us can begin to comprehend. Watching someone you adore be tormented by a disease you don't understand and can't repair changes your perspective on life forever.

My brother and sister-in-law have been kind enough to share their precious children with me. Our families are extremely devoted, sharing in each other's pain and triumphs, wanting nothing more than to love and support each other unconditionally. Knowing your family loves you completely and will always have your back allows you the courage to stretch and to heal.

—An aunt

6

Overwhelmed? Simplify!

> I heard the fear in your voice: the torment of wondering
> what the future has to bear, of questioning how you
> are going to balance your life with that of your family.
> You will find your way. We did. No matter how strong
> we are perceived to be, the skillful roles we perform
> in life, our accomplishments, or our significance,
> when we see our own children in pain, we can
> become momentarily incapacitated and paralyzed
> in the fear. Simplify. It will help with the balance.
>
> —One mom to another

Families come in all different dimensions, with varied bandwidth and experiences, never looking identical to others. What works for one may not work for another. By *family*, we mean the immediate family who lives with you, adult children whom you see often, and those who have close contact with the person who is struggling with an eating disorder.

When raising a child with an eating disorder, there are some common family dynamics that seem to cross over most boundaries. For example, family meals feel stressful, relationships between siblings are strained, and siblings can feel frustrated with the child who is struggling. Everyone seems to be walking on eggshells; the person fighting the disorder becomes more and more withdrawn from family members; parents can be more argumentative and short with each other; and the overall tone of the home is far more tense.

Bluntly put, you will need to find effective ways to cope with stressors and prioritize the things that are vitally important in your family's life. You are now not only a parent but a caretaker to a sick child; this can feel very overwhelming. We will discuss three areas of importance in helping you to simplify and make dealing with life easier:

- Learning coping skills
- Prioritizing family time
- Balancing work and life

Next Steps to Take Now: Putting One Foot in Front of the Other

Make Your House a Home

You have the ability to create an inviting space. We are not kidding when we say to turn on your music! Help create the ambience you want to feel upon entering your home, whatever your space may be. Your children will notice! Create smells, sounds, and sights that are welcoming and warm and feel safe. This is an opportunity to lighten up the mood a bit. There is a difference between a house and a home. Anyone can live in a house, but a home is the sacred space a family creates that helps everyone feel nurtured, safe, and relaxed.

I've always wondered whether other people rush around at the end of the day, right before their spouse, partner, or family comes home, to do a quick tidying up. I do that! It just makes me feel better. I hope it makes our house feel orderly and welcoming and comforting. Sounds so conventional, but it makes sense, right? When you walk into any space, you make an immediate judgment about it depending on what you see, feel, hear, and smell. It was important to me that our children felt good about the home they walked back into every day after school. My efforts were never perfect and sometimes went unnoticed, but they freed space up for me to focus on how their days had gone, what headaches or heartaches they were carrying around, and what challenges we were facing as a family.

—Mom and wife, never perfect

Pause and Write

What can you add to your home and to your daily routine that can create a more welcoming, warm, and safe atmosphere? Please refer to *Working by Their Side* to write your thoughts and ideas. We have given you some suggestions and prompts to consider.

Learn Coping Skills

Every one of us who has contributed to this book has had to learn and relearn coping skills when caring for our loved one. It is our responsibility as caretakers to create a safe place for our loved one by setting an example. This requires vulnerability and a willingness to engage in coping skills continuously.

Stabilize Your Mental Faculties

Your emotional state will set the tone in your home, most especially if you are scared or sad. Be conscious of your body language and the energy you project; react mindfully, calmly, and without judgment. Get help from a therapist if necessary.

Commit to Being Honest

Be honest with yourself about what you need in order to operate at your best. By honest, we mean be sincere, honorable, vulnerable, and free of deceit or blame. When communicating with your spouse, partner, children, and loved ones, practice speaking with honest sincerity. It will cut through the misunderstandings and help stabilize your mental faculties, reasoning, reactions, and judgment.

In retrospect, the experience did provide a huge knowledge of sensitivity to my other children, though not always at the time. Their frustrations and resentment then were valid. Being honest with each other did validate us, and we could work from that baseline.

—A mom of five, one of whom
suffered from an eating disorder

Gain Respect by Giving Respect

Treat your loved one with respect, and they will learn to respect you. Be patient. Listen. Forgive, and ask for forgiveness when you make a mistake. Brainstorm problems; don't yell; don't demean or embarrass your child in front of others; and ask that they treat you with respect, like the respect you demonstrate. Respect is a vital component to any relationship.

Open, raw, laid-bare honesty is the only way to gain someone's respect. You can't hide anything. Our girls have seen it all—the good, the bad, and the ugly, in both me and my husband. And being able to talk through *all* of it as a family is so very important. Sometimes our girls say, "OK, Momma, enough honesty. TMI!" Establishing that dynamic in your family as early on as possible is not easy, but it can be so beneficial. Making sure you know when to share and how to share is equally as important—delivery is key. And know your audience. If you have a child who needs to hear things slowly or in bits and pieces, not all at once, gaining the respect of that child means delivering messages in a way that works for him or her.

—A mom of two adult children

Spend Time Alone with Your Spouse or Partner

Remember: you are the adults in the family, and you need time alone. Have a date night!

Communicate

Set aside time to talk as a family and address what's going on with each member. Be honest, be appropriately open, and be the adult in the conversation! Straightforward talk with appropriate boundaries can relieve tension and fear. Do not constantly talk about the disorder! Talk about other meaningful and important topics as well.

If communication is part of the issue, we highly recommend you engage in family counseling to have a safe place to discuss the family's dynamics.

Educate Your Family about the Eating Disorder

Have no doubt; the family is in for a challenging ride. If you are a parent of more than one child, keep the other siblings in the loop. Help them understand what is going on and why things feel different right now. Knowing what their sibling is fighting helps them prepare for the future without as much confusion or anger.

Recognize Quality Time versus Quantity Time

The reality is that with a sick child, there is no equality of time in terms of quantity. The sick child needs more. With your other children and family members, do your best to focus on *quality* of time. For example, try to attend the other children's important events, such as sports, school, arts, life celebrations, and other occasions outside unrelated to the disorder that are important to them. When you must let them down by not being present, help them understand the current situation by communicating lovingly and including them when appropriate. It is common for siblings and other family members to initially resent what the illness does to the family. Time and open, loving communication with your children and family do help with sensitivity. Remind them to fight the disease, not their sibling.

Put Your Children to Bed at Night

Make them feel safe and loved as the day winds down into night. A young adult or older teen might not actually want you to physically tuck them in bed, but saying goodnight in a loving way matters.

Don't Lose Yourself. Remember Who You Are!

As we have repeatedly stated, you are more powerful than this disease. Who are you, and how do you choose to maintain your sanity?

Say Yes When Possible

Add some lighthearted fun to your lives.

Say No When Necessary

When saying no to a child, remember that the delivery of the message will substantially affect their reaction! A loving no with a fair explanation, even if it is short and to the point, will be received far better and will create mutual respect.

Let Go of Nonessential Activities

Let go of the obligatory events and activities. It can be difficult to set boundaries and say no, especially if other relationships—like people from school or work, neighbors, or your faith community—are involved. But remember, this is temporary, and giving your energy to your family and what matters most right now can make all the difference to turning things around.

Fight The Battles That Are Truly Consequential

For example: the length and dyed color (sometimes purple!) of a teenager's hair will change with time. Let go of arguing about how you want them to present themselves!

Ask for Help from Loved Ones outside of the Family

These are friends you trust immensely. Learn to let these others in; they want to help. Nor is asking for help a reflection of failure on your part. Being able to receive support is a strength.

Accept Help from Friends, Extended Family, and Neighbors

You cannot do it all, so if someone offers to lend a helping hand, consider saying yes and thank you! We have seen so many family members and friends who feel helpless. Allowing loved ones to help gives them the gift of helping, and that feels purposeful.

I realized these out-of-control emotional breakdowns from my grandchild were not going away. From the outside (and I had *never* been kept on the outside), it looked like something my grandchild needed to get a grip on and just get over. And then I watched my own daughter completely change, going from open to secretive. I realized the problem was both overwhelming and consuming her. She watched helplessly as her daughter's condition deteriorated. Maybe I could have helped my daughter more if I had been brought into the problem of my granddaughter's eating disorder earlier and been allowed to feel a part of this problem.

—A grandmother

Listen

What are the needs and wants of your family members? You might learn something you were not aware of, and one of them just might have a wonderful idea or solution to an issue.

I regret that it took me a long time to notice how important it was to wait for my older daughter to express her thoughts and emotions. She always needed time to process and prepare before launching into an important conversation or answering a question that was a bit layered. I labeled her as shy when she was younger, and I probably said that a little too often in her presence. She *was* shy, and I assumed—wrongly—that she needed me to answer for her when an adult asked her a question and she didn't respond right away. This was one of my biggest mistakes as a parent, because I think she adopted that term, applied it to herself, and grew to believe it, in turn making certain social situations difficult. Once I recognized the need to give her space and wait patiently for her to respond, our dynamic changed for the better.

—A parent who learned to listen

Share Family Meals

Taking the time for regularly scheduled family meals can actually help children with self-esteem and with building relationships in the family. Two critical keys to sharing a fun and peaceful meal with the family are positive conversation and affirmative body language. As adults, we can help implement both of these, especially by modeling them in ourselves! Consider asking the professionals on your loved one's treatment team for specific suggestions on how to make mealtime pleasant. Begin with a smile, light positive conversation, and maybe even pleasant background music. Mealtime can be extremely difficult; you know your family best, so think of ways to mindfully keep the experience positive. For more information on the benefits of family meals, we recommend the suggestions given by Pam Myers, BSED, in the article "8 Reasons Why Sharing Family Meals Is Important."[1]

Hold Family Meetings

Several of us contributing writers have discussed the successes (and frustrations) of arranged family meetings. Choose a day and time that is most suitable for everyone. Sit down in a comfortable place, and discuss upcoming plans. This is a good time to set up a family calendar, listen, respond to your family's concerns, and share your thoughts. Keep the peace, and remember that your disposition will help to set the mood of the meeting. Do your best to be even tempered.

Schedule Family Therapy

Does it fit in your schedule? Probably not, but we highly recommend family therapy. When you schedule, know that your treatment may require several weekly visits to the family therapist for an extended period of time, perhaps even three to twelve months. You can decide whether private therapy time is most helpful or try participating in a family support group.

Help Yourself Too

Make an agreement with yourself that you will take care of yourself. Mentally and emotionally settle into the journey. Evaluate your priorities, and be

---

1   Pam Myers, "8 Reasons Why Sharing Family Meals Is Important," Child Development Institute, November 8, 2015, https://childdevelopmentinfo.com/family-building/why-sharing-family-meals-is-so-important-2/#.XD5UzC2ZNhA.

willing to shift if and when necessary. Sometimes, when these shifts occur, you just might find peace in releasing what you once deemed so important and realizing that life's design feels more rewarding and meaningful when you focus on the consequential.

> Many years ago, I was told, "Mind your tone, mind your words, mind your body language, and remember to empower her without judgment. All the while, create a comfortable, loving home, give attention to other loved ones, work to get out of the obsessive thoughts, maintain your individuality, and put your creativity on paper to eventually share with others!" I did not do it all well at first, but with time, I was able to balance most of it. Certainly with flaws and not perfectly. Once I realized perfection was unreasonable, I began to focus on and logically implement the most important things my family and I needed. It takes patience!
>
> —One regrouped from chaos

Worship Together as a Family

Serve Together as a Family

Deal with Stressors in the Family Head On

Find effective ways to fairly deal with the most obvious stressors in the family. Family therapy is recommended.

> ### Open Book
>
> I am a blessed grandmother to a close family who has always been open with each other. But when my own daughter (then in her forties) was dealing with a child with anorexia, she pushed me way. I did not realize how deep the problem was, and I wish

now I had done what my intuition was telling me to do—*step in*—instead of letting my daughter's fears hold me at bay. I wish my daughter had been more open from the beginning. If I could change anything about my role as a mom and grandmother, it would have been to press my own daughter about what I could do to relieve her of her family duties. Looking back, I think she was trying to protect me by leaving me alone and not asking too many "favors." She was trying to handle it all quietly to protect her child from the stigma of the label of anorexia. The open-book policy is the only way to go. Yet I realize that when it is your own child, you do not want the rest of your friends, or your friends' children, to say she has an eating disorder. Once my grown daughter was able to be open and honest with others, the clarity with which she handled the problem was wonderful, as she no longer feared what others would say.

—A grandmother

Cut the Screen Time in Half, and Spend Time Together

Along with sleep and physical activities, cutting screen time has been linked to improvements in cognition.[2] Less screen time enhances a child's ability to recognize emotion and interact with others more significantly.[3]

Seek Out Community

This could mean making friends with other families in your neighborhood, going to your place of worship as a family, getting involved in the local YMCA, participating in school activities, and more.

---

2   Brett Molina, "Study: Limiting Kids' Screen Time Improves Brain Function," *USA Today*, October 1, 2018, https://www.usatoday.com/story/news/nation-now/2018/10/01/screen-time-study-less-than-2-hours-day-kids-boosts-brains/1484765002/.

3   Juana Summers, "Kids and Screen Time: What Does the Research Say?," *NPR*, August 28, 2014, https://www.npr.org/sections/ed/2014/08/28/343735856/kids-and-screen-time-what-does-the-research-say.

Pause and Write

Please refer to *Working by Their Side* to answer some important questions about defining your current needs.

Recognize That There Are No Perfect Answers

When mistakes happen, give grace and forgiveness both to yourself and to family members. Mistakes *will* happen; it is inevitable. However, they most always open the door to learning opportunities. Take advantage of mistakes, and learn together, all the while standing firm in your wisdom to avoid making the same mistake over and over again.

Choose Joy

There's a saying: "Choose joy." It's not that easy for some, and I totally get that. However, in our circumstance, this was our only option. It helps that I was raised by two amazingly loving and joyful parents who taught by example. I watched how they navigated life's ups, downs, disappointments, and thrills. I learned all I know about love and joy from them. I am blessed. So, each morning on the thirty-minute drive to the hospital, my daughter and I *chose* joy. It did not mean it was easy, but it helped make it bearable. It was our only option. We sang, prayed, and even laughed some. It might have been nervous laughter, but we consciously chose joy in the blessing of recovery. God is so good. We got through it. She got through it and is better than ever.

—A loving mom who fought for her child's freedom

Mind Your Expectations

Does this need an explanation? Please refer to chapter 7's discussion on celebrating a B rather than demanding an A+.

Say Kind and Encouraging Words to One Another

*The tongue has no bones but is strong enough to break
a heart. So be careful with your words.*

—Unknown

Prioritize Family Time

Find the time to review your priorities. Write them down if need be, and begin a sequential list from critical to less important. Balancing both your priorities and your family's takes time and cannot be done overnight. Be patient with yourself, but try to calculate your decisions.

Above all, I am a mother, and mothers believe that we can restore and mend what is broken, especially in our very own children. Each child is different, and thus each journey must be different and customized to that child's needs. No one really understands the plight of the parent-child relationship except one's own self. I have a connection some don't understand. We've been told it is too deep, too close. I don't believe that; all I care about is that my little girl understands who we are as mom and daughter. What does it take for her to feel safe and unconditionally loved? What will it take for her to understand us? Am I willing to put in the hours it takes to prioritize my child's needs?

—A mom

Pause and Write

Follow the prompts in *Working by Their Side* about recognizing that there is no such thing as perfection. Mistakes are inevitable!

Share Responsibilities with Your Spouse/Partner

Take turns tending to your children's needs and household tasks, especially when the children are young. Parents and guardians are most successful when they take the time to discuss these responsibilities and consider whose personality is best at what: financial tasks, cooking, emotional nurturing, the morning routine, the late-night routine, or spontaneous decision-making. Prepare yourself by knowing that you will have to take care of areas in which you feel inadequate in order to cover for your spouse. Serious lessons in give and take are easiest when communication is respectful.

Engage Your Children, and
Teach Them to Fend for Themselves

For example, set up chores, and have the children clean their rooms, make their school lunches, help with errands, drive younger kids to events, help cook meals, etc. If you have preteens or teenagers, it is so important to give them responsibilities in the home. This makes them feel purposeful and ultimately helps them become independent and capable. Once they get used to the responsibilities, they will actually like the independence. Hopefully, they will feel a sense of purpose and will enjoy helping relieve you of the constant family duties. Reward them with gratitude.

Keep a Family Calendar for
Everyone to See Daily Schedules

Do you work better with a schedule? If so, keep a family to-do list, and post it where all can see and respond to it. Have your children keep lists of what they are responsible for accomplishing each day of the week. Organize, to the best of your ability, a structured routine that feels steady and prudent when it comes to responsibilities in the home.

Keep a Conscious Mind Regarding
Which Chores Are Actually Important!

For example, if a bed does not get made in the morning, decide whether that is worth an exchange of harsh words. Could it be made in the afternoon?

If Financially Able, Acquire Educational Assistance

Do not hesitate to get school tutors to help with homework and projects, especially if you have children in high school. We believe this is an important suggestion, as we are moms and caretakers, not our children's high school or college professors. Ask for help from counselors, teachers, coaches, and, if necessary, the administration. You want your children to feel supported in their studies, but, honestly, education is a demanding area that requires a lot of time from parents. We suggest getting outside help if possible.

Organize Ahead of Time

My family has a drawer in our kitchen full of shoes. These are the shoes dropped on the floor after school or left under the homework table, in the yard, or on the floor the night before. That may seem silly, but in the rush of the morning, our kids always get out of the door on time and with a pair of shoes on! We also have a toothbrush drawer in the kitchen, as well as lockers by the back door for backpacks and a coat rack. A smooth morning looks something like this: eat breakfast, brush your teeth at the kitchen sink, get your shoes from the shoe drawer, grab your backpack (which you packed the night before), get a coat, and the kids are off for school! The point is that we have had to create staging areas that may not seem typical but that work great for our family. And, by the way, I too had to learn how to be more structured and organized!

—A mom who is not typically organized

Balance Work and Life

Work is important for your well-being and your family's. Your income is potentially what supports treatment for your loved one. Maintaining the balance between work and life can be very challenging, and it's a delicate balance, particularly in terms of fulfilling the needs of the individual suffering from the disorder.

Leave your work at the office so that when you are at home, you can focus on your relationships with those you love. This is much easier said than done, especially if you are a creative type, are the sole breadwinner, or work from home. But, willfully and with purpose, do your best to give full attention to your family when you are home.

If you're the creative type, include your family in your work when possible, and ask their opinions. For example, ask for advice on the title of the book you're writing or help with art projects.

> Some of the happiest memories occurred in my messy art studio. The kids were allowed to freely explore with paint, charcoal, and markers. I did not know it then, but that was our *art therapy*.
>
> —An artistic parent

- Leave for work stress-free. Do your best to set the atmosphere of the morning rush, making it as peaceful and organized as possible. Try playing relaxing music rather than the news. Consider preparing the night before, especially if you have young children, in order to start the workday more relaxed.

- Use your time efficiently.

- Understand your company's policy regarding medical leave, time off, and flextime. Talk with your HR manager, and review company policies.

- Communicate. Consider talking to your boss, business partners, and colleagues up front to explain your loved one's situation. Be honest, but don't be overreactive or catastrophic in your explanation. We hope you will receive moral and emotional support.

- Review the office insurance plan. If you are covered by insurance at work, set up a meeting with the person or people in charge of the plan. Educate yourself on your insurance coverage and how best to approach filing claims. Please refer to chapter 12 for more information regarding insurance and benefits offered or carried by your employer.

- If you are the boss, let your assistants know, with integrity, that more will be required of them during this time. Ask colleagues whom you trust to fill in when you are absent.

- Confirm times away from your job for therapy. In other words, if you need to take three to four hours off once or twice a week, set it up to the best of your ability from the beginning. Get it on your schedule!

- If your work is portable, take it with you. You will have downtime while waiting on your loved one—waiting to pick them up as they finish a therapy session, for example, or during travel if you have to go elsewhere for help, or sitting in the waiting rooms of therapists, doctors, or nutritionists.

- Say no. Respectfully decline extracurricular work-related events and activities. Spend time at home instead, or spend some time alone to rejuvenate, in whichever way works best for you.

- Be prepared for emergencies. When dealing with eating disorders and mental health, there will potentially be emergencies that pull you away from work. Have a backup plan in place should you have to suddenly leave.

- Connect with your family during downtime at work. If possible, check in with your children and loved ones during lunch, coffee breaks, travel, etc. A simple but thoughtful and encouraging text feels good to receive.

- Use technology to meet your needs. For example, videoconference with therapists and doctors when necessary using Skype or FaceTime. When possible, telecommute to work at home, providing the same performance you'd give at the office. Consider less time at the office and more time at home.

- Encourage your child to work! In some cases, a child can work for or with a parent, caretaker, or mentor. This is a personal choice for you to make. Sometimes, getting a paid job outside of the home or family—of course, this is dependent on age—can bring about a sense of purpose and responsibility. It can also help the individual abstain from obsessing. Be wise in helping your child choose a job or volunteer work.

Therapy is a lifesaver for so many millions of human beings, and I would never discount its purpose in this world. But I sometimes believe therapy, especially talk therapy, can become part of the problem. The constant discussions about "me" have to make a child continually think about "me"! So why not come up with solutions for "me" that aren't necessarily about "me"? This is why I wonder whether work is one positive solution. Often, I say to my kids, "Go volunteer," but that often is self-gratifying and becomes a "me" subject again. Work, though, is a place where you have responsibilities and where people depend on you to do your part. In a sense, it's required of you.

—A mom

Work may mean using your acquired skills, finding a creative outlet for your mind, providing a purposeful benefit to our world, or perhaps just working a job that pays the bills. For many, success is measured by the amount of money one makes, but not everything should be measured in economic value. True, bona fide success is measured in relationships. Life is sorely lonely without relationships; it's important to take a step back and reevaluate our relationship with work and the relationships in our families. Fulfilling our responsibilities to family is necessary both financially and emotionally.

One of the things I found interesting is that my sister received disability for her anorexia. Because of this, she did not work. That was a curse! If she had worked, she would have been forced to get out into the world and would not have been so isolated. It would have helped her feel a sense of purpose!

—An adult sister

It's an intricate balance. The stability of work helps sustain the equilibrium of the family structure, yet it cannot buy love. Love is free to give.

Love is free to receive. Love outweighs any paycheck, and the return is invaluable. Parenting a child with loving deliberateness will potentially be your most important life's work. The effects play out for generations to come!

The parent-child bond is the foundation on which all relationships are built. In and through the secure parental connection is where children learn how to love themselves and internalize how they deserve to be treated by others. Treasure and nurture this bond like no other. Let your children know that you can make room for imperfection—yours and theirs—and that the very things that make them beautiful are their flaws and their unique essence. Measure your love not in numbers but by character and intrinsic value. Form a reflection that they can be proud of when they look at themselves in the mirror and see what you have helped to create.

— Therapist Miki Johnston, MSW, LCSW, a mother, wife, daughter, and psychotherapist for teens, adults, and families

Pause and Write

Go to *Working by Their Side*, and create a to-do list. Use a short-term list and a long-term list to decide which tasks are urgent and which can wait. Share with family, and, depending on your kids' ages, delegate responsibilities.

Does This Feel Familiar?

That was then; this is now.

Then, my family was overwhelmed and confused. I believed being on the other side of this disease to be a burden. *Now*, I see it as a blessing—something I find my strength in and a large part of my story.

Then, written by the seventeen-year-old version of myself:

Growing up as the sister to a victim of anorexia was no fairytale, to say the least. In many cases, and certainly in my life, when one family member is taken down, everyone suffers alongside their loved one. As a family member closely bound to my once-victimized sister, I am here to tell you what it is like. I too struggled hand in hand with my sister's eating disorder. Although I did not have anorexia, her eating disorder placed a burden on my childhood because it affected every aspect of my world. Some days, I felt so scared that I felt like giving up. I could sense that my parents were scared too. You may feel that way at times too. But when we dare to love, we allow ourselves to be engulfed by this powerful emotion. We are agreeing to be there through thick and thin. "Till death do us part" is how I like to put it, and for my family, that is oh so true.

Much like my mother, you, as a mother or guardian, are seen as the caretaker. When your children are in trouble or need, you are looked at to come to the rescue. Although I was aware my mom wasn't perfect, sometimes it felt like the disease won when, really, I wanted to feel like I deserved to win, like my sister deserved to win. To help us feel safe, show up for soccer games, and let us tell you about our day—even if you only have five minutes to talk. Doing your best to be present allows us to feel more important than that atrocious disease and more important than the distraction of an eating disorder.

Anorexia has a tendency to skew our views and make the disorder the main focus. Yes, healing your sick child and giving them the attention they need is crucial; however, the effect this illness places on the ones who love the victim are crippling. I, a child of seventeen who watched my sister struggle for a decade, can tell you parents that we need you to watch us too. Balance is my advice, as simple as it is. Tuck us in at night, tell us we are smart, and put notes in our lunch boxes so that we know you think about us too.

I reckon that you feel guilty, as I'm sure my mom and dad did at times, but the reality is that these disorders demand attention. Regardless of how hard you try to spread the love to all of your children, eating disorders are selfish. Talk to us; tell us enough to alleviate our fears, even if we don't really understand everything. I needed to believe my sister was going to be OK. If you are overwhelmed, just tell us the simple version—that's always better than nothing.

So, as a parent who wants the best for their children, love the sick, and love the healthy as purposefully. We need your love just as much as some eating disorder that wants to take that love away from all of us.

This is now, written by the twenty-four-year-old version of myself:

One of the most frequent questions I get asked is, "What got you into social work in the first place?" After having been asked more than a dozen times, I have come to the conclusion that my sister's eating disorder gave me a glimpse into what my patients go through every day, thus giving me the ability to relate to people on a deeper level. I was given the chance to experience pain, go through hardships with loved ones, and see healing. Had I not been exposed to anorexia, I would have never known what a psych ward looks like, how family therapy works, or what it's like to be around mentally ill patients. I wouldn't have learned that in pain, there is more hope than is imaginable. I would not have found my passion; I would not have found myself.

I am now, six years later, a LMSW (Licensed Master Social Worker) who works as an inpatient therapist in a psychiatric hospital with chronically psychotic patients. I can confidently say that my profession is a reflection of the skills and experiences that I began to develop during those crucial years of my sister's illness. I look back now and see those years, although confusing at the time, as the building blocks for who I am now, who I always wanted to be. I see my sister's disorder as a blessing, and eventually, you may too. I can remember my mom saying to me over and over again, "One day, we'll look back and be better because of all of this," and I reckon that she knew what she was talking about.

Now I see my mom and dad's efforts as unconditional, inspirational, and somewhat outrageous. My mom believed in me all along. My dad was consistent. Yes, I felt alone at times, but looking back, I feel remembered and loved and known.

My advice is: Believe in your children. Tell them you do; tell them they matter, and maybe they will begin to believe in themselves too. Believe that, one day, they will be better because of all of this and that their heart will be gifted with empathy and the capacity for forgiveness. Believe that both the sick and the healthy will heal, more likely than not into something spectacular.

Let your children feel; let them be sad and upset; it is healing when people let us live where we are in our journey. I remember the times I felt the most at peace were when my parents stopped faking it, were honest, were open, and felt with me. Be present with your kiddos; let them see you; let them know you. There is nothing as powerful as feeling connected to your parent through honesty and vulnerability; it saved me at times.

I tell you this to give you hope in healing. To ensure that your children, both the sick and the healthy, have the capacity to heal, to learn, and to find worth because of this experience. Believe that they will.

Then, I believed being on the other side of this disease to be a burden. *Now*, I see it as a blessing—something I find my strength in and a large part of my story.

—A grateful sister

Self-Reflection

Honest questions we must ask ourselves.

This chapter is geared toward parents but can be useful for anyone who loves someone struggling with an eating disorder. As we have shared throughout this book, it is beneficial to seriously look at our own actions and motives. As we shared earlier, the people writing this book have all had to look into our own mirrors over the years and, at times, make changes. We've had to seek personal help from therapists and counselors. Sometimes, it was difficult to see our own fallibility, yet we are grateful and better for that work. Self-reflection is a beneficial exercise.

> What gets us from experience to understanding is reflection. With the aid of a simple question like "what did I do well in that situation?," "what could I do differently," we can make small but cumulative steps to doing things better. Reflection also helps to provide deeper learning by looking at situations through a different lens and by asking yourself searching questions that challenge one's assumptions about the world around you.[1]

There are few things in life that are guaranteed, but two absolutes are (1) no one is perfect and (2) everyone experiences pain. We make mistakes, fail, and disappoint ourselves and others. No matter what, this is the human condition. And though we are not perfect, we do have free will and the ability to make choices and respond to the pain of life. Holding

---

1   Jo Ayoubi, "The Importance of Reflection," *TrainingZone*, January 30, 2013, https://www. trainingzone.co.uk/develop/talent/the-importance-of-reflection.

on to a prideful ego, refusing to learn from our own personal mistakes, is debilitating. Maybe it is not ego, but fear!

If we look at self-reflection as learning more about who we are, doing it should help us decide the best ways to handle pain and disappointment. It should help fill in the blanks to the blind side of a life we do not currently understand. Reevaluating our own actions, motives, and personal characteristics will feel vulnerable, and yet these steps toward a happier life are freeing. We know—all of us have been there! We, the writers of this book, are parents, aunts, uncles, children, sisters, brothers, and grandparents. We are you. So please be honest with yourself, with your closest loved ones, and with the professionals you work with in helping you help yourself—thus helping your children to help themselves!

> I had never been to therapy; I had no friends or family with an eating disorder. I was totally in the dark and ignorant in this very unfamiliar world of anorexia. Within a few months, it came to my attention that the way I spoke about my body and referenced my size, my looks, and my eating habits set an unhealthy example for my child of twelve. It was maybe done unconsciously, but my comments were said with a bit of sarcasm. Sadly, she listened, she heard, she saw, and she reacted.
>
> —A mom who wishes she could do it over

Next Steps to Take Now: Putting One Foot in Front of the Other

Below, we have answered some self-reflective questions, but you know yourself best and must answer in good faith, being accountable to your own self. Once you finish this chapter, please refer to *Working by Their Side* to answer the questions.

Am I Grateful for My Body?

Do we really have to love everything about our bodies? Do you actually know anyone who loves everything about their physical body? Learning to respect and be grateful for the gift of breath and body is far more conse-quential and impactful than spending our lives trying to improve or change our looks. Your body is a gift and, yes, it is your responsibility to take care of it with respect and a daily practice of healthy living. But this does not mean we need to obsess over our looks! There is no perfect body, and your vision of a perfect body is based in what you've been taught according to the culture you were born into. Do you respect your own body?

For more information on this topic, we recommend you consult the work of Renee Engeln, PhD, a professor, speaker, and body-image activist and the author of *Beauty Sick: How the Cultural Obsession with Appearance Hurts Girls and Women*. She has also written for *Psychology Today*, including an article entitled "You Don't Have to Feel Beautiful to Care for Your Body."[2]

As a grandma, one of the things I noticed as a model for my own daughters and granddaughters is how we talk about our own image of ourselves. I have never been overweight, but I do have a tummy, and I have often fixated on how I look in clothes. This is based in our culture and what we perceive to be the right way to look. This perception is taken in from childhood and reinforced by ads in magazines and models or movies. I wish I had been less concerned about body shapes, but I've realized I, too, am affected by the culture of what a woman's body is supposed to look like!

—A grandma who's still learning

Do I Continue to Add to My Child's Eating Disorder?

You know from chapter 2 of this book—"What Causes an Eating Disorder?"—that none of us *caused* our loved one's eating disorder. But yes, we can amplify the issue. Most likely, adding to your child's problems was not intentional. For example, dieting and high expectations might not be

---

2   Renee Engeln, "You Don't Have to Feel Beautiful to Care for Your Body," *Psychology Today*, June 29, 2018, https://www.psychologytoday.com/us/blog/beauty-sick/201806/ you-don-t-have-feel-beautiful-care-your-body.

triggers for you, but they might be for a sensitive person fighting an eating disorder. All human beings have a blind side, and that is why it is critical for all of us to self-reflect and educate ourselves. We all have actions within our parenting style that need attention, and getting advice from a professional on how to more suitably deal with your child's emotional issues—as well as your own—is well advised. Be open to personal adjustments and the time necessary to evolve into the parent your child needs. Obtaining the parent-child relationship you desire takes work from both you and your child.

Be an advocate for your child, as a role model, dependable adult, listener, and constant yet boundary-conscious parental caretaker. Be non-judgmental, unbiased, and an educated parent. Fight the disease, not the child.

> Mom, what I really want is to know that at the end of the day, I can come to you with anything, and you will still love me.
>
> —A teenager to her mom

Does My Spouse, Partner, or My Family Unit Add to the Eating Disorder?

As we discussed in chapter 3, research suggests that people can be born with genetic predispositions that make them more susceptible to this type of illness. Many, many people around the world who are in dire circumstances do not develop eating disorders, yet people from happy, healthy homes full of love and support do.

A troubled family environment can also contribute to an eating disorder, as discussed in chapter 2, as can a recent divorce, a death, or toxic, unhealthy relationships. Look at the interactions within your family and the way your loved ones behave toward one another. There is absolutely no excuse for abuse, be it sexual, physical, or verbal. That is an absolute.

How do you speak to one another? Are you careful not to favor one child over another? Are you and your spouse or partner setting a caring, loving example? Do you respect each family member? Do you smile? Do you touch? Do you offer up kind words? Are you grounded in your decisions about self and family? When you're angry, do you lash out, or do you mindfully construct your words and actions so they are not hateful?

How do you deal with confrontation? With anger and frustration?

Do you push back when you know a situation is wrong? Do you allow cruel behavior from yourself or others? Have you truly focused on making the atmosphere of the home safe and comforting?

Hateful, demeaning, neglectful, hostile interaction is never useful.

How Can I Be a Benefit to My Child's Healing Rather Than a Hindrance?

Have patience! Listen, and then stand firm in your compassionate parental discipline and boundaries. The family unit is always complex. Good parenting should be based in love, and with experience, we do get better. Do not settle into believing that your child will always have an eating disorder or that your family cannot evolve into a more functional, loving unit. Everyone in the family has to do the work. The work begins with knowledge. It should always be based in love, not in ego or control.

Try not to be defensive or resist new ideas. Relinquish the guilt, and keep moving forward, understanding that you might take three steps forward and one step back. Sometimes you level out, and sometimes you might even go backward. Always keep your eyes locked on the bigger picture: a healing, well-adjusted, and healthy child. Set it in your mind's eye now that healing will happen. How you see yourself in your role as parent will affect the way your child responds to you.

- Set boundaries intended to keep your child safe. Positive boundaries are not a parental power play, and we know the difference within our own selves. Safe, positive boundaries take more explanation and more time. Your child will eventually recognize that your intentions are on their behalf, and they will feel safe.

- Speak with firm but loving words. Mind your words in a mature and reflective way. Your voice is powerful—both positively and negatively.

- Establish a relationship of respect. Respect is a two-way street.

- Listen without judgment.

- Be an example. We hear this all the time, but how do we really implement being an example? Body language is the first impression; a frown, an unhappy expression, a lack of touch, and crossed arms say it all in a second. Being an example begins with how we manage our adult demeanor.

- Often, our children's anger, grief, frustration, or pain can trigger our own, and when that happens, we are no longer present or able to give room to the emotions others want to express. Find help managing your own emotions so that you can make space for your child's.

Do I Celebrate the B or Demand an A+?

It is critical that our children know perfection is unrealistic. We keep saying this because perfection is a driving force behind eating disorders. Therefore, it is important to be very aware of your expectations and the standards set upon your loved ones. We must ask ourselves: Is it our journey we are expecting our children to forge, or is it their own? If you are raising a preteen, teenager, member of Generation Z, or a millennial, you might already understand that almost all of them see the world differently than we do. They are the first global-citizen generation, and success is more about meaning than it is about money or stature. Do you agree, and do you see this in your own children? Are you meeting them where they are?

When your child comes home with a B, are you disappointed? If so, why? Is average not good enough? Frustration is fair if your child is simply not trying, but inevitably, there is a reason for that. Is the bar set too high? No one sets the bar higher for themselves than individuals struggling with eating disorders—they're perfectionists. When you set goals for your children, are you telling them you believe in them, or are you setting up a mandate that is rigid and often unattainable? Discernment in accountability and ethical standards is different than adhering to our society's competitive standards. No one can be the "ideal child"—be it in terms of what they look like, how awesome they appear on paper, or how they manage their emotions. Just like us, our children continue to learn, all the while preserving their place in the world and where they fit. By no means should we enable apathy, self-hatred, or harmful behavior, and there are times it is our responsibility to intervene. Helping them navigate their journey, both in failure and in victory, includes loving them despite their human flaws.

Perhaps the most important question is whether your child's performance somehow reflects upon you as a parent or person. If we are honest, the answer is yes, and not only for you. We have all felt this judgment, especially when our child is the one with the disorder.

Under Pressure

I always knew it was my responsibility to look the part, to be the personification of my parents' hopes and dreams. The unnatural battle between being me and pleasing them was not apparent to me until years after I left my eating disorder. I say *left* because for many years, it was my trusted life preserver, keeping me afloat while anchoring my emotional growth and self-knowledge. My relationship with food was dependable when nothing else was. I could control something, and the scales measured my success.

Women living without fear of judgment were a mystery to me. Realizing I could set my own goals, cultivated from personal instincts and desires, was the first step toward reclaiming my lost childhood. The greatest challenge was deprogramming the alarm bells telling me to care more about how others viewed me than how I did myself.

If you love someone struggling with anorexia, listen to them. Actively seek knowledge about who they are, and help them learn to dream their own dreams. Look into their eyes and smile; make sure they believe it is their perfectly unique self you love, not an image. Encourage and celebrate authenticity. Try not to offer unwanted advice. We are hyperaware of our faults, fighting to trust our inner voice. You can hardly imagine the burden. Don't value thinness. We know when you are faking it, so truly take the time to examine your relationship with appearance. Appreciate the gift this person is in your life, and become their champion. Say you are sorry if you wish you had done things differently. Own your part, and help them know their mistakes are of the past, useful only as a launchpad for a journey toward new strength. Mend wounds with laughter, tears, and forgiveness. Stumbling is natural. We are just humans doing our best to be real.

—Now a loving mom of teenage boys

Am I Using My Child's Successes to Make Up for My Own Lack of Purpose?

Your child does not want to be your trophy. Nor does a child need a parade for every so-called accomplishment. Average can actually be very good, even in this highly competitive world. Consider reframing your understanding of success, both for your child and yourself. Many of us were taught that success was based on how much money we made and on our status within society. As we stated above, our children desire meaning and purpose.

If you feel a lack of purpose or boredom with who you have become, again, you are not alone. Sometimes we lose our way and forget who we were before the childrearing years. But do not use your child's potential achievements to fulfill your lack thereof, be it in sports, artistic talent, or academics. That kind of conveyance puts undue amounts of pressure on children. Instead, go recreate yourself, and rediscover who you are and who you want to be.

See my soul, not just my body. I am a human *being*, not a human *doing*. I need to know that there are no conditions required of me to be loved by you. I need that, Mom, I really do.

—From a child recovering from an
eating disorder to her mom

Have I Asked for Support from My Family?

You will personally benefit from the support of a spouse, partner, and mentally healthy family members.

Loving Someone Right Where They Are

I truly never saw my role in the healing of the eating disorder as anything other than being supportive and loving the person right where they were. I listened. I learned. And I am still learning. I think I just wanted to be there. And sometimes that meant sitting in silence or providing a few minutes of space and breath—a presence. I never felt I contributed much. But less can be more. And silence can be golden. There is relief—however brief—in knowing that another human is there, feeling your pain, loving you and your child unconditionally and nonjudgmentally. At times, presence in the moment says much more than all the words one can string together.

There is a definite ebb and flow with this disease. A forward movement, then retreat, then growth, then a complete standstill. No two people heal at the same pace or in exactly the same way, but they heal, given the right tools, environment, support, and time—lots of time. Have patience.

Being a wingman—that was my role in all of this. I was a small part of the support team. No one gets through this anorexic journey alone. We all have a part, a role to play, and all the roles are important.

What doesn't kill us makes us stronger—and all of those surrounding us stronger too!

—An aunt

If you have other children, they will be affected. For many of us, it is challenging—and often taxing and unnatural—to ask for support. In loneliness, we stay stuck in feeling like we have failed. The truth is that being a parent does define us—perhaps not entirely, but it does—and we are innately programmed to fix problems within our families and solve issues. So asking for help can feel negative. But once you say it out loud, the disease becomes real. You are freed. Try to embrace an eating disorder as a disease, not as parental failure. Honesty and family therapy are recommended.

Have I Built My Village of Support?

As with the instincts of animals, we feel the urge to carry the burdens of our offspring upon our shoulders. The arduous weight often transfers into pain and fear. Yet we do have a choice in how we perceive and react to our child's burdens. No matter how strong you are, none of us was created to live alone. Confide in others who love you, especially those who love without judgment. Find a place to release your frustrations as well as people to bounce ideas off of. Build your own village of support.

> When our child was diagnosed with clinical depression and began expressing suicidal ideations, I felt as though I were the only dad who ever encountered such a gut-wrenching, disruptive challenge. As the father of the family, I was supposed to know what to do—but I didn't. Quietly, so as not to alert our friends and neighbors, I set about trying to blindly solve the problem on my own. It did not work. In fact, the circumstances worsened. Our child's condition deteriorated, my marriage struggled, and our family unit began to unravel. Fortunately, I was led, albeit reluctantly, to talk to others—first to professionals, then to other dads and moms with similar experiences. I eventually opened up without reluctance and began aggressively seeking help. It was only then that the feelings of hopelessness began to diminish and the path that ultimately led to the wellness of our child emerged.
>
> —An initially reluctant dad

Do I Love Myself?

In Jen Sincero's *New York Times* best-selling book *You Are A Badass: How to Stop Doubting Your Greatness and Start Living an Awesome Life*, she helps the reader identify how to create a life they really love.[3] Of Jen's twenty-seven chapters, she ends twenty of them with the same two words: *love yourself.* It is that easy, and it is that hard! When we sincerely love ourselves, we

---

3   Jen Sincero, *You Are A Badass: How to Stop Doubting Your Greatness and Start Living an Awesome Life* (Philadelphia: Running Press, 2013).

become the most efficient caretaker possible, as well as an empowering, positive example to our loved ones. *You Are a Badass* is a good read for young adults and above.

Can I Love Unconditionally?

We define unconditional love as the choice to model a consistent love without judgment. It sometimes requires tough love, but never prideful love, nor love given in return for actions of approval. Are you capable? Can you make a conscious decision (and commitment) to love your child no matter the circumstance, outcome, or conditions, both good and bad? Can you love your own self unconditionally? If not, seek help in understanding what this means and how to bring unconditional love into play. It is a choice, a clear decision we make, when we commit to loving unconditionally. It sounds romantic and easy, but in reality, unconditional love is a learned behavior, a patterned habit. Sometimes the most loving things you do for your child are not the easiest things.

I Need You, No Matter What Today Feels Like

Dear Mom,

First of all, let me start by saying I need help. I need you to be my advocate because I am currently incapable of being my own. I am scared and depressed. I am captive to my own mind and am imprisoned by this disease. Here are a few things I want you to know.

Don't let anyone tell you that I will deal with this for the rest of my life.

Set my weight much higher than you think is necessary. Doctors give you the bare minimum weight and call it healthy. However, metabolism, muscle, the thyroid, hormones, medication, etc. all influence weight, and I will forever be a prisoner to the scale if you set my weight too low.

Don't let me count calories. This is adding fuel to the fire that is destroying me. If you want me to be happy and healthy, you will keep me from this addictive habit. If I start counting now, I will still be counting the calories in my wedding cake and feeling guilty rather than focusing on the joyous celebration. That is hell, and I don't wanna ever be there. Protect me, please.

Help me to accept my body. Whether I'm ten pounds heavier or lighter, my body's shape is the same. The sooner I recognize that my body is the way it is, the sooner I will be one step closer to recovery and healing.

Do not let me replace obsession with food for obsession with exercise. This is simply another method of controlling my body and will simply replace another unhealthy obsession that already exists. Help me to find my worth in different places and to have a healthy and balanced relationship with exercise.

I am not myself, so please don't take anything personally. This disease will change me into someone you don't know. Do not worry; this is temporary. Know that I love you.

Please don't let me stand in front of a mirror. It does nothing good.

Throw away the scales in the house.

Keep me accountable, and set boundaries. I will be pissed at you initially, but I promise I will thank you later. This is actually how I am going to feel the most loved and valued by you. I need you to be firm and stand strong.

Set a healthy example. I watch everything you do. If you aren't loving your body, why would I love mine?

Help me to redefine health. Health and strength come in every size. Help me to let go of Americanized ideals of what being healthy looks like, and help me to learn that size is predetermined at birth, separate from my physical health.

I need your tough love, Mom. You are going to have to make some really difficult decisions regarding my health. *Fight* for me. Ultimately, I want freedom, so do not give up on me. Please. I will give you hell as you try to help. Know that this is not me. It's the disease. I love you so much. Please keep loving me. Please fight for my freedom . . . and ours.

—A teenager who is now a recovered, healthy woman

Do I Need to Engage in Therapy for Myself?

Yes, we recommend it. We all have been to therapy. Be open minded in the therapeutic setting with the personal therapist you choose. There is blindness to all of us, and learning to see ourselves fully is rewarding. Your openness will allow for further knowledge, change, and new experiences. There may be behaviors that you can adjust. These adjustments will aid your growth as a parent and also benefit your child. Find a therapist who agrees to have a relationship with your child's therapist. Be honest, be open, be unguarded, and, above all, be genuine. This includes being vulnerable. For more information, please see chapter 9, "Getting Professional Help for Yourself."

A Mom's Issues with Body Image Affected Her Daughter's

A new client sat across from me. She was fourteen, blonde haired, blue eyed, a freshman cheerleader with a long history of gymnastics and dance. The mother made the appointment due to her teenager's "moodiness." (Doesn't that come with the teenager territory? I kid . . . sort of.) After a few minutes with the daughter, I learned of her rampant body-image issues, her restrictive eating, her excessive exercise routine, and her anxiety regarding the constant competition she felt pressured to keep up with. She was depressed and bordering on an eating-disorder diagnosis. Mom minimized the symptoms, brushing these behaviors off as "normal teenage worries." One day, when leaving my office, the daughter asked, "Can we get a sandwich on the way home?" The mother softly responded, "Oh, honey, you know I'm not eating carbs right now. If you're so worried about your weight, then maybe you should do the same." She gently touched her daughter's arm and walked toward the elevator. In that moment, between the daughter's expression and the seemingly innocent mother's matter-of-fact attitude toward the shaming statement she had just projected onto her daughter, it became clear that the teenager didn't feel pressure only from her peers but from her parent as well. These seemingly subtle comments became more and more frequent in my presence. Mom minimized her daughter's symptoms because she, too, experienced them. Instead of empathizing with her child, she denied the severity of her child's feelings in an attempt to normalize her own. Mothers often forget that they can project their own body-image issues onto their children. Parents, often unknowingly and unintentionally, create an environment where children learn to criticize, even hate, their own bodies. I no longer view body image as an individual issue. It's a systemic issue.

—Mary Grace Mewett, licensed professional counselor, MS, LPC, NCC

Am I Fighting This Battle Alone? For What Am I Fighting?

You will find yourself fighting for your own sanity as well as your child's freedom from the terror of an eating disorder. Fight for health, and do not get lost in the battle of worrying what others think, of saving face, or of covering up something you feel portrays you as weak. It's not worth your energy. If you are fighting this battle alone, ask for help. Do you think you are a control freak? Someone who thinks they know all the answers? If so, you are not alone. It seems to be common, especially among us parents. Consider surrendering to the importance of consulting a certified eating-disorder specialist, then implement their professional suggestions. Together, the fight is easier, more productive, and not as scary.

When I'm asked what it was like, what I did, what the signs were, I take a deep breath and try to convey that this is not your fault; you did not cause this. Your child is struggling, conflicted, confused, likely pissed off, and in their attempt to deal with these overwhelming emotions, they seek control. It becomes about helping them face what they are trying so desperately to conceal. They have the key; they just don't know it's in their hand. Research, ask questions, and seek professional help, but above all, reassure them, and remind them how fiercely they are loved.

—A mom who knows love is victorious

Am I Taking Time out of the Day for Myself?

Self-care practices are not selfish! Contrary to what most people assume, creating a habit of prioritizing self-care is often the most selfless thing you can do for a loved one. When we deplete ourselves, there is nothing left to give. When you do the opposite and take time for your mental, spiritual, and physical well-being, you then have an immensely greater capacity to take care of others. Ask yourself: What do you need to do to sustain positive self-worth, a calm heart, and a clear mind daily? Take a walk, read a book, write, spend time with a friends, spend time alone, listen to music, share a favorite meal, worship, be creative, take an interesting class, etc.

Journal

Perhaps you will never share the words you write in a journal with anyone, or perhaps you will share those recorded feelings with a therapist, a loved one, or a stranger. At the very least, writing clears the mind and gives you a place to express your thoughts and feelings. Throughout your journey, you can always go back and reference past events, milestones you've experienced, and lessons you've learned. We've found getting feelings and frustrations out on the page to be very therapeutic and beneficial in therapy. Please take the time to write in this book's accompanying workbook, *Working by Their Side*.

Does it take a lifetime to fully know ourselves? With every turn of events and new challenge, will we always respond the same way? Do we continue to evolve through our lives, and if so, what does that feel like? The power of introspective work allows us the time to consciously increase our purpose and become the individuals we aspire to be.

Pause and Write

Please take some prayerful or meditative time to think through the questions in this chapter. Then, with intention, write the answers to the questions in *Working by Their Side*.

Some of the questions posed in self-reflection might feel invasive, complicated, or potentially difficult to answer. Self-reflection does not mean you are "doing it wrong," nor should you feel belittled by this request; it is a healthy process. If you have not dealt with mental or emotional disorders, learning how to respond, react, and get motivated in a positive manner will help minimize frustration and miscommunication.

You know yourself best and must answer in good faith, being accountable to your own self.

Does This Feel Familiar?

#StopMindingYourOwnBusiness

What a controlling, conflicting, confusing relationship humans have with food and body image. It is a love affair, a battle of wills, a best friend, a worst enemy, and a force that can take us to our knees. That's what it has done to me: it has taken me to my knees. This is a difficult piece to write. Although I regularly write about coping with difficult topics like depression, substance abuse, addiction, and suicide, I admit that I am almost speechless when addressing the topic of eating disorders. For weeks, I have contemplated why this topic is so difficult, and the conclusion I have drawn is that EDs are the beast of all mental health issues. Obviously, I would not be contributing to this book if I had not been directly affected by an ED.

What happened to the stripped-down purpose of food as fuel for our bodies? What happened to self-love? For me, it became a tangled mess of biology, psychology, and distorted thought. I do not personally have an eating disorder, but we do suffer alongside our children when they are struggling. One of the reasons this subject is hard for me is, once again, because I have to look at myself with forensic glasses. In other words, what has my loved one's struggle with an ED forced me to face about myself?

Pain and loss are not foreign to my life's path. My four daughters were born in the late eighties and early nineties. Precious, beautiful girls. So many blessings: a beautiful home, healthy children, a golden retriever, plenty of food on the table. Then, in 1995, an implosion of nuclear proportions occurred in my life. The father of my four daughters died by suicide in our home after years of struggling with alcoholism and depression. For years, the five of us bounced through life, trying to get our bearings. Following his death, I was so stricken with grief that when I looked at myself in the mirror, all I saw was a shell of a person. I had so many questions, so many whys, and since he could not answer them, I had to seek the answers for myself. That meant working with a therapist, attending peer-support groups, taking medication for depression, and engaging in a comprehensive forensic investigation about . . . me.

Then, in 2004, I received the call each and every one of us parents fears. At the age of forty-seven, I had accomplished a long-term goal and entered law school. The desire to practice law had begun while I was covering the courthouse as a news reporter twenty-five years earlier, but no one really knows the secrets that lurk behind closed doors. Two weeks into classes, on a Wednesday evening, my phone rang, and with it came news that shattered my heart . . . My fourteen-year-old daughter had taken her life. I withdrew from school and went to therapy twice a week for nine months. I took medication to boost my depleted serotonin and dopamine, and I joined support groups. Grief shattered my confidence. I was distraught, overwhelmed with sadness for myself and devastated for my three girls. It affected my concentration, retention, and focus.

Time passed. I lived in a realm of loneliness and uncertainty, and one night, I found myself sharing my fears during a therapy session. The counselor's words changed my life. She said, "I'm not in the business of telling my clients or patients what to do, but I am telling you—you are going to law school. You are going to take it one semester at a time, and in three years, when you walk across the stage and receive your hood and diploma, you will know there is nothing you cannot accomplish." Two months later, with fear and trepidation, I reentered law school. Three years later, when I walked across the stage, the loudest cheers came from my three daughters.

Self-reflection, for a person like me, is ridiculously difficult. When I grew up, the environment in which I lived triggered coping mechanisms of learned behavior I cultivated my entire life. I became a master at reading people's moods, body language, and feelings, and I adjusted my behavior either for self-preservation or to please those around me. Over time, I lost who I was; I became the person I thought others wanted me to be. I was an overachiever, perfectionist, and superstar. My self-worth was about how I looked, what I accomplished, and how many people liked me. The burden of such an existence took its toll on my mental health; I bit my fingernails, I pulled the hair from my part, and I spent immense energy hiding my true self from others. Along the way, I lost who I was, and I was easily molded into the person I thought others wanted me to be.

I wish that was the end of my story, but it is not. Therapy and education taught me that traumatic events can trigger behaviors and negative coping skills that temporarily remediate the pain trapped in the consciousness of the sufferer. When disordered eating in my family became an eating disorder, the game changed. I know about depression, suicide, substance abuse, alcoholism, and addiction, but I had no idea about the beast known as an ED. Every instinct to act, confront, reason, persuade, and challenge was counterproductive and harmful. At a complete loss, I remembered what I'd done many years ago when my experience with mental health began: I'd reached out to people who knew exactly what I was going through. The gentle love, kindness, and understanding they shared touched my heart. Their experience, strength, and hope were the compass that helped me navigate the unknown and dangerous waters of EDs. They introduced me to professionals specializing in EDs. Those professionals welcomed me into their offices and explained the nature of the illness, suggested I receive my own counseling, and provided resources in case the disease progressed and more intensive treatment was needed. Dr. Tyler Wooten, the affable medical director of a residential treatment center in Dallas, described EDs in a way that I will never forget. I asked whether EDs are genetic or environmental. His answer: "Genetics loads the gun, and the environment pulls the trigger."

Our secrets keep us sick. I learned that long ago. I also learned there is a respectful way of purging the secrets without harming our loved ones along the way. I have to keep the focus on myself and stay out of the professionals way; I am not God, and I cannot heal my loved ones. Recovery from an eating disorder is bigger than I am. I do not have the answers; I do not have the solutions. I love and support the sufferers in my life, and I never judge their failures or struggles. When my loved one opens up and expresses fear and hopelessness, I stop what I am doing, and I listen. I thank God that my sweetheart trusts me enough to express her feelings and to share them with me. I do not talk about her food intake or lack thereof; I ask her about her feelings, and then I close my mouth, and I listen. You see, that is new behavior for a mother like me—someone compelled to "solve" everyone's problems and "fix" their sadness. Some of the best advice I ever received is that when fear is surging through body, when I feel helpless and hopeless, when my heart is racing and I cannot sleep or function and am paralyzed and terrified, I must remember to let go and let God. There's an action to letting go; it is naming the fear, writing it down, and putting it in my God box. He is the mighty healer. I have learned to do my best in the moment and then let God do His job! That might sound cliché, but it has been the most pivotal piece to my healing.

—Terry Bentley Hill, a Dallas attorney with a criminal defense practice. In 2011, the State Bar of Texas awarded her a Presidential Citation for assisting lawyers dealing with addiction, anxiety, and depression. She is chairman of the Peer Assistance Committee for the Dallas Bar Association and a TLAP volunteer. She is married to Tom Krampitz and is the mother of four daughters, one of whom lives in heaven.

8 Strengthening Your and Your Family's Emotional Health

> This being human is a guest house.
> Every morning, a new arrival.
>
> A joy, a depression, a meanness, some momentary
> awareness comes as an unexpected visitor.
>
> Welcome and entertain them all! Even if they are a
> crowd of sorrows, who violently sweep your house
> empty of its furniture, still, treat each guest honorably.
> He may be clearing you out for some new delight.
>
> The dark thought, the shame, the malice.
>
> Meet them at the door, laughing, and invite them in.
>
> Be grateful for whatever comes, because each
> has been sent as a guide from beyond.
>
> —Rumi

As you are surely aware by now, this journey to recovery is an incredibly emotional one for all involved. As the caretaker, it is easy to allow the vast range of emotions we and our loved ones experience to overwhelm us. It is also easy to take on the feelings of our loved ones in an attempt to change, fix, or alter their unpleasant experiences. However daunting or overwhelming the emotional experiences may get, it is critical to work toward the emotional wellness of all involved. This wellness requires that sentiments and feelings are processed, understood, and expressed. We must remember that emotions are sent to us as informants that we can learn from; invite them in, and welcome whatever lessons they may carry.

Pause and Write

Take a minute to write what you are feeling currently in *Working by Their Side*. Writing it down will be helpful in providing clarity and aiding you to move forward.

Next Steps to Take Now:
Putting One Foot in Front of the Other

Break and Reset

Give yourself permission to not be OK. Allow yourself to cry, to break emotionally, and to process your frustrations. Therapy is a safe and private place for that. A trustworthy friend who just allows you to emote and experience your emotions with no judgment and no intention of fixing you is always helpful. Those of us who are parents tend to believe that we must always be strong. It is not weak to cry; it is healthy, as it releases the disappointment, anger, and resentment you potentially harbor when dealing with this merciless disease. Then reset!

It is also fair to discuss your frustrations with your loved one, but not in a cruel or mean-spirited manner—especially if you are a parent. You are the adult and need to put restrictions around how you present your feelings and what you tell your child. Love prevails. Love is why we get so frustrated.

Forgive and Learn

This does not suggest you forget, and by no means should you bury your head and pretend something did not happen.

We think it is critical, however, to forgive. You will make mistakes. Forgive yourself. Do not hold yourself captive to self-ridicule, resentment, or grudges. Your loved one will make mistakes. Forgive them. Shaming others, especially your own child, is destructive. They are already feeling ashamed of themselves. Together, forgive, and learn from the experience. Drop your guard, relinquish your pride, and calmly discuss the mistakes. Then be proactive by applying the knowledge learned in the mistakes to change future happenings.

Nurture Your Family

When one person in a family has an eating disorder, everyone suffers. Parents, especially mothers, often feel like the cornerstone to the emotional health of a family and are concerned with questions like, How do I deal with the intense emotional states this is building in my family? Undeniably, it is a challenge. We have discussed the need to prioritize, educate yourself, and listen to your intuition, but how do we nurture the other children who do not have an eating disorder? Begin by making them feel safe. Be nonconfrontational, speak lovingly, spend intentional quality time together, physically hold and touch them, put them to bed at night, try to be there when they wake, be honest, and ask them to be patient during this unsettling time. Try your best to continue the behaviors, endeavors, or activities that are special between you and each of your children. Children need reassurance. Make sure they know you love them equally and that the attention given to the child struggling is not favoritism. Sadly, it is often the siblings who go unnoticed because we are hyperfocused on the ill child. You will find yourself spending an inordinate amount of time, energy, and mental anguish dealing with the one loved one who has the eating disorder. The great dichotomy is also tending to your healthy children while responsibly supporting the recovery of the one afflicted. Remember, neither you, the ill child, nor your other children are at fault. They simply want love and attention, but you have a child being strangled by an eating disorder.

I am a brother, and in my eyes, a relationship among siblings is based on one important characteristic. That characteristic is known as love. This sounds cliché, but it is the core of sibling relationships—at least, for me it is. My sister has found her way after beating a wicked eating disorder, and she has discovered how to sincerely love herself. That was not always the case. Today, our relationship comes with ease, and I believe it is based on her capability to love herself, not in a selfish way but in a healthy, positive light.

Am I pleased with my relationship with my sibling? Yes, but pleased is not the word I would use to describe my feelings toward her. Very simply, I am infatuated. She not only beat an eating disorder but now has the ability to share the experience with others. She confidently provides a sense of *help* and redeeming *hope* for other individuals who are struggling, depressed, and feel a sense of hopelessness. My sister is powerful, she is talented, she is fun, and she is not controlled by an illness. My relationship with her really is based on love. A devoted type of love that makes a little brother wake up every day impressed with whom she has become.

—A brother

Communicate Honestly and Openly with Your Spouse, Partner, or Significant Other

If you are married or in a committed relationship, getting on the same page with your spouse or partner from the beginning will help you both stay grounded. We have witnessed marriages and partnerships where spouses support one another and thus stand stronger together. They help balance one another by fairly discussing issues surrounding the eating disorder, compromising, asking for help, offering help, and covering each other's responsibilities, especially when they have more than one child. This is preferable, helpful to your child's recovery, and a good example for the whole family. If you are in sync with your partner, that is fortunate.

We understand that life is not always smooth. Please know you are not abnormal if you and your spouse or partner feel a sense of discord. Of course, all adult relationships are unique, and no matter the status of your relationship, even a healthy relationship can deteriorate under this kind of stress. Often, the pain of the situation will uncover issues in your marriage or relationship that need to be dealt with. When you are able, deal with the discrepancies. By nature, we are all created differently; thus, our opinions come from our personal points of reference and life experiences. This does not make you right or wrong, and it does not make your mate right or wrong. It confirms that your individual thought processes are different. Agreeing on best-case scenarios for your child is complex. Congruency takes patience, time, effort, and an open mind. Ask for help, tenderness, and love from your spouse, and in return, try offering it. Do not hesitate to get involved in marital counseling or parent support groups or to meet with and learn from other couples who have experience with the death grip of an eating disorder.

To the best of your ability, work diplomatically with your spouse or partner. Blaming one another for your child's issues is common, but don't be fooled—it is destructive and can lead to resentment. We know this from experience!

If your spouse or partner is not interested, overwhelmed, or simply cannot grasp the effects of the disease, do not freeze. We suggest you actively move forward and be intentional in informing them of the course of action you have chosen. Communicate honestly, and remember that being kind and boldly honest with your spouse or partner will be much more effective than being hateful.

Realistically, being in union with your partner is beneficial, but sometimes it does not seem possible. You know your partner best, and ultimately, it is you—and often only you—who will know what steps to take to help yourself and positively aid in your child's healing.

Pause and Write

Please refer to *Working by Their Side*, and follow the prompt to write about breaking and reseting, forgiving and learning, nurturing your family, and communicating.

Does This Feel Familiar?

A father's perspective.

It is with great humility that I attempt to explain a father's perspective of caring for and helping to raise a child with an eating disorder.

In the summer of 2005, my perspective on our family would have read like a storybook. Family of five, living in an upper-class neighborhood with good schools, lots of friends, well-adjusted children, and what I perceived to be a better-than-average marriage. I was thinking we were truly blessed and that, other than the normal trials and tribulations involved in raising young children, we were the luckiest people on planet earth.

In September of that year, our daughter was diagnosed with anorexia. Scared and uninformed, Mom and Dad sprung into action, however in very different directions—Mom with her emotional, nurturing, kind way, and Dad convinced that it was only a matter of time until he found the solution to the problem. Initially, I discounted by wife's concerns, as I was convinced that the entire situation was being blown way out of proportion. However, one month later, our daughter was hospitalized. It was then that we began to organize a well-educated and informed team of medical professionals to assist and educate us with regard to this traumatic problem. As we listened and learned, we both began to formulate our own ideas and opinions, which created a growing divide between the two of us. This divide and lack of communication developed into a change in what we had grown to know as normalcy in our family order and in our marriage. Eventually, as things worsened, all fingers were pointed at me, and I became the cause of the problem and the underlying cause of the eating disorder. The divide grew wider!

Through numerous hours of individual and family therapy, I began to realize I could not change the past. I needed to let go of hurt feelings, join hands with my family, and be an unselfish part of the solution. Throughout the therapy, I began to understand that some of my parenting behavior was surfacing as an important factor in our daughter's insecurities. It took me a while not to take these realizations as personal attacks, for I knew that I would never hurt what I loved the most on this earth: my family.

Though I know I did not cause the disorder, with the help of my wife I did apologize and ask our sick child for forgiveness. We, our entire family, all asked forgiveness from each other and learned the importance of that. I now think that this willingness to be vulnerable and to ask for forgiveness provided us the ability to move forward.

A turning point for me was finally being convinced that an eating disorder is a mental illness and that every case is unique and different. We continued to push forward with unrelenting devotion to our daughter and her brother and sister. Finally, with the understanding that I could not solve the problem, I began to soften and let go of the resentment I had formulated toward my wife. In hindsight, it was her intuition and incredible drive that had identified the issue, and she had gotten us the help that we were all in need of. She dealt with and observed this problem all day, every day, for weeks on end, for months, for years. During those early years, I would come home at night and profess to have a better idea or a different approach.

To the fathers out there struggling, confused, or angry: listen to your wife. When you question the intuition of a mother, do it gently, and be as supportive and as noncombative as possible in times of crisis. Participate in therapy, listen, and open your mind to a new world that you cannot initially understand!

Be fully engaged and supportive of your spouse, your sick child, and your entire family to the best of your ability. Communicate with your children such that they can begin to understand the shift in parental attention and time. Most importantly, set your ego aside, recognize your limitations, and tell your wife how much you love her each and every day. You have to be a team! We dads tend to get caught up in our jobs and outside responsibilities, and we lose sight of how important it is for our children to feel the security and safety of a father's unconditional love.

Dads are trained to lead and to channel our energy into being logical thinkers and problem solvers. Unfortunately, this disease does not fit that strategy. I encourage each of you to recognize this fact early on and join hands with your spouse to learn how, together, you can best cope with the situation. Additionally, it will take the combined effort of you both to maintain some sort of normalcy in your family life at home, which, by the way, is just as important as the resolution of the medical problem.

To the mothers and wives in the daily grind, connect with your spouse, and recognize that fathers don't always have the innate intuition or understanding that mothers do. Communicate with your spouse, and attempt to unite in every aspect of fighting this disease. Thinking your spouse does not understand or isn't emotionally capable of dealing with it causes resentment and has negative effects on the marriage and the children. I beg you to work together. Allow one another to voice your opinions, concerns, and thoughts, and focus on listening, such that the best of Mom and the best of Dad will be exposed. Given the differences in the male and female psyche, this is easy to say and extremely difficult to put into action. If there were ever a time to put egos aside, now is the time. Move forward as a united team. This will provide the best support for your sick child and will provide the family environment your other children so desperately need, not to mention that this unity will provide the foundation that your marriage needs to fight off the attack. Following a tormenting ten-year journey with a daughter who was victim to an eating disorder, I can successfully report, with great humility, that you can and will learn to cope with and control this horrible disease. Our daughter graduated from an arts magnate high school, moved completely across the United States, graduated from college in four years with honors, and is now working and supporting herself. My sincere advice is to understand at the onset that there often is not a logical approach or definitive answer to dealing and coping with this mental disorder. Often, we learn what *not* to do.

I wish I'd known in 2005 what I know now, but I encourage every dad who finds himself in this predicament to stay in the fight, stay involved, get educated on the disease, and, most importantly, to support your wife and her motherly intuitions. Your relationship with your wife, your sick child, and your entire family will be better for it, as humility and support breed respect!

—A dad

9
Get Professional Help for Yourself

[
You can't help them if you don't help
yourself! It's courageous to seek help.
]

First and foremost, we believe a person can recover from an eating disorder, and we know the "therapeutic work" is worth the effort. Recovery is about discovering the authentic human being you were uniquely created to be by learning to love yourself (and thus to love others). This discovery is about you as well as your child. Don't we all want to be happy with who we are and who we are becoming as a person? Therapy can help you discover, recreate, develop, and mature certain aspects of your nature and character. As parents and guardians, we tend to give all our attention to our kids and often deprive ourselves of the exact processing we are asking of our children!

For ten years, I was so consumed by the state of my daughter's eating disorder, 80 percent of my focus was on it—not myself, my husband, my other children, or my friends. It was not until the joy I felt with the birth of my first grandchild that I realized what I had missed out on. I had been physically present at the important events with my family, but due to the worry about my sick daughter, I wasn't emotionally invested. How sad to waste so much energy on something I loathed and had no control over. Take care of yourself and your loved ones. It's important for them to see that the eating disorder is not going to take you down as well. It's a destructive behavior that just gives the ED more power.

—A mother and grandmother

There are benefits in going through therapy at the same time as your child. It provides a common thread and helps you become a relational human being with your child. Sometimes we need to know ourselves better in order to be what our child desires us to be and what we aspire to be. The common thread is about relationship. Do you really understand your innate temperament? Your loved one's temperament and personality?

1. Why is it important to understand our own innate temperament/personality?

    Really effective communicators don't use a "one size fits all" approach. Rather, they adjust their communication style to match the preferences of the person with whom they are communicating. For example, based on the preferences of an ISTJ (Introverted, Sensing, Thinking, Judging) person, one would do best to use a straightforward, logical, calm approach. Conversely, if communicating with an ENFP (Extroverted, Intuitive, Feeling, Perceiving), the preferred communication would be energetic, empathic, and optimistic, with a focus on building rapport.

    Knowing and understanding our own personal style preferences—and those of our loved ones—not only helps with effective communication but also helps us understand what pushes our buttons. Our natural tendency is to use our own preferences to gauge how we behave and communicate with others. The more effective gauge would be based on the preferences of others. Similarly, understanding personal style differences can help us distinguish the intent of others' behavior from the impact of that behavior.

Most of us know the Golden Rule: "Do unto others as you would have them do unto you." An upgrade to the Golden Rule is the Platinum Rule: "Do unto others as they would have you do unto them." Simply put, treat others the way *THEY* want to be treated, which may be different from how we want to be treated. In order to do this effectively, we must first understand what the other person wants.

2. Is there a tremendous upside to therapy for a caretaker? If so, why?

Yes. The importance of self-care for the caretaker (more appropriately called "caregiver") is often underestimated. Caring for a loved one can be emotionally, physically, and financially draining, particularly when the timeframe is more of a marathon than a sprint. When flying on a plane with someone needing assistance, we are instructed to put our own oxygen masks on first, in order to be able to then assist others. When we first take care of ourselves, we can provide better care to others. Sometimes we are so busy giving that we don't realize we have nothing left to give! Caretakers who acknowledge their own vulnerability and the need to process their own feelings are more able to provide valuable support and are more aware of the impact of ongoing stress.

—Dana Beer, LPC, MHSP, PCC, JD, executive leadership coach, DanaBeer.com

When you do have this knowledge of another person, you can address them with the words and certain behaviors that are most favorable! Have you ever taken a personality test to better understand yourself and how best to relate to others? Below are six examples. There are others, should you choose to research.

• The Enneagram: EnneagramInstitute.com. There is a cost for this test.

• Free Enneagram testing can be found on several sites, including:

> » LonerWolf.com/enneagram-test/
> » EclecticEnergies.com/enneagram/test
> » GrowthMarketingPro.com/enneagram-personality-test/

- DiSC: 123test.com/disc-personality-test

- How To Fascinate: Howtofascinate.com/about-the-personality-test

- The Big Five: Truity.com/test/big-five-personality-test

- The Myer-Briggs Type Indicator (MBTI): MyersBriggs.org/my-mbti-personality-type/take-the-mbti-instrument/. A shorter version of the MBTI is available for free at HumanMetrics.com/cgi-win/jtypes2.asp

- 16Personalities: 16Personalities.com

Do you know your "love language" or that of your loved ones? Gary Chapman's affirming book *The Five Love Languages*[1] describes the five categories: words of affirmation, quality time, receiving gifts, acts of service, and physical touch.[2] Discovering your love language and the love languages of others helps with communication. *Working by Their Side* contains more information about love languages and how to take a simple love language quiz.

> Knowing your spouse or child resonates with specific love languages provides a valuable insight into their emotional world. But how do you figure out your partner's or child's love language? Listening to and observing how they respond to specific actions can reveal their love language. For example, if your spouse or child often asks for hugs and wants to cuddle or sit in your lap, you can bet that receiving touch is a primary or secondary love language for them. Does their face light up when you compliment them? Then chances are words of affirmation is their love language.[3]

---

1   "Discover Your Love Language," 5 Love Languages, https://www.5lovelanguages.com/.
2   Brianne Hogan, "What Are the 5 Love Languages?," SheKnows, January 23, 2019, https://www.sheknows.com/love-and-sex/articles/1059295/what-are-the-5-love-languages/.
3   Jon Beaty, "Build Stronger Family Connections by Speaking Love Languages," *Gottman Relationship Blog*, May 5, 2017, https://www.gottman.com/blog/build-stronger-family-connections-speaking-love-languages/.

> ### Pause and Write
>
> Please go to *Working by Their Side*, and follow the prompts about taking a personality test and the quiz revealing your love language. It might sound trite, but learning communications skills is vital to helping your loved ones and yourself. It's very telling and constructive.

Too many people who refuse therapy say things like, "I don't need it," "It's weak to have to get outside help," "They don't know me and can't understand," "It's too expensive," "Of course a therapist wants to help, because that's how they make money," and "I don't have time!" The list is endless. It is sad because this kind of self-pride stagnates healing for everyone involved. Afraid to open Pandora's box? Scared of being different? Scared of being the same? Understandable—many of us were too! But if your loved one is willing to try, you should be too. If you are open to learning, there is a tremendous upside.

> ### Pause and Write
>
> If you are not already in personal therapy or counseling, perhaps it is time to secure a professional who has knowledge and experience with eating disorders. Please go to *Working by Their Side* to make a list of referrals.

Next Steps to Take Now:
Putting One Foot in Front of the Other

Secure professional help for yourself, and educate yourself in these four areas: personal therapy, marriage/partner/couples counseling, family therapy, and self-help therapy. Below are five steps to consider.

Ask for Referrals

Word-of-mouth referrals seem to work the best. If you know someone who has dealt with or is dealing with this issue, call them, and ask for help. If not, get a referral from your child's therapist, your primary-care physician, friends, acquaintances, colleagues, or family members.

If you are truly stumped and cannot find a therapist, please see the appendix for referrals from the National Eating Disorders Association (NEDA), the International Association of Eating Disorder Professionals (IAEDP), and EDReferral.

Secure a Personal Therapist

Your personal therapist should educate you on the disease as well as open your heart and mind to proficient tools that are helpful in both your personal life and your parenting style. There are several reasons we recommend you find a licensed therapist who is trained in eating disorders. They have specific knowledge and should be up to date on the newest issues with eating disorders. They are trained in this field and know how to deal with the emotional issues that lie beneath the surface. They are also trained in coexisting illnesses and are connected to other professionals who can assist in your loved one's treatment. The following are some questions to ask when selecting a therapist.

- Are you connected to other professionals whose involvement will benefit my loved one's healing, such as a treatment team, licensed dietitians, medical doctors, family therapists, local school counselors, current workshops, retreats, etc.?

- Will you consult with my child's therapist? Though confidential, will you help me understand the unperceived issues consequential to both my child's healing and my own?

- Do you work with the family unit?

- Do you do couples therapy? If not, do you have a referral with whom you work? Will you consult with them with?

- Will you help me discern personal issues such as codependency, anxiety, low self-esteem, etc.?

- What types of treatments do you practice? For example: cognitive behavioral therapy, psychoanalysis, etc.?

- Can you prescribe medication? If not, can you give a referral to someone with whom you work who can diagnosis and prescribe medication if necessary?

- Will you give me "assignments" to complete before the next session?

- What do you expect from me as your patient?

- Would you consider working through *Working by Their Side* with me?

Engage in Marriage/Couples Counseling

Many of us have opted for marriage counseling during the years we dealt with our loved one's eating disorder. Some of us are not married or in a committed relationship, so individual therapy was sufficient.

We all have our strengths and weaknesses, and learning how to communicate more clearly and understand each other's feelings and positions helped define appropriate actions we needed to take in our families. It is essential to the longevity of recovery that you understand your spouse or life partner as soon as possible and that you become a team. There are also times when only you can decide what must happen in your marriage or relationship, not only with regard to the destructive eating disorder but also with regard to your life.

Some people prefer to start with personal, one-on-one time with a therapist. It can help ground you, especially if you are new to therapy, just starting the journey, or in conflict with your spouse and need advice on how to communicate with them fairly. Again, reach out, and ask for referrals.

For others, couples counseling works best. These people are fulfilled by doing therapy sessions together and do not want individual therapy. You will need to make a personal decision as to what serves you best—personal therapy or couples therapy—at this particular time in your life.

Engage in Family Therapy

We recommend family therapy. If your loved one is currently in treatment, family therapy is often required. For many of us, family therapy has been extremely beneficial, especially when additional children are involved. An eating disorder never affects just one member of a family. It is a problem for every member, and it needs to be addressed and dealt with together.

There are two incredibly important aspects to family therapy. First, everyone learns coping skills, both for themselves and for dealing with the disease. Secondly, even if family therapy is painful, learning to communicate, listen, respect, and respond thoughtfully is healthy for the family unit. The goal is to get beyond any pain and learn about one another.

> Family therapy allows everyone to be heard, from the pain and despair of the parents to the fear and anger of the siblings. The entire family is affected, and everyone needs to know that they can contribute to the recovery of their loved ones. Family therapy helps us understand our roles and, in some cases, defines triggers that we may not be aware of. Through therapy, we can learn how to make changes for a healthier, more supportive environment. Equally importantly, standing strong on a unified front with your family and holding the disordered person accountable for their actions gives the illness less control and power. Commitment and determination from every member of the family will help save your loved one's life.
>
> —A mom who knows that every voice
> in her family is important

Engage in Self-Help Therapy

By "self-help," we mean being proactive in getting an education from others or accessing more affordable or free information. It is wise to learn from others who have "been there, done that." We realize taking care of a loved one battling an eating disorder is expensive, but be careful—there is misguiding and false information on the internet. And there are so many opinions that it can be completely overwhelming! If you feel you cannot afford therapy, please see chapter 13 for more information.

There are many workbooks for patients but few for caretakers. Listed below are three self-help resources; new workbooks may come on the market at any time, however, so feel free to do your own research. Please see the appendix for more information on these resources.

1. Around the Dinner Table: AroundTheDinnerTable.org. This forum is an online community of parents from all around the world. We recommend this because you can have a live conversation with other parents.

2. *When Your Child Has an Eating Disorder: A Step-by-Step Workbook for Parents and Caregivers* by Abigail Natenshon is thorough, educational, and self-paced.

3. *Working by Their Side.* This is the guided journal that accompanies the book you are reading.

A good therapist is an unobjective third party who unemotionally helps you dissect and restructure issues that are currently destructive. The therapist is on your team as an advocate who helps you think, decipher, and negotiate new beginnings. Think of therapy as continuing education. Learning more about who you are helps you direct your way in the world. It also helps you become a better caretaker.

Destroying the false image of perfectionism and surrendering to the fact that we can't do it all opens us up to the relationships we yearn for with our loved one: relationships that are honest, real, respectful, and authentic. This may take some humility.

Therapy looks different for each individual and each family, as it is tailored to specific needs. Are there any areas in your life in which you feel confused, inadequate, or like you simply need a more thorough education? Could you and your family use some professional help in learning to communicate more candidly without the discomfort of being misunderstood? Is your child shut down and not sharing their self with you? Therapy could be the perfect catharsis that you and your family need in order to strengthen and grow.

As you go through the process of finding a therapist, don't forget to answer the questions in *Working by Their Side*. Notate any research, list questions that arise, and take the notes to whichever therapist you choose to confide in. In those initial meetings of therapy, you will be months ahead if you have done the exercise of journaling in advance.

> **Pause and Write**
>
> Please go to *Working by Their Side*, and follow the sequence of questions, thoughts, and ideas from the categories discussed above.

Does This Feel Familiar?

Puzzle Pieces

My husband and I have raised two girls. I guess we are still raising them, in a way, but they are both over twenty now, and so technically adults. I *love* having adult "kids." They are so darn much fun! And like jigsaw puzzles, things are starting to fit for both of them. It hasn't been easy. Lots of twists and turns and putting pieces in the wrong place.

When we had girls, I thought, *Wow, how easy this will be! I "get" girls. I know how to talk to girls, how to parent girls, etc.* I could not have been more wrong! Just as my husband and I are different, our girls are also individuals. Same gene pool, but drastically different personalities.

We've done our share of thinking that our girls needed to fit into different shapes, if you will, guiding them in directions that were not the path they needed or wanted to take. There were times my husband and I did not agree and sought out help. Raising kids can feel like a circus act most of the time. Sometimes the best advice comes from friends who are in the same stage of life. It's so incredibly helpful to have access to a community of parents who are struggling with similar issues. But sometimes therapy is necessary. I believe in *any* therapy that can heal wounds, build bridges, and keep your family together.

So my husband and I participated in couples therapy. I was leading the charge, and my husband went dragging his feet and dreading each session. As uncomfortable and painful as it was for both of us at times, we believe we came away from the experience with tools that have been very helpful to us even years later. We most definitely understood each other better. That was half the battle. As we age, we most definitely change, and learning to accept the differences in each other was a big hurdle for us. Sometimes it takes a third party to help uncover the real issues causing the anger or fear one or both of you are experiencing. Finding the right fit is critical, however. If the first one or two therapists you try out don't feel right, it's OK to keep looking. It's a little like dating. You want to feel comfortable and free to express your fears and concerns in an environment that is supportive, caring, and free of any judgment. The right therapist can help you learn to communicate your needs and express those needs to your partner in a fair and loving way. We discovered that a lot of our struggles stemmed from our different parenting styles and from the pressures of raising kids while working, paying bills, and just keeping our heads above water. We learned that good, effective communication skills are critically important and that knowing how best to communicate with various individuals can be an exhausting effort. But there is no perfect!

We are all kidding ourselves if we think perfection is an attainable goal. There is no such thing! And we can't expect that of our children either. Making our kids feel that they have to "measure up" to a certain standard that is not realistic is completely unfair. It actually helped our girls to see us try and fail on occasion. And it helped them to see us have conflict and work to find a resolution. If we don't model that for our kids, they will not learn it any other way. We are their teachers, whether we like it or not. Don't be afraid to be real with them. As different as my husband and I are, I admire and appreciate him for so many reasons, mostly because he is very measured and contemplative. Like our older daughter, he does not rush into conversations or decisions. He loves our girls dearly and is totally stoked when they come to him with their concerns.

Our girls have taken advice from us and either used it or transformed it to create their own tableau. They have also sought advice from academic advisors and friends and made their own determinations about what will work best for them in life. *That*, in our opinion, is a win-win. Our hope has always been that our girls will find their passion. I attended a parenting seminar when the girls were young. The gist of the information presented was to let your children make their own mistakes. Don't always give them the answers. We all learn through failure. It's hard to sit back and let failure happen when you are a parent. But there is so much personal strength and self-confidence to be gained from falling down, picking yourself back up, and trying again . . . and again, and again, and again.

When the girls were young, being there to help pick up the broken pieces was something we felt we needed and wanted to do as their parents. Putting those pieces back together, however, was something *they* needed to do for themselves. Early on, I realized my reactions to them were also very different. Our older daughter is quiet—a thinker. She takes an inordinate amount of time to make a decision. She weighs all options, evaluates outcomes, and then carefully, slowly makes up her mind. Our youngest is loud—a talker. She makes knee-jerk decisions. She picks the best, prettiest, brightest, shiniest options and makes up her mind in a nanosecond. This caused me to speak and listen to them in very different ways.

With our older daughter, I have to ask a question or plant a seed and wait for her to process the information and eventually react or answer. When I am communicating with my younger daughter, I have to be a little more proactive and quick on my feet. As she matures, however, she is showing more signs of thoughtful consideration of various issues. That growth is fun to watch!

What pleases us the most is watching them build their own puzzles.

Our girls are as different in personality as night and day, so we had to learn on the job how to react to them and support them, each in their own way. Guess that's what keeps it interesting and keeps us on our toes. They are their own puzzles. Different shapes, different pictures. Both beautiful.

—A dad and mom putting the puzzle together

Treatments and Therapies

The cycle is self-obsession, for I think the world is looking at me, but I suppose this is simply how I interpret it to be. No matter if hatred or narcissism, it is one and the same. Self-abuse, a form of self-obsession, is a trepidation-inducing game. Fear will keep you locked in the castle of your mind . . . waiting for a Prince Charming to tell you that you're worthy of his time. But this life is *not about me* . . . No. So my proposition is as follows: filling body, mind, and soul with self-hate leads to nothing but an existence that is hollow.

—From the diary of a teen battling anorexia

10 Treatment and Various Options

> Securing treatment and accepting help from professionals reduces the burden and worry. We become more clear minded and more powerful advocates.

It felt excruciating. I was scared, afraid, and upset. I hated every single aspect of treatment, and I was surprised by the amount of anger I felt toward my parents for having admitted me. I thought that they were overreacting. I had convinced myself that I wasn't *that* bad. In the midst of an eating disorder, I was truly incapable of understanding my need for treatment and professional help. I now feel immense gratitude for my parents' bravery and commitment to my recovery. Their tough love saved my life, and their willingness to make the tough decisions ultimately led to my recovery.

—One who has recovered

How does a guardian know when it is time to move forward with treatment for their loved one? This is a difficult but defining question. First and foremost, if your child is in medical danger, take them to the nearest emergency ward. The staff there will walk you through the next steps and options regarding treatment.

Knowing the right moment to move forward with treatment is often complicated, not always a strategic plan, and sometimes a repetitive effort. Do not delay the decision to get your child help.

Parents should seek treatment for their children when a need is identified. Delaying treatment for the child can be damaging not only physically but also mentally. Having a good understanding as to how the eating disorder is affecting the child and those around them can determine how soon one will initiate treatment. The first conversation between the parents and child regarding treatment can be uncomfortable. There are many reasons as to why, such as a lack of education related to eating disorders, treatment facilities, and recovery; being in denial; and fear of the unknown outcome. It helps when facilities offer a comprehensive intake to help patients and parents gain a better understanding as to what to expect from their program. When I encounter families struggling with the decision to place their child in a higher level of care, I recommend they educate themselves on all treatment options, research local and regional facilities, envision what ideal treatment would look like, and then accept what the reality of treatment will look like based on the options they have. It is vital for parents and children to find a practitioner with whom they are able to build a rapport and develop a trusting relationship. A strong practitioner will educate the family and allow them the appropriate space to begin the process of healing the pain experienced through these disorders. Sometimes it helps just to talk to the child about how much their disorder is affecting them in everyday settings, such as school, church, social clubs, family events, and affecting their health. This will assist with making a decision, especially if the child is on board. I also find that parents who seek processing and supportive groups within their community composed of others who are experiencing the same challenges tend to become more confident in their decision to leave their child behind for treatment. Having the ability to understand that you are not alone can help put your worries at ease.

—ShaQuaila Burrell (LCSW), a psychiatric social
worker at Parkland Health & Hospital System with
more than ten years of experience in public health.

Her patient population includes those struggling
with mental illness, such as eating disorders.

When considering treatment, there are many variables to think about within the structure of the loved one's current lifestyle. You will know when the time is right, but that does not mean it will always be a smooth transition. Interrupting life for treatment is never a fun and exciting adventure, but it may be the deciding factor in saving your loved one's life. Always—and we mean always—the earlier you choose to address an eating disorder, the higher probability of restoring health.

So how will you know? Listen to that true, internal voice that we call intuition. How do you really feel about the behavior and symptoms you are witnessing from your loved one? Are you in denial that there is a problem? Are they in denial? Are you making excuses for new patterns of behavior, weight loss, or odd food habits? Are they making excuses for themselves? Very honestly, is there just something that is not right, but you can't put your finger on it? Do you know treatment is needed, but you are too intimidated, worried, or just downright scared to send your loved one away? If so, you are not alone. Many of us writing in this book have had to send a loved one away for treatment. It was difficult. It was necessary.

I went to the office of a friend whose firstborn child had battled an eating disorder in her teens, and through my tears of fear and frustration I said, "I do not know what to do." My friend then explained the taxing days and nights of her worry and frustration, her fear that her child would never get past the eating disorder and die a pitiful death. She said they'd come to a crossroad and had not known what to do. They changed therapists four times and finally found a fit and a treatment center. They admitted their precious teenage child into full-time residential care at an eating-disorder treatment center.

"It was against the will of my child, who screamed, cried, and begged me not to do this to her. We had to engage a social worker to come and physically take my child from our home. I wept, threw up, and felt a physical pain that tore the heart right out of my chest. But our decision saved her life."

Their child, now a healthy adult and a mom herself, eventually thanked her parents profusely for making her go to the treatment center. My friend still feels the pain and anguish from that day and was teary eyed to relive it in words. She went on to explain the tender heart of a mother and that there are times you have to guard your heart in a steel cage. Then my friend looked at me and said, "Do the hard thing. You have to do the hard thing!"

—Parents who did the hard thing and took their children to treatment

Next Steps to Take Now: Putting One Foot in Front of the Other

Let's begin with a general guide to standard types of treatment options. The options begin with critical condition treatment, then infrequent outpatient needs, then aftercare. According to NEDA, "Getting a diagnosis is only the first step towards recovery from an eating disorder. Treating an eating disorder generally involves a combination of psychological and nutritional counseling, along with medical and psychiatric monitoring. Treatment must address the eating disorder symptoms and medical consequences, as well as psychological, biological, interpersonal, and cultural forces that contribute to or maintain the eating disorder."[1]

The name and definitions of treatment options vary between different consortiums, but here are the five basics:

---

1   "Treatment," National Eating Disorders Association, 2018, https://www. nationaleatingdisorders.org/treatment.

- **Inpatient hospitalization.** The patient is critical enough to be hospitalized for medical stabilization. Restoring weight, dealing with medical complications, and treating coexisting illnesses like depression and anxiety are common. The length of time is determined by the patient's progress. Once stable, the patient is released to a residential care program. When a patient is suicidal or in medical danger, take them to the nearest emergency room. The doctors and staff will stabilize the individual and offer treatment suggestions.

- **Residential care.** The patient is stable enough to live in a twenty-four-hour facility or residential care program and does not have an acute medical condition. All treatment, physical and psychological, occurs under one roof. A personalized treatment plan is created with a team consisting of (but not limited to) a psychiatrist, therapist, dietitian, group therapy, and, when ready, family therapy. A patient learns behavioral changes and coping skills. They deal with past traumas and emotional pain, work to eat intuitively, identify triggers, and restore one's love of self and others. The patient works full time in an effort to restore mental and physical health. The length of one's stay is determined both by insurance and by how the patient reacts to healing. It could be thirty days, or it could be two years. When people refer to a "treatment center," most often they are referring to residential care.

- **Intensive outpatient (IOP).** The patient is enrolled in a treatment facility or hospital setting but sleeps at home or wherever they are living. Most of the time, the patient maintains partial activities outside of treatment, like limited school or work. Outpatient can be taxing on caretakers, but if sleeping at home stabilizes the patient and feels safe, we recommend it, especially for younger children. The learned skill sets and treatment plans are similar to residential care but less restrictive. They meet in a group and are therapeutically led by a trained professional. The length of stay varies depending on the success of balancing daily living while positively contesting negative behaviors. Individuals in IOP meet with the group one to four times a week for several hours at a time until released by their doctor. Depending upon the age of the individual, parents most often participate in IOP. We suggest you get involved; it's a wonderful learning tool for you as well.

- **Outpatient.** Outpatient care is less frequent and a less restrictive level of treatment employed as the patient integrates back into daily life. The patient is medically and psychiatrically stable and able to function comfortably as they continue to make healthy decisions. The individual may still be a patient of the IOP team or engage in individual treatment with a licensed professional such as a therapist and dietitian.

- Aftercare. Before a patient is "discharged" from treatment, it is important to secure a nurturing aftercare scenario in order to maintain support in hopes of successful long-term healing. Sometimes this plan is put in place and loosely monitored by the treatment team, but it can also be an actual place of residence. Depending upon the age of the patient, the aftercare location may or may not be at home. Because relapse is a reality, an aftercare program feels essential for both accountability and productive healing. There is not a 100 percent guarantee that your loved will overcome the disorder once they go to treatment. Aftercare helps prevent relapse. Please see chapter 13 for more information on extended care and aftercare treatment.

Unfortunately, it's the curveballs in life that continue to bring our daughter back into a terrifying, unhealthy state. Whether it be the loss of a loved one, anxiety over a new job, or transition into new living conditions, some of these major changes in her life have caused the eating disorder to rear its ugly head. After two treatment centers in a three-year period, we're very aware that relapse is not uncommon. We will continue to encourage continued outpatient therapy, praying that she's gaining strength and tools to deal with whatever the future holds.

—A fighter

Below are six thoughts to help you move forward in your decision-making. You will have to weigh your options with honest conversation, evaluating the stage of life your child, your family, and you are currently in. You are not alone in this fight. Please know that good, positive treatment can be beautifully life-altering. Be creative, be persistent, and, above all, be honest with yourself and your loved ones.

Ask for Help

Ask for help and referrals from anyone you know who has walked (or currently is walking) this path before you. We say this over and over in this book because you are not alone and you do not have to start from scratch. There already is a square one—and much, much more! Reach out for help.

Collaborate with Professionals

How do you choose which treatment is right for your loved one? Set up a consultation with a licensed specialist in eating disorders, and meet with them face to face. If you are not in the same city, try FaceTime, Skype, or a similar program. Explain the situation, and as they offer opinions, ask yourself: "Does this feel right? Is there hope in the message? Is this professional understanding our needs? Are we communicating fluidly?" When choosing which treatment option seems best for your loved one, your family, and you, collaborating with the potential professionals is critical. When you make a final choice, be prepared to work together, pool resources, participate by offering your understanding of the current circumstances, and communicate openly. Then be prepared to listen and learn. And if your choice of treatment does not work as planned, change it.

Do Your Own Research as You Seek
Treatment for Your Loved One

We recommend you do some research on your own to find the most affordable and suitable treatment for your family. All family dynamics are different, so you must be realistic with what works for your loved one, you, and your family. For instance, it is important to consider the center's location, how appropriate it is for your child's age, and whether it has a religious affiliation or not. There are hundreds of treatment centers; here are some good sites on which to start your search.

- EDReferral: EDReferral.com

- Eating Disorder Treatment Reviews: EDTreatmentReview.com

- National Eating Disorders Association (NEDA): NationalEatingDisorders.org

- National Association of Anorexia Nervosa and Associated Disorders (ANAD): ANAD.org/our-services/treatment-directory

- Eating Disorder Hope: EatingDisorderHope.com

- The Treatment Specialist: TheTreatmentSpecialist.com/mental-health/eating-disorders/

- Multi-Service Eating Disorders Association (MEDA): MEDAInc.org/services/heal/find-a-treatment-facility/

Stay Within Your Financial Means

You must try to be realistic and know there are limits to when, how, and how much one can spend on treatment. We will do almost anything in the world to help heal our loved ones, but we try to be as reasonable as possible. You, as the adult, are responsible for making the monetary decisions; your child is not. Do not discuss cost or any problems associated with this expensive venture, especially if there is financial strain. It will trigger shame and put undue burdens upon your child. Do what you can financially to help your child, but recognize and respect your monetary limits.

If you have a self-sufficient adult child living outside of the home and carrying their own insurance plan, then you can, and should, talk financial details. If they are invested financially, they will be more serious about the treatment.

Mind Your Physical and Mental Health

There will be times when you are maxed out. Be considerate of your own physical limits, and react accordingly. Take care of your physical health, however that works best for you. There will be times when you are emotionally spent. Again, stop and assess your needs for clarity of mind. Please know that there are times when you have to say, "I can't," either physically, emotionally or financially. Do not torment yourself over feeling inadequate or unable to spend a particular amount of money on treatment. You might be doing your absolute best, but you are human. We do have limitations.

Seek Your Own Worth

Often, much emphasis and devotion is spent on teaching patients to "love your body." This is a common theme in treatment. It is great if you love your body—few really do—but what if we accept, appreciate, and feel gratitude for our body, but love our soul?

> Now that my daughter has been taught this healing concept of loving your body, she's finally asking, "Why do we have to love our bodies? Why can't we put the emphasis and attention on other things that have nothing to do with our looks or our bodies—like our talents, our hearts, our interests, our future? Taking our minds *off* of our bodies is the most beneficial thing to help with our recovery!"
>
> —A listening mother

A decade ago, there were twenty-two treatment centers for eating disorders. Today, there are more than seventy-five in America alone.[2] Is this because eating disorders are rampant in our Western society? Yes, that's one reason. Additionally, in 2008, the Mental Health Parity and Addiction Equity Act[3] was passed, requiring insurance companies to cover mental illnesses, such as eating disorders, and addiction treatment. Then, in 2010, Obama's Affordable Care Act furthered the cause.[4]

This burst in growth gives parents and caretakers options, as treatment centers have different philosophies toward restoring the health of their patients. It also makes choosing treatment more complex. Location,

---

2   Erica Goode, "Centers to Treat Eating Disorders Are Growing, and Raising Concerns," March 14, 2016, https://www.nytimes.com/2016/03/15/health/eating-disorders-anorexia-bulimia-treatment-centers.html.

3   "Mental Health Parity and Addiction Equity Act (MHPAEA)," Centers for Medicare & Medicaid Services, https://www.cms.gov/CCIIO/Programs-and-Initiatives/Other-Insurance-Protections/MHPAEA.html.

4   Cecilia Muñoz, "The Affordable Care Act and Expanding Mental Health Coverage," August 21, 2013, https://obamawhitehouse.archives.gov/blog/2013/08/21/affordable-care-act-and-expanding-mental-health-coverage.

financial wherewithal, in-network facilities, the patient's health condition, and the patient's age all play a role in the decision. It is a personal decision that depends on your desire for faith-based treatment versus secular, inner-city locations versus rural acres in the countryside, or a hospital setting and philosophy versus a comfortable center that offers fun activities. We cannot recommend the best option or comment on what we perceive to be the worst treatment centers, but we can assure you that the earlier you get help for your loved one, the higher the probability of full and comprehensive healing. We can also tell you that relying on professionals to help your loved one reduces the burden on a caretaker. If you think it is time (or past time) to send your loved one to treatment, please know that hundreds of us have endured the dilemma, and you will get through to the other side. You will.

Please refer to the appendix in this book for more details on the MHPAEA and the Affordable Care Act.

Doing the hard thing can be momentarily painful, but the payoff for your loved one's future is worth it.

Pause and Write

Please go to *Working by Their Side*, and follow the sequence of questions, thoughts, and ideas from the categories above.

Does This Feel Familiar?

My best college friend.

She had been back from inpatient treatment for about three weeks the first time we ventured out to dinner together. The act was familiar enough for both of us: picking our path across the campus lawn in the fading light, navigating around a group of kids playing touch football. The air was still so warm that even she couldn't be cold, and as we walked, we talked about the unremarkable items of the day in a remarkably ordinary way. Surely it had been just a handful of months, but it seemed so incredibly long ago that we were last this at ease in each other's company.

In truth, her downward spiral had been a very quick one—and probably not entirely unpredictable. We met as fresh-faced freshmen girls, both the furthest from home we had ever been for any significant period of time, both so excited to finally be there. Our connection was pretty much immediate, and in the way of dorm life, we became inseparable in what, in retrospect, seems like a matter of minutes. There were several months of relative normalcy—just long enough to forget there was ever a time when we weren't friends. Long enough to be convinced we knew each other better than anyone else knew us. And then, before I even noticed what was happening, this sweet friend of mine became a different person altogether. This girl, widely known for her belly laughs, for her buoyancy, her light . . . Even with our special brand of best-friend humor, I couldn't coax a smile from her.

Ever the fixer, I tried my damnedest to break through the wall that seemed to have gone up around her. I had dealt with eating disorders before; I knew how this worked. I figured persistence was key. I tried to make her talk any chance I got. Worse, I tried to make her eat. I barked orders, I pushed, I chided, I threatened. She withdrew further. I redoubled my efforts. I labeled her behaviors. I studied the smallest details of her life, trying to micromanage any stressors but somehow only adding to her pain. And eventually, inevitably, everything good about our friendship evaporated, leaving nothing but bitterness behind.

And so it felt like an unexpected gift that evening, as we walked to dinner, as we ordered our matching salads and embraced our return to normalcy, when I felt a streak of hope reach up through my chest. I was going to get her back, and it was going to be exactly what it had been before. That perfect, sunny relationship we'd had, where we just "got" each other, and all we ever did was giggle. I think she must have felt bold that evening, too, perhaps encouraged by a similar hope, because when I suggested we cap off the night with an old tradition—a soft-serve cone from McDonald's—she agreed.

I knew she was trying. I knew she wanted to eat that ice cream. I even knew that she knew how much it meant to me that she eat it. But she couldn't stomach it, and suddenly, I was livid. Eat the freaking ice cream already! After two bites, she was sick.

We walked back to the dorm in a shattered silence, disgusted and disappointed in ourselves and in each other, and we didn't speak again for several months. I couldn't look at her without feeling this terrible mix of simultaneous frustration and anger, overlaid with embarrassment at my own lack of empathy or understanding. I knew about eating disorders. I knew how this worked. So why was I so mad at her?

I learned a lot about myself in trying to process those feelings. I learned that I am not a particularly patient person. Further, my patience is at its most limited when dealing with those closest to me. I learned that I am controlling, and I detest situations I cannot manage. I realized I am not the great listener I'd envisioned myself to be. I've been working on all of that. I also learned I cannot fix someone else. I've learned that I have a tendency to be very unforgiving when it comes to my own bad behavior, a trait that has yet to prove itself helpful. I learned that no amount of reading or talking or researching could ever really make me understand what it is like to have an eating disorder—that there's a big difference between saying, "It's about control," and actually having any clue what that might mean. I realized how easily disappointment and fear turn into something else entirely, and as a result, I'm much more likely to step back and inspect my feelings nowadays, just to be sure I'm dealing with what I think I'm dealing with. I have also learned that time is an impossible concept when you've been hurt and that healing consists of many shades of gray. Years later, I can say we salvaged the relationship. I can say we are friends who made it through a really terrible thing. But we are not the same friends we were, and I know now that hoping for that was hoping for too much. We are friends who have spent a great many hours and an immeasurable quantity of tears trying to sort out just how we got so hurt by each other, how we can let go of that, how we can make an eating disorder that never totally went away stop steering our friendship, and how we can accept this changed and flawed version of our relationship as enough. But we are friends, and for that, I am grateful.

—A friend

11 Registered Dietitians and Nutritionists

$$\left[\begin{array}{c} \text{Nutrition is critical to the chemistry of the brain.} \\ \text{Without proper nutrition, brain chemistry is altered} \\ \text{and does not perform in its optimal range.} \end{array} \right]$$

Lack of nutrition can decelerate thoughts, causing both physical and emotional dysmorphia. Dysmorphia is when a person sees and feels abnormalities that are not real except to them.[1] For example, have you heard your underweight child say, "I feel fat"? It makes no sense in your mind, but due to lack of nutrition, the mind of someone struggling with anorexia literally sees his or her body as different from the physical reality. The grip of an eating disorder is much more prevalent when the mind and body are malnourished.

For those suffering from anorexia, a starved brain makes it difficult to engage in therapy, so nutritional weight restoration is critical to the recovery process. With this said, a dietitian or nutritionist is an important part of the success of the treatment team.

Sadly, we have seen a substantial amount of harm caused by alleged dietitians and nutritionists who do not have expertise in eating disorders. An exorbitant amount of time is wasted unwinding the misguided information. For example, calorie counting is a negative learned behavior. Today, there are many dietitians and nutritionists who do not ask their clients to keep a count of their caloric intake. Once a person masters calorie counting,

---

1 "Body Dysmorphic Disorder," Diseases & Conditions, Mayo Foundation for Medical Education and Research, last modified 2019, https://www.mayoclinic.org/diseases-conditions/body-dysmorphic-disorder/symptoms-causes/syc-20353938.

they cannot reverse the issue later in life. Like unwinding your ABCs or the simple math of 2 + 2 = 4, it is impossible to unlearn the patterns. That is only one example of why it is critical to hire a licensed dietitian or nutritionist who is experienced with eating disorders.

> I have this story in my head—a script of how it's "supposed" to be. Filtered, edited, revised, and photoshopped—producing the ideal image of me. I have this story in my head of how I ought to look. A Barbie image, objectified to the media's perfect picture from a never-ending book of rules, regulations, and policies to follow, teaching me that if I do not fit into their definition, I am nothing else but unlovable. So, bleeding, aching, hurting, I strive to stand up to this perfection. Allowing myself, my body, my appearance to become my one obsession.
>
> —Former victim of an eating disorder

Next Steps to Take Now:
Putting One Foot in Front of the Other

Focus on the big-picture goal of your loved one's freedom. Visualize them cured of negative and distorted thoughts about food and about themselves. Support your loved one's efforts to normalize their eating and to learn to listen to and trust their body's internal hunger cues. The ultimate goal is intuitive social eating. Sharing meals is a social bonding activity in all cultures. Therefore, choose a dietitian or nutritionist who knows that eating is not just about food.

There is no such thing as perfection when it comes to eating and food choices. Every single culture has rituals around eating, specific foods that are preferred, and traditional foods for celebrations. Many people have peculiar food habits; some are vegetarians, gluten-free, or nondairy, and though their habits might be odd or their choices narrow, they do not have an eating disorder that constantly interrogates their thoughts, projecting negativity, self-hatred, and shame. There is a difference—a difference so vast that the disorder is actually trying to kill the sufferer in the form of a slow suicide. Though that sounds harsh, it is true. An eating disorder is a mental illness that controls the mind, behaviors, and perspectives. Comprehensive healing happens when the disorder no longer controls the person's thoughts. Then, there are no more hateful thoughts discrediting their existence. It truly is not just about the food, though at first, the intake of food is critical to restoring health. Learning to be comfortable with and around food is also critical and a difficult step for many people struggling with an eating disorder. Comprehensive healing, however, is about alleviating the mental illness that constantly degrades, humiliates, and finally convinces people they are not worthy of living.

It is important that you engage a dietitian or nutritionist who understands eating disorders, as there are consequences to what your loved one learns. Please hire an accredited and qualified dietitian or nutritionist. If you would like to investigate this subject, see the updated articles at the Nutrition.gov website for more information.[2] Below are eight things to consider to help you move forward when hiring a dietitian or nutritionist. (Note: if your loved one is in a treatment center, they will be assigned to a staff dietitian or nutritionist.)

Understand the Options and Differences between Dietitians and Nutritionists

Dietitians and nutritionists should always be part of a multidisciplinary team including physicians, psychiatrists, and therapists. It is considered unethical if one is the only health professional treating a patient with an eating disorder.

> The management of an eating disorder requires a multi-disciplinary team consisting of a medical doctor, a psychiatrist, therapist, family members, and a nutritionist (or R.D.) who specializes in eating disorders. If a nutritionist decides to take on the task of working with eating disorder clients, it is essential that they work as a "team player". In fact, one might consider it unethical for

---

2   "Eating Disorders," Nutrition.gov, last modified May 8, 2019, https://www.nutrition.gov/subject/nutrition-and-health-issues/eating-disorders.

a nutritionist to be working alone and treating a client with an eating disorder. Being part of this team allows each team member to be the most effective in their role, minimizing "triangulation and splitting," and allows continued communication between all parties involved. While each team member's role within the team can often overlap, and the goal of recovery for the client remains cohesive, it is important to remember that each team member has specific boundaries.[3]

The different titles, certifications, and acronyms change with new development in the field and can be a bit confusing if you are just starting the journey of seeking help. Find someone both you and your loved one jell with. If your loved one is over eighteen years old, helping them find a satisfactory fit is wonderful, but ultimately, they get to choose. The relationship should always be professional. Though you always have to trust your doctors, it is usually not the case that you will form a friendship. Please be cognizant of choosing a person who is well trained, for an unaccredited/unlicensed individual can unintentionally harm the psyche of a person struggling with negative body image. Time, training, and knowledge will give way to new and various titles for dietitians and nutritionists. Please do additional research until you feel informed.

A friend suggested I take my athletic child to a "nutritionist." Naïvely, I did, and within twenty minutes of conversation, the nutritionist had suggested my child was too heavy and her BMI was unhealthy. What my daughter heard was, "You are fat!" She was only twelve years old. It was the final tipping point, and she began to starve herself. It took her almost eight years to get beyond anorexia and the self-loathing feeling of "I am fat." So sad. If only I had known.

—A once-naïve mom

3   Karin Kaplan Grumet, "The Role of the Registered Dietitian/Nutritionist on the Eating Disorder Team," Gürze-Salucore Eating Disorders Resource Catalogue, June 5, 2014, www.edcatalogue.com/role-registered-dietitian-nutritionist-eating-disorder-team-2/.

Registered dietitians (RDs) and registered dietitian nutritionists (RDNs) have completed the rigorous academic and experiential prerequisites required by the Accreditation Council for Education in Nutrition and Dietetics (ACEND). A RD or RDN is a specialist who has expertise in nutrition, foods, nourishment, their effects on the body, and the science of nutrition. Many of us writing this book have been happy to work with RD/RDNs, most especially when they are experienced with eating disorders. These professionals have met all national and international legal standards, completed an accredited internship, and passed the registration exam; they are registered, licensed, and legally protected, they carry the professional title of RD or RDN, and they are required to maintain their educational requirements.

Nutritionists have varying definitions. Unlike an RD or RDN, the law does not protect the title of "nutritionist." Individuals who refer to themselves this way may or may not have nutritional education, a four-year bachelor's degree in nutrition, or a master's degree. Not all nutritionists are dietitians, so be careful when choosing a qualified professional.[4]

A certified nutrition specialist (CNS) is an accredited nutrition expert who must complete a master's degree or doctoral degree, complete a thousand hours of supervised experience, pass the certification exam, and maintain their certification by continuing professional education. If you choose to hire a nutritionist, please ask about their experience with eating disorders and professional education.[5]

A holistic nutritionist promotes an integrative approach to eating by emphasizing optimal health for mind, body, and soul. There are several educationally proficient holistic nutritionist programs. Holistic nutrition seems to have a bright and promising future as an emerging field, but many states do not regulate the use of this title. Again, if you choose to go

---

4   "What Is a Registered Dietitian Nutritionist," eatrightPRO, Academy of Nutrition and Dietetics, last modified 2019, https://www.eatrightpro.org/about-us/what-is -an-rdn-and-dtr/what-is-a-registered-dietitian-nutritionist.

5   Federal Trade Commission, *Table I: Comparison of CNS, RD, and CCN Board Certification Requirements*, https://www.ftc.gov/system/files/documents/public_comments /2014/03/00012-88800.pdf; "How to Become a Certified Nutrition Specialist® ™," NutritionED.org, https://www.nutritioned.org/certified-nutrition-specialist.html.

the holistic route, please make sure the individual is experienced in eating disorders.

> Holistic nutrition is the modern natural approach to developing a healthy balanced diet while taking into account the person as a whole. Holistic nutrition is considered to be part of holistic health. . . . Food not only provides the energy needed to function in our daily lives but constantly supplies the nutrients which are required to build and regenerate body tissue, bone, muscle, fat and blood. The nutrients in food are also necessary to produce substances for the chemical processes that take place in our bodies millions of times a day.[6]

Naturopaths are licensed doctors of naturopathic medicine (ND, NMD) and have completed a four-year graduate-level program accredited by the Council on Naturopathic Medical Education.[7] They are very well-educated, as the first two years of a naturopathic medical degree are the same as for traditional medical students. Naturopathic doctors take a holistic approach when possible, yet most NDs are willing to work in conjunction with medical doctors (MDs). Licensed naturopaths can assess your child scientifically (through blood work) and deal naturally with imbalances in the brain and body through science. They are also seen as nutritionists and educators on the subject of health. Please refer to the "Therapies, Practices, and Innovative Treatments" section of the book for more information.

Nutritional therapists are popular and individualized. A registered nutritional therapist desires to administer the right foods and nutrients to link physical and mental health. Nutritional therapists attempt to rehabilitate behavior regarding food in hopes of stabilizing, and eventually normalizing, a client's eating pattern; however, this is not the same as nutrition counseling. When dealing with eating disorders, most nutritional therapy is overseen by an RD.

---

6   "Holistic Nutrition," Holistic Nutrition: A Nutritionist's Guide to Holistic Health, http://www.holisticnutrition.com/.

7   "The Council on Naturopathic Medical Education," Council on Naturopathic Medical Education, 2019, https://cnme.org/.

Nutrition therapy is a critical component in the recovery from an eating disorder. Therapy with a qualified nutritionist will include discussions on current food intake and its adequacy to maintain health. Counseling also includes discussions of food restrictions, self-imposed food rules and personal attributes ascribed to foods. Locating a nutritionist with both knowledge and compassion for recovery is essential.[8]

Beware! Traditional eating-disorder dietitians or nutritionists are specialists who meet with the client and devise a structured plan to monitor food intake with "food logs" while sticking to a certain meal plan with caloric boundaries. Asking a patient to count calories in an attempt to get enough nutrition each day is a dangerous and very slippery slope, especially for teens. Once a person starts monitoring food by keeping count of calories, they cannot unwind their knowledge of numbers. We believe counting calories keeps a patient in the eating-disorder mind-set. It becomes an obsession and makes comfortable, intuitive social eating much more difficult to reach. We absolutely do not endorse calorie counting.

Having said that, here are other controversial—yet common—methods we recommend you avoid:

- Calorie counting. You cannot unlearn this once learned.

- Weighing clients. The number on the scale can keep a person in the disorder.

- Body mass index (BMI). This is not measurable for everyone on the charts, and some people do not fit the "averages."

- Low-weight acceptance.

- A stigma of "being in shape."

- Eating only "healthy" foods. Restricting the diet to only so-called healthy foods can be confusing for someone struggling with an eating disorder. Of course, eating healthily is important, but an anorexic can intentionally (or unintentionally) abuse this notion.

---

8   "How Can I Find a Nutritionist Who Treats Eating Disorders?," EDReferral, https://www.edreferral.com/nutritionist-near-me-for-eating-disorder-help.

Get a Referral

A referral from a friend or acquaintance who has hands-on experience with a specific dietitian or nutritionist is the best way to move forward. You might also check with any doctors or therapists with whom you are currently involved, such as your child's school counselor or school nurse, the local health clinic, or a college advisor. If you do not have access to a referral, please do some research online. Try searching the International Federation of Eating Disorder Dietitians[9] by entering your zip code to find help near you. Also search EDReferral.com[10] or Eating Disorder Hope.[11] For more details about these organizations, please refer to the appendix.

Consult with Your Child's Therapist or Doctor about Whom to Hire

If your child is currently in therapy, ask the therapist whom they recommend as a dietitian or nutritionist or whether they are familiar with the person you have hired. It is imperative they work together. Your therapist takes the lead in helping put the treatment team together.

Your child's therapist and dietitian/nutritionist are most constructive when working together and both communicating with you. It is unethical for a dietitian/nutritionist to work solo with an eating-disorder client.

Ask the therapist's thoughts and recommendations on licensed dietitians, holistic nutritionists, traditional eating-disorder dietitians/nutritionists, naturopaths, and nutrition therapy. If they are not well versed in the answers, ask them for a referral to speak to someone who is experienced.

Ask the Potential Dietitian/Nutritionist Questions

If possible, set up a consultation with the dietitian/nutritionist before you hire them and before they meet with your child. Ask questions like:

---

9   "Treatment Finder," Federation of Eating Disorder Dietitians, http://www.eddietitians.com/treatment-finder/.

10 "Nutrition Therapy and Eating Disorders," EDReferral, www.edreferral.com/nutrition.

11 "Eating Disorder Hope™ - Resources for Anorexia, Bulimia & Binge Eating," Eating Disorder Hope, 2019, https://www.eatingdisorderhope.com/.

- How much does a session cost?

- Do you take insurance?

- Are you licensed? If so, what is your education?

- What is your experience with eating disorders?

- Will you communicate with me? How often? With my child's therapist? How often?

- Can I contact you, and should I expect a return response?

- What are the boundaries between us?

- If my child is eighteen years of age or older, what is to be expected of me as the parent? Will you still communicate with me?

- Do you weigh your clients? How often, and why?

- Do you measure BMI? Why or why not?

- Will you grocery shop with my child or share a meal? (Some dietitians will shop for food and help prepare and eat meals with patients and sometimes with their families. We have found this to be very helpful but not common.)

- What is your opinion on traditional eating-disorder dietitians/nutritionists—in particular, the practice of things like calorie counting and keeping food logs? (As a reminder: we do not recommend these traditional methods.)

- Are there any new and innovative treatments you apply that have been successful?

Understand Refeeding

Refeeding is the act of reintroducing nutrition/food to patients who are severely malnourished. Refeeding is most common in the treatment of anorexia or of a person who suffers from a severe medical issue. It seems easy enough to say, "Just eat!" but refeeding is a serious and methodical process that should be monitored under the care of a doctor. If not done slowly and monitored correctly, complications such as "refeeding syndrome" can occur. When starving, the body is in a catabolic state, breaking down tissue for nutrients. Once an individual begins eating again, the body shifts to an anabolic state of rebuilding. Due to the change in metabolism and because the body is hungry, a release of hormones occurs that can cause severe imbalances and complications. If your loved one is severely starved, take them to a hospital or treatment facility.

We highly recommend you work with an accredited dietitian or nutritionist who understands eating disorders and refeeding.

If your loved one is currently in treatment, the treatment team will know how to handle this issue. Let them do their job; refeeding a body is an intricate balance. As a caretaker, this is a good time to learn and be educated. It is also the time to be the most loving advocate possible. Refeeding is very emotionally hard for those suffering from anorexia or starvation; your children will need your support.

Understand Intuitive Social Eating

The ultimate dream of health when it comes to nutrition is intuitive social eating, and sometimes, freedom must be allowed to manage this. Remember, eating disorders are about underlying emotional issues; they are not just about the food. Intuitive eating is about becoming both familiar and in tune with natural hunger signals. We also include the word *social* because eating comfortably with others is essential to the balance of life. When it is achieved, intuitive eating becomes an effective way of maintaining healthy weight rather than keeping track of the amount of calories. It also feels more normal in the social bonding that occurs when eating with others, which is very important for the rest of a person's life.

In their newly revised book *Intuitive Eating: A Revolutionary Program That Works*, 3rd ed., doctors Evelyn Tribole and Elyse Resch give the reader a complete understanding of this concept. They reference ten principles of intuitive eating:

1. Reject the diet.
2. Honor your hunger.
3. Make peace with food.
4. Challenge the food police.

5. Respect your fullness.
6. Discover the satisfaction factor.
7. Honor your feelings without using food.
8. Respect your body.
9. Exercise—feel the difference.
10. Honor your health.[12]

Learning how to train the brain to think positively about food helps us to use food to both nurture and satisfy the body without fear or false hope.

For more information on *Intuitive Eating*, please refer to the appendix.

Make a Change if Necessary

Remember, you, as the caretaker, are an important advocate for your loved one. If the relationship with the dietitian or nutritionist is not compatible for your loved one, make a change. Personalities often play a part in the success and potential failure of the work. If you feel the need to employ a different professional, consult with your loved one's therapist or doctor, and ask for a new referral.

Not Sure if You Can Afford a Dietitian or Nutritionist?

Dietitians and nutritional therapists can be very expensive. If you are insured, ask your provider what they reimburse. Please refer to chapter 13 for more information.

If you are currently tight on money and this component is not in the budget, consider the following options.

• Ask the other doctors on the treatment team for help.

• Look for scholarship opportunities.

• Negotiate pricing with the professional, and ask for a sliding scale.

• Consult with a NEDA Navigator. These are trained volunteers associated with the National Eating Disorders Association who have firsthand knowledge and experience with eating disorders. Ask for advice and help.

---

12 Evelyn Tribole and Elyse Resch, *Intuitive Eating: A Revolutionary Program That Works*, 3rd ed. (New York: St. Martin's Press, 2012).

- For a list of virtual IFEDD member dietitians, use the treatment finder on the International Federation of Eating Disorder Dietitians website at EDDietitians.com/treatment-finder. These specialist work by phone, video chat, or online.

- If you live in the UK, connect with Nutritionist Resource at Nutritionist-Resource.org.uk/articles/eating-disorders.html.

For more information on how to connect with a NEDA Navigator, please refer to the appendix.

"Registered dietitians," "nutritionists," and "eating" are pretty sticky subjects and involve a variety of options. By no means are we being negative about the extremely important work of these skilled professionals, but once again, trust your intuition, and make the best decision you can on behalf of your child, your family, and yourself. You want a dietitian or nutritionist who helps alleviate the burden of constantly monitoring your loved one's food intake. It is best to be led by the professional. Let them do their job so you can be an advocate for your loved one rather than the food police!

The value of the work can be found in the practical balance of mind, self, and food!

Pause and Write

Take a minute to look at the websites listed in this chapter and in the appendix. Make notes in *Working by Their Side* in hopes of ultimately finding the most suitable fit for a nutritionist or dietitian. This takes time, and you might have to refer back to this part of the workbook several times. Be patient with yourself!

Does This Feel Familiar?

My precious twin, lost to an ED.

The love my sister and I shared was deep, constant, and unconditional. We were soul mates. We were identical twins. We often knew each other's thoughts and feelings without speaking. My sister was energetic, outgoing, positive, and caring. She made you feel important and special.

Both type A pleasers and achievers, my twin sister and I did not really do conflict well. Instead of voicing our negative feelings, we got busier. When I made cheerleader and my sister didn't is, I believe, when she clearly began to feel less popular and less loved than me. My sister was always a little bit of a stronger athlete, a little higher in her grades, yet she never felt the approval of others like she needed. She saw herself as very capable but not necessarily as well liked or as attractive to boys or men. Ironically, she was very well liked. Everyone loved my sister. She was elected class president, was best pledge in her sorority at college, and was in Phi Beta Kappa. These were all things she could achieve—even "control," per se. Yet they were not enough to validate her.

As we grew into young adulthood, she would say that the real issue that caused her eating disorder was her relationship with our mother. But in reality, her addiction started to manifest itself in college. There can be a "blame game" that goes on for ED patients. Perhaps it is easier to cast blame on others or on circumstances rather than own up to our own issues.

She married and had children, but sadly, she could never seem to let go of her ED. And for women with children, the issues of an ED can be transferred to the children. She would want desperately to control their food, their decisions, etc. Her children have never known a well mom. Time after time, they heard, "Mommy is going away to get well." She would come home from treatment centers not well, then go again to "get well." The ED also became a type of parent, in a way. *It* decided where they would go, when they would go, with whom they would go, until finally my sister went nowhere, choosing to stay home with her lover—the ED— instead of engaging in relationships with others. As her health and her ED worsened, her relationships with her husband and boys worsened. This caused more guilt and shame and self-loathing. For more than half of our lives, my "normal" was helping not only her but also her boys and being the go-between for her and her ex-husband. This, too, probably added to her feelings of being incapable. But she was my sister, the twin I so dearly loved, the other part of me.

I resented her illness and hated her ED. I raged at how it had stolen my sister, her boys' mother, our parents' daughter, and her friendships. Everything was stolen by her eating disorder. I felt guilt at my anger. Shouldn't I be more compassionate, more supportive? As my husband or others offered advice, I was angry with them. How could they understand? I became distant, closed off, tired, and sad.

As the ED became more severe and she tried to fight it, she turned to another addiction—alcohol—and cast blame on it for her problems. I don't really remember when she started going to AA meetings, but I do know that she went to two treatment centers for alcoholism. They both sent her home, saying that they could not treat her because her primary addiction was the ED. I believe she used the alcoholism as a red herring so she would not have to address the ED. Yes, she wanted to get well, and she craved community. Alcoholism is accepted—even worn as a badge, sometimes, in our society. People readily tell us they are off to their AA meeting. This is *not* so with an eating disorder. It is a shameful disease, one we do not like to share or talk about. It is ugly, frightening, confusing. There are no twelve steps to recovery!

She would easily talk about her struggles with alcohol. It became a way of keeping me at a distance from her ED. She blamed all her issues on alcoholism. This infuriated me. I found myself resentful of AA and even of her AA friends. I thought, *Those people are so naïve to not see that her biggest problem is her ED!* So I came to a point where I couldn't stand it! I confronted her, telling her that I knew that her ED was the root issue and that I did not want to hear any more about her alcoholism or AA. I was setting a boundary, hoping that this would encourage her to get more help for her ED. I wonder if this caused her more shame, more self-loathing, more disgust with herself at her allowing her ED to rule her life.

Toward the end, she was very self-focused. Almost like she had imploded. She was truly unable to believe that my life had challenges or pain. And let me assure you, though I feel very blessed, my life is not perfect. I am far from perfect. I do have a type A personality. I like a routine. I like to feel in control. But I was never held hostage, and I guess the difference is that I do love my blessed, imperfect life and myself. I realized I did not have to be in control and understood that my Lord didn't compare me or ask me to earn my worthiness. He simply asked me to trust Him and promised that even when life looks completely out of control, He is in control, promising strength and growth and beauty out of life's messiness. My sister knew this, but I wish my sister had learned to surrender to the unequivocal power of God's mercy, not to the power of an ED.

I went through a type of survivor's guilt as I watched the sister I knew and loved disappear. I thought, *Why her and not me?* I often wondered what I could change to help her. I now realize that it was not me—or any of us—who needed to change to help her; it was her perspective that needed to change. Yes, we need to be sensitive, encouraging, and good listeners. But we also need to set boundaries and even to do the hard thing, which can feel like the cruel thing.

In the end, the ED won. The morning my sister died, I felt I knew when she slipped away. I had a strange peace sweep over me. I then received a call that she had died from complications of an eating disorder.

After her death, I realized I had spent more than half of my life caring for her and her ED. I kept hearing from others, "You will find your new normal." I continue to find my new normal, but I do have peace. It is well with my soul. You see, I grieved my sister during the twenty-five years of her illness as she slipped away from me because of the ED. I know that now she is at peace, healed and whole—something she was not here on earth. This is what comforts me; that is what carries me. The ED robbed us of so much, but it never stole our love.

—A sister who lost her twin to an eating disorder

12 Medical Health Insurance for Eating Disorders

[
Currently confusing and seemingly
ever-changing scenarios!
]

Yes, we have to deal with this too. Educating ourselves on insurance can be monotonous, so try to be patient. This is a good time to recruit a knowledgeable friend, family member, associate, or acquaintance for up-to-date help. We have all had to deal with insurance companies—some of us having good experiences, and others very, very, very frustrating experiences. In the end, you alone (or with your spouse or partner) will have to make personal decisions regarding money. By no means do we claim to know everything about the fast-changing world of policies and coverage, but we will share with you what we do know. Note that hospital emergency rooms, inpatient care, treatment centers, and some professionals will guide you through the insurance protocol.

Advocates continue to fight for more sufficient coverage. Sadly, it is frustrating to discover that insurance often covers only a small portion of the expenses for treating psychiatric conditions, but that is changing. For example, the Eating Disorders Coalition (EDC) has advocated for the recognition of eating disorders as a public health priority throughout the United States as they work with Congress on federal policies. (For more information on the EDC, please visit EatingDisordersCoalition. org.) Though many insurance policies come with restrictions regarding mental-health coverage, they are required by law to treat mental illnesses in a way equal to medical illnesses. Finding doctors and treatment in network is less expensive.

If the doctors and treatment you prefer are out of network, you can personally submit expenses and file out of network with your insurance carrier. Out-of-network help is covered at a lower percent or not at all. Learning how to work within the system and obtain adequate coverage is possible.

Next Steps to Take Now:
Putting One Foot in Front of the Other

Talk Directly to the Treatment Center

If your loved one is in treatment or going to treatment, you need to speak directly to that treatment center about health insurance, protocols, and how to obtain the most sufficient coverage.

Review Websites with Insurance Knowledge

The simple answer is for you to investigate online and read about insurance coverage for eating disorders. Start by reviewing insurance advice from the resources listed below; you can also find more resources in the appendix. Please also do your own research, as the world of insurance changes regularly.

- National Eating Disorders Association: NationalEatingDisorders.org/learn/general-information/insurance.

- Center For Discovery: call 800-760-3934, or visit CenterForDiscovery.com/blog/does-your-insurance-plan-cover-eating-disorders/.

- Eating Disorder Hope: EatingDisorderHope.com/search?q=insurance.

- Eating Recovery Center: EatingRecoveryCenter.com/families/insurance. This site's Parent's Guide to Navigating the Insurance Appeals Process is thorough and very informative, should you ever need to appeal and insurance issue: EatingRecoveryCenter.com/ERC/media/global/Families/Guide-Appeals-Process.pdf.

```
┌─────────────────────────────────────────┐
│              Pause and Write              │
│                                           │
│   If you do not understand insurance—and, │
│   admittedly, it is very confusing—please │
│   refer to Working by Their Side to take  │
│   notes from the four websites suggested  │
│   above, as well as any additional research│
│   you conduct.                            │
└─────────────────────────────────────────┘
```

Review Your Insurance Policy

Is your insurance policy an indemnity policy (few are), a preferred provider organization (PPO), or a health maintenance organization (HMO)? Eating disorders are covered under the mental health section of your insurance policy. Review your policy, and understand what percent of coverage you have and how it works. For example, are there deductibles in your policy? Is there a defined number of visits allowed per year? Is there an annual cap to expenses for mental health?

There is a number on the back of your insurance card. Call the number, and ask about your coverage and benefits. Ask any and all questions you want to understand. Write down the answers for future reference.

The Mental Health Parity Equity Act of 2008 mandated the same coverage for mental illness as medical illness, but this applied only to employers with at least fifty employees offering health plans with benefits. Then the Affordable Care Act was passed. Now mental-health coverage is mandated for individuals, and the individual cannot be discriminated against if they have a preexisting condition.[1]

For more information, please refer to the appendix.

Recognize What Your Insurance Company Needs from You

Your insurance provider does not know you individually, and big carriers have thousands of patients. Insurance companies are required to confirm and seek answers regarding your request, so to determine coverage, they must confirm

---

1   Judith Graham, "New Insurance Policies Must Cover Mental Illness," *Kaiser Health News*, January 9, 2014, https://khn.org/news/mental-illness-an-essential-benefit-sidebar/.

the legitimacy of the illness and pay for reasonable treatment. There is no standard from carrier to carrier; policies vary depending on the negotiation. Large companies are able to negotiate insurance to best fit the needs of their employees, whereas private insurance is not as flexible. To better help them assess your situation, we recommend taking the following steps.

- Gather letters from professionals validating the diagnosis and the need for treatment.

- To the best of your ability, supply your insurance company with proof and evidence of the patient's diagnosis and treatment needs.

- Keep copies of everything.

- Take fastidious notes.

- In your persistence, be as professional and levelheaded as possible. All calls are recorded, so keep your cool. Treatment for eating disorders is not as easy to evaluate as medical needs like broken bones.

Contact Your Insurance Company (the Earlier the Better)

Contact your insurance provider before your child starts formal treatment. (Unless your child is in medical danger—in that case, go to the nearest emergency room for help.) You will most likely be assigned a case manager, sometimes referred to as a nurse case manager. If you're not assigned to a case manager, ask for one. Ask to speak with someone who has experience with eating disorders. Get to know your case manager by name. If you truly do not connect with their personality, ask for a different case manager. Ask as many questions as you find necessary to understand your policy. We suggest you:

- Get comfortable up front, knowing you will have to be persistent. Continue to call, and do not hesitate to ask for a supervisor.

- Ask for help and advice from your insurance agent.

- Ask for a copy of your policy. Have the insurance company email, fax, or mail the policy for your review. Make sure, up front, that you understand the coverage for mental health. Get a hard copy (a printed version) or digital copy of the benefits from your insurance company.

- Get a signed waiver if your child is eighteen or older. This allows you to work with the insurer on your child's behalf.

- If you are married and covered under the same policy, engage your spouse's help. Often, one spouse is the primary insured, so help each other navigate.

- Communicate and ask questions of the professionals you, your loved one, and your family have committed to working with. Most professionals and treatment centers are very helpful.

Educate and Update Yourself and Your Insurance Provider

When having a discussion with your insurance agent, insurance company, doctor's office, HR department at work, etc., be appreciative for their help, and be easy to work with in hopes of making the process as smooth as possible. By no means are we suggesting you be a pushover, and please do not give up trying to get what you want or need. Be an advocate—and a stern advocate—but to the best of your ability, do not be difficult or rude. Entitled, offensive behavior causes more problems. Share information about regulations, guidelines, and new laws currently instated or currently being reviewed.

The emotional toll that is felt when caring for an unhealthy child is exhausting, and adding the financial burden onto what all are going through is an added stress that none of us wish we had to experience. But illness in any form costs money. For those of us who are insured, we are fairly knowledgeable and accustomed to pulling out our insurance card at the doctor's office when our child is sick. If our child has an injury and needs an X-ray, that is an understood process that we know. But when one is faced with the reality that their child has a mental disorder and that the need is for psychological services, then we are thrown into a world of things we hoped to never hear: "We don't accept insurance," "You pay in full," "You're out of network," "Good luck getting your insurance company to reimburse you," etc. Ongoing therapy is expensive. I always like to lighten things up by saying that we will continue to grow more "money trees" in our backyard. Although that is a fabricated pipe dream, we do often exceed our monetary capacity in our desperation to help! All of us will do anything we can to help a child who is hurting, and that includes paying for treatment. I would like to share with you that all is not lost when it comes to medical insurance. I recommend that you call your insurance company and specifically ask what your policy might cover. Secondly, always get a receipt or statement from every doctor you see, whether it's a therapist, psychologist, psychiatrist, etc., and always remind them to put their code numbers on the receipt. We send every charge to our insurance company. Sometimes, we actually do get a partial reimbursement. It never hurts to try and collect; after all, you are paying for your insurance whether it's used or not. It's a shame that many disorders that fall into the psychological category are usually not covered, whereas if your child breaks their leg, then all is easily processed. There are currently efforts underway to improve this, and my hope is that the day will come when mental and psychological disorders are proportionally equal in coverage to any illness. Until then, I encourage you to submit and stay with it.

—A determined mom, navigating complex insurance

Get a Confirmed Diagnosis

Most insurance companies require a confirmed diagnosis by an eating-disorder specialist. Get a diagnosis so that the eating disorder and associated mental and physical health issues are properly documented. Ask the doctor for the diagnostic paperwork or digital assessment so that you can forward it to your insurance company. In some cases, the doctor will file with your insurance company.

Get Preauthorization

Inform your insurance provider about doctors or treatments you are planning to see, and try to get prequalified. Some doctors will not be in your network. You'll have to make a personal financial decision regarding this issue. Remember to ask for a list of in-network professionals in your area. This step could potentially take a while. If your child is in medical danger, seek help immediately, or go to the nearest emergency room.

Confirm Billing Codes Used by Doctors and Professionals

Billing codes are something we have found to be very important in regard to validating payouts from an insurance company. Confer with your professionals to ensure the diagnosis is filed under the correct billing code. These codes are used to medically describe the disease, the symptoms, and the condition. It is not important to fully understand the coding system, but it is important that your doctor assigns the code that corresponds to the eating disorder and all coexisting illnesses. According to the National Eating Disorders Association, there are certain rules and government regulations about who can perform services and how those services must be coded. Ask your doctor about the billing codes they have assigned to your case. For more information, please refer to the appendix.

If You Are Employed

If you are insured through work, go visit with your HR department, and obtain a copy of benefits for your review. Get an education from them about the coverage possible and how to go about obtaining the best possible treatment for your loved one. Remember, since the employer pays for the insurance, it is actually the employer who has control over what benefits are provided by the PPO or HMO.

Understand the Laws in Your State

Laws and regulations regarding coverage for eating disorders vary from state to state. Learn the laws in your home state of residence, and communicate with your insurance provider to review new and existing state laws. Interestingly enough, some states have better coverage for eating disorders than others, so be sure to do your research. For more information, visit the website of the National Conference of State Legislatures (NCLS).[2] This site

---

2   "Mental Health Benefits: State Laws Mandating or Regulating," National Conference of State Legislatures, December 30, 2015, http://www.ncsl.org/research/health/

is very dense, but informative. Also see chapter 13 for more ideas about affording treatment and obtaining insurance and affordable help.

Overwhelmed? So were we! Dealing with the insurance company and trying to get coverage for the illness while dealing with so many emotions seems impossible. It does take time and patience. Please ask for help. If you know your insurance provider or if they live in the same city, consider meeting with them face to face.

The Parity Laws and Affordable Care Act (ACA) have been intentional in helping citizens obtain more adequate health insurance for "behavioral health coverage."[3] For more information on the Affordable Care Act, go to the official website, HealthCare.gov.

As we write this book, times are already changing. The future of health insurance is unpredictable. New legislation is being reviewed, conversations are being had, and activists are trying to get more adequate coverage for mental health. Insurance is personal, with both fluctuating and immovable policies, so you must deal directly with your carrier. Take notes during your research, and record your questions and answers about medical health insurance. Our hope for you is that your doctors or treatment center of choice will be insurance advocates for you and your family. Many have personnel well trained in coverage for all mental illnesses; we hope that person becomes a part of your village!

Pause and Write

There is room in *Working by Their Side* to take notes about this chapter, keep track of information, and keep your findings all in one place.

---

mental-health-benefits-state-mandates.aspx.

3   Louise   Norris,   "How   Obamacare   Improved   Mental   Health   Coverage,"
HealthInsurance.org,   July   5,   2018,   https://www.healthinsurance.org/obamacare/
how-obamacare-improved-mental-health-coverage/.

Does This Feel Familiar?

Differences between the lies she was hearing and the truth.

I am the mother of four daughters, married to a wonderful man who is very involved in raising our children and shepherding them into adulthood. My husband and I were deliberate and focused on never having any of our girls battle an eating disorder. I had heard what that looked like, and we were not going there. As my girls neared their preteen and teen years, I read as much material and attended as many lectures on eating disorders as possible. I thought I totally had a handle on this one. Our home was a safe place where we didn't focus on our bodies or food. We played "catch the lie" when we watched movies or TV or read magazines—pointing out the lies the culture puts out. Then, one day, a friend who had walked that road with her daughter mentioned that I might want to carefully watch one of my daughters. She was growing painfully thin right before our eyes, and we hadn't noticed. As she entered her sophomore year in high school, we started paying very close attention. True, she was not eating much, but we assumed it was part of her body changing as she matured. Her spirits seemed happy and content. It wasn't until we read a poem she had written that it hit us. She wrote that she felt like she was trapped in chains and couldn't break out.

There was no mention of food—just the feeling of being in bondage to something unspoken. When I asked her about the poem, she broke down and admitted that she was indeed in a battle that was bigger than her. She couldn't find her way out. She was terrified. So were we.

I am so thankful my husband was determined to understand the pain our daughter was feeling and to walk every step of this road with us. Some fathers cannot handle it. With his support and her honesty and desire for victory over this, we sought a counselor who understood eating disorders. We didn't want to overreact, but we sure didn't want to ignore this either.

How did this happen? What caused this? Where did we go wrong? Like any parents, we just knew that if we understood the cause, we could fix the problem. As our daughter continued to be honest with us about her emotions and her constant battle, we saw that we needed more help than just weekly counseling. As a side note, I must mention that there are so many treatment options that it is overwhelming. It is critical that you do your research to find the best fit for your child and your family. Determining what type of treatment is affordable, who offers services in network with your insurance carrier, and what treatment is needed takes tenacity. If you find it's not a good fit once you are in, don't be afraid to move on. We made the sober decision to enter our child into an outpatient program at our local children's hospital.

It was there that she began the process of getting healthy physically so she could get healthy mentally. It was also there that our entire family entered into deep introspection about who we were, individually and as a family unit. As the saying goes, you are only as healthy as your least-healthy family member. We were all hurting as we fought to understand her pain and struggles. This was especially difficult for her sisters.

We began a combination of family therapy and therapy for my husband and I alone. I think both were critical in helping us better understand our family dynamics and how they may have played a role in her pain and confusion. It was vital for the three sisters to get involved so they could learn how to support and love their sister along the way, as well as work through their own pain. The two older sisters could totally engage. The youngest daughter was still too young to fully comprehend what was going on, but we included her as much as was appropriate. Thus continued the delicate balance of guiding each of our girls in an age-appropriate fashion. As for me and my husband, counseling on disordered eating was critical. I will say, in the beginning, we felt like all of the "professionals" were overly aggressive in trying to determine where the fault lay. It felt like they assumed it was a parenting issue, or perhaps a mothering issue. Through the process, though, we were all able to slowly understand each other better. It was humbling—and worth our daughter's hope for healing—to be honest and vulnerable. We attended counseling while she was in outpatient care; then she continued weekly counseling once she was discharged. She continued meeting with the therapist regularly throughout the remainder of her high school career and periodically through college. She also saw a certified nutritionist on a weekly basis. We didn't realize at the time that most ED patients can be dishonest and deceptive. We quickly learned to appreciate that she was being sincere and honest with us and that she didn't want to be in that situation any more than we wanted her to be in it. This mind-set greatly enhanced her recovery.

Were we scared? Absolutely. Perhaps we always will be, a little. We walked on pins and needles around her for years, and I think to this day we all still treat her a little more gingerly out of fear of a relapse.

Was it my fault? You always hear about "mother's guilt"; it is a very real thing. I'm sure childhood issues that I brought into my adult reality didn't help. Having grown up in a large family with a small mother and an obese father, my biggest fear was that I would end up like my dad. There was often family conflict that included a dose of sarcasm and hurtful condescension. I have determined to raise my own children with more grace.

My husband and I are so thankful for our house full of girls, but it is a balancing act of roller-coaster emotions on a constant basis. We have always fought for our girls and our family as a whole. We always will. One of our mottos is "Sisters are closer than friends." Some days, it didn't feel true, but we persevered in teaching them to love and forgive. Families are fragile and need extra love and grace.

My job as a mom was to be her safe place. The more consumed she was with the ED, the more she pulled away from her friends. It seemed to us that the ED was her best friend, but that was a relationship based on lies. The key was for her to learn how to differentiate between the lies she was hearing and the truth she knew in her soul—the truth that she was good and worthy and perfectly knit together. God didn't make a mistake when He made her just the way she was.

We had a team of professionals that advised us through the battle, and my role in her recovery became clear. Love her, support her, hold her accountable with a touch of grace, and encourage her to keep moving forward. When she was overwhelmed and in tears, struggling to fight, I learned not to push her with comments like, "Just change! Just stop restricting!" Instead, I hugged her and told her it was OK to feel what she was feeling. I encouraged her to lean into her feelings, talk about them, and write them down. We approached the ED as a lie she was hearing. She had to learn how to identify the lies and then how to replace them with the voice of truth—even if she didn't believe it yet.

On a practical level, planning meals was overwhelming. I helped her plan her meals and made sure I provided all the resources she needed to succeed, such as a variety of healthy food options and miniature food scales (which her nutritionist suggested). We would go through her food plan and talk about it. During meals, we did not talk about food or put pressure on her to eat her dinner. As a mom, I needed to be a safe place. I made it a practice to tell her daily that I believed in her. She told me, much later, that knowing we believed in her gave her the necessary strength to fight and win. I was in awe of her courage in fighting the battle.

I want to mention the importance of finding a trusted set of friends whom you can lean on and who will support your family. We were fortunate enough to have that. This allowed us to be totally honest and not feel the need to keep secrets. Not only were they there to love me and my husband, but some of their children were also purposeful in loving and supporting our three other daughters, as well as encouraging our child who was sick.

Don't lose hope. Don't give up. Believe in your child and their ability to fight.

There can be victory.

Ten years down the road, our daughter is thriving. She is healthy, peaceful, and happily married to a wonderfully supportive young man. She is our hero.

—The mother of a fifteen-year-old
daughter, a sophomore in high school

13 Other Ways and Means to Afford Treatment

[
Learning how to take advantage of available resources.
]

Worried because you are not insured? You are not alone, and there are ways to get help. Treatment is expensive, and we all have worried about the cost. To find free (or low-cost) help, you will need to be diligent as you advocate for your loved one and family. According to the Elisa Project (TEP),[1] which is dedicated to developing healthy children and adolescents by promoting awareness and prevention through education, support, and advocacy, treatment does exist for those who have no money or insurance benefits. It is often difficult to locate, though. The Elisa Project recommends options such as counseling centers at work, school, or community facilities, as well as psychiatry departments in medical schools. TEP also has a helpline. When someone calls, they will receive a return call from a live person to talk to.

Accessing ED resources for recovery with little or no financial resources is tough, but not impossible. It takes diligence, persistence, creativity, and a loud voice. Remember, you are fighting against a disease that is smart, cunning, and does not want you well. In seeking treatment, you'll hit many walls, but you must not give up efforts or hope. That's what the ED wants you to do. Help is out there, but it's like mining for diamonds or panning for gold.

—Kimberly Martinez, executive director at the Elisa Project

---

1   "Fighting Against Eating Disorders," Elisa Project, 2019, TheElisaProject.org.

For more information on the Elisa Project, please see the appendix.

Next Steps to Take Now:
Putting One Foot in Front of the Other

You will have to educate yourself and dig deeper in your research, always asking for help. Whatever treatment center or doctor you speak with, ask them directly up front whether they will consider taking your case for free—many do pro bono work. It does not mean they will say yes, but it does not hurt to ask.

Below are suggestions on how to potentially receive financial aid for the treatment of eating disorders, along with suggestions on free consultations, blogs, apps, and podcasts. You can find more information and links to these organizations in the appendix.

Low-Cost Health Coverage

If your loved one requires treatment and has no medical insurance, we suggest you look online at sites for low-cost heath insurance. This is a constantly moving target, so please do your own research. Consider checking out eHealthInsurance.com to find affordable health insurance in your state.

You should also consider studying short-term health insurance under the Affordable Care Act[2] or HealthCare.gov.

Cannot Afford to Pay for Help?

If you cannot afford professional services for your loved one or family, call the National Eating Disorders Association Helpline at 1-800-931-2237. Ask questions, and they will guide you through their website if necessary.

Free Consultations

Free consultations are available online on many websites. There are toll-free phone numbers that direct you to an eating-disorder specialist and short forms you can fill out to receive a response by live chat or email. We want

---

2   "Short Term Health Insurance," Obamacare Facts, last updated March 17, 2019, https://obamacarefacts.com/insurance-exchange/short-term-health-insurance/.

to reemphasize the importance of contacting an *eating-disorder* specialist! Search online for "free consultation with an eating-disorder specialist," "free consultation for eating disorder help," or a derivative with similar key words.

Most treatment centers and national eating-disorder websites offer a variety of free consultations. Please look online for free consultations, help, and helplines, as you may find something new that will be helpful to you and your loved one. Here are suggestions for free consultations.

- **Eating Recovery Center.** The ERC is the largest network for eating-disorder treatment in the US. Schedule a free consultation by filling out a few questions, or call and visit with a master's-level clinician. Locations and hours available for consultation are listed on the site, EatingRecoveryCenter.com.

- **Positive Pathways.** Dr. Dorie McCubbrey, MSEd, PhD, LPC, CEDS, is the owner and clinical director of Positive Pathways, as well as the creator of Eating Disorder Intuitive Therapy (EDIT)™. Visit DrDorie.com/positive-pathways/.

- **The Center: A Place of Hope.** Offering a free initial consultation, the Center can be contacted at 1-888-771-5166, 425-771-5166, or APlaceOfHope.com. Financing is available.

- **Eating Disorder Recovery.** Joanna Poppink, MFT, is a psychotherapist based in Los Angeles and the author of *Healing Your Hungry Heart.* EatingDisorderRecovery.net offers free phone consultations as well as guidance, information, inspiration, and recovery advice, primarily for the patient but also for family and friends.

- **TreatingEatingDisorders.com.** Abigail Natenshon is a consultant for parents of children with eating disorders. She educates and supports parents while helping to define their ever-changing role in their child's recovery. As mentioned elsewhere in this book, Abigail has a great workbook for parents called *When Your Child Has An Eating Disorder: A Step-by-Step Workbook for Parents and Other Caregivers.*

- **Center for Discovery.** This site offers free assessments, potential scholarships, and up-front insurance verification at CenterForDiscovery.com/eating-disorder-scholarship-program/.

- **The Elisa Project.** On TheElisaProject.org, first click on the "Resources" tab; this will take you to "Support and Guidance for Caretakers." If you want to personally talk with someone there, call the Texas Eating Disorders Helpline at 866-837-1999.

Pause and Write

Take notes in *Working by Their Side* on the websites listed above that are applicable to you and your loved one's current situation.

Blogs to Read

We have tried to give you a variety of choice when it comes to blogs, sites, and posts that focus on caretakers.

- Lorri Benson, "'Parent Talk': Tips on How to Parent a Child Struggling with an Eating Disorder," National Eating Disorders Association, https://www.nationaleatingdisorders.org/blog/%E2%80%98parent-talk%E2%80%99-tips-how-parent-child-struggling-eating-disorder. This article provides information on how to fill your role as a parent.

- Jenni Schaefer, JenniSchaefer.com/blog. Jenni's best-selling book *Life Without ED* is for the person struggling with ED. Her blog and website has lots of good information for caretakers.

- Amy M. Klimek, "Siblings and Eating Disorders: What We Teach Each Other," Eating Disorder Hope, last updated May 6, 2017, eatingdisorderhope.com/information/eating-disorder/brothers-and-sisters-and-eating-disorders-they-play-a-crucial-role. This article contains several discussions about the crucial role brothers and sisters play in their loved one's eating disorder, as well as family dynamics and importance of involvement.

- Boys Get Eating Disorders, Too: AnorexiaBoyRecovery.Blogspot.com. This blog by Bev Mattocks Osborne contains discussions on boys and eating disorders.

- Eating Disorder Blogs: EatingDisordersBlogs.com. This site contains posts for both caretakers and patients.

- Project HEAL: TheProjectHeal.org. This blog is primarily for the person fighting or in recovery, but it has important, relevant information to help caretakers understand where their loved one is coming from in thought and action.

- "Getting through Tough Times," Healthy Place: HealthyPlace.com/blogs/toughtimes. This site has several posts on getting through tough times.

- Wear Your Voice: WearYourVoiceMag.com. This site offers articles on identity, race, LGBTQ issues, and what is trending now in the news.

- Jennifer Rollin's blog: JenniferRollin.com/blog. Jennifer Rollin, MSW, LCSW-C, is an eating-disorder therapist, founder of the Eating Disorder Center, and chairwoman of Project HEAL's national network of eating-disorder treatment providers

- "YouTube Recovery Channel," National Association of Anorexia Nervosa and Associate Disorders: ANAD.org, ANAD.org/education-and-awareness/youtube-recovery-channel/. Visit this channel for videos and educational programs focusing on awareness and prevention.

- Kartini Clinic for Children & Families: KartiniClinic.com, KartiniClinic.com/blog. This is a good site and blog for parents of young girls and boys fighting an eating disorder.

RSS Feed Readers

The suggestions below are for browser-based RSS feed readers; you choose the websites and blogs you want sent to your email for reading. You can add unlimited websites, blogs, YouTube channels, and RSS feeds for free, or choose the premium membership for a cost. To get updated information pared down to the sites you want to review, we suggest the sites below.

- Feedspot: blog.Feedspot.com
- G2Reader: G2Reader.com
- CommaFeed: CommaFeed.com

Pause and Write

Check out the blogs and RSS Feed Readers above. In *Working by Their Side*, list which ones seem interesting and applicable to you and your loved ones current situation.

Seek Out Free Services and Care in Your Community

Ask for advice or referrals from individuals in gratis positions. For example, consider meeting with:

- Moms, dads, and caretakers who are dealing with the same issue
- School counselors
- School nurses
- Youth ministers
- Local YMCA leaders
- Local teaching hospitals
- Community mental health agencies in your city
- Leaders in medical schools and universities in your city; often, there are free clinics operated by residents in training and supervised by faculty

Consider also searching the internet for free clinical trials in your area.

Negotiate with the Doctors or Treatment Centers Regarding Cost

Explain your situation, and ask for assistance. Inquire about scholarship programs. Some treatment centers are supplementary—funded by county, state, or federal funds—and potentially required to make care available. You will never know unless you ask.

Mentor Programs, Scholarships, and Resources

There are programs and scholarships all over the country. Search online for eating-disorder scholarships, and research scholarship opportunities on websites such as:

- "Overview of Current Programs That Offer Scholarships for Treatment," Eating Disorder Hope: EatingDisorderHope.com/blog/scholarships-treatment

- "Scholarship Foundation," EDReferral: EDReferral.com/blog/scholarship-foundation-182

- "Treatment Access Program," Project HEAL: TheProjectHEAL.org/treatment-access-program-1/

Here are mentor resources and scholarships we are familiar with. Do your own research as well, as more programs become available frequently.

- "Finding a Mentor in Eating Disorder Recovery," Eating Disorder Hope: https://www.eatingdisorderhope.com/blog/finding-a-mentor-in-eating-disorder-recovery

- OutshiningED: OutshiningED.com

- National Association for Males with Eating Disorders (NAMED): NAMEDInc.org

- "Mentor Program," National Eating Disorders Association: NationalEatingDisorders.org/mentor-program

- "Family, Friends and Carers," Eating Disorders Victoria (located in Australia): EatingDisorders.org.au/getting-help/for-family-friends-and-carers

- "Recovery Mentor," National Association of Anorexia Nervosa and Associated Disorders: ANAD.org/volunteer/opportunities/recovery-mentor/

- Manna Fund: MannaFund.org

- Jennifer Mathiason Fund, Moonshadow's Spirit: MoonshadowsSpirit.org

- Gail R. Schoenbach FREED Foundation: FREEDStat.org

- Clinical Trials: ClinicalTrials.gov

- Lisa's Light of Hope: LisasLightOfHope.com

- Mercy Multiplied: MercyMultiplied.com

- Eating Disorders Anonymous: EatingDisordersAnonymous.org

- Rebecca's Eating Disorder Foundation: RebeccasEatingDisorderFoundation.org

- "Eating Disorder Scholarship Program," Center For Discovery: CenterForDiscovery.com/eating-disorder-scholarship-program/

Online Parent Forums

The following are online forums geared toward parents and caretakers.

- Around the Dinner Table: AroundTheDinnerTable.org. This fabulous resource is an online forum of parents from all around the world. It is run by Families Empowered and Supporting Treatment of Eating Disorders (FEAST). Visit FEAST at FEAST-ED.org.

- "Eating Disorders Forum," Mental Health Forum: MentalHealthForum. net/forum/forum32.html

- Forums at Psych Central: Forums.PsychCentral.com/eating-disorders/. This site is not exclusive to eating disorders; it deals with a variety of topics, including coping with emotions, spiritual support, and affirmation. You can ask questions specific to your needs.

- "Forums," Eating Disorders Victoria: EatingDisorders.SaneForums. org. This site deals with mental illness and is moderated twenty-four seven by professionals. It is not specific to eating disorders but is a good place to ask questions, as many eating disorders are accompanied by other emotional challenges.

- "Free & Low Cost Support," National Eating Disorders Association: NationalEatingDisorders.org/free-low-cost-support. The NEDA forums are available for individuals and loved ones wanting to connect about eating disorders in a safe space. Topics covered include ones relevant to siblings of suffers, partners and spouses of sufferers, parents of sufferers, friends in support roles, and more.

Support Groups

To find a support group in your area, visit Eating Disorder Hope at EatingDisorderHope.com/recovery/support-groups. For more information, please refer to appendix.

Workbook

Our first suggestion is to complete *Working by Their Side*, the workbook that goes with this book. Whether you are able to actively partake in therapy or not, we also recommend *When Your Child Has an Eating Disorder: A Step-by-Step Workbook for Parents and Caregivers* by Abigail Natenshon. It is a good place to start or restart.

Online Funding Platforms

Medical expenses can be outrageously expensive, and many people are turning to the internet for help. Use technology to your advantage. Raise treatment funds by crowdsourcing, a popular way of getting financial support from large groups of people around the world who donate through an online platform. People donate because they want to give. There is no paying back. There are many crowdfunding sites to explore, so please do so. Below, we've suggested a few medically minded sites.

- GiveForward: GiveForward.com
- GoFundMe: GoFundMe.com
- YouCaring: YouCaring.com
- FundRazr: FundRazr.com
- Kickstarter: Kickstarter.com
- DonationTo: DonationTo.com
- JustGiving: JustGiving.com

Pause and Write

Educate yourself, and make a list of free mentor programs, scholarships, resources, online parent forums, and support groups. In *Working by Their Side*, write down which options seems interesting and applicable to you and your loved one's current situation.

Podcasts

You may choose to do your own research on podcasts; you will also find podcasts associated with some of the resources mentioned in this chapter. We recommend *ED Matters*, the podcast of the Gürze-Salucore ED Resource Catalogue, which interviews experts in the field on a wide range of topics, including conversations with Jenni Schaefer, Claire Mysko (the CEO of NEDA), and many more experts in the field.[3]

Online Therapy and Therapy Apps

With the existence of the internet, most anything can be found online—even therapy for eating disorders. The field of eHealth delivers health care, and eTherapy provides online treatment for depression, anxiety, and now eating disorders. One such therapy is called CBTe (cognitive behavioral therapy online). It is free, personalized, and intriguing! We do recommend you research further and see if online therapy for eating disorders suits your lifestyle and pocketbook.

Many sites have compounded lists of the best apps for mental health or eating disorders, including Psycom, Healthline, and *Medical News Today*.[4] BuzzFeed has also reviewed apps for people recovering from an eating disorder.[5] These apps are either free or accessible with a small fee. When reading about these apps, check to see whether they are compatible with your particular phone. Some work on iPhones, others only on Android, and a few cross over between different smartphones. Research on your own, and discover which apps are applicable to your lifestyle. Some apps, like Recovery Record, are for the patient struggling and working toward recovery. Others, like Headspace, Happify, and Calm, are applicable to caretakers as well.

---

3   "Podcast Archives," Salucore, 2015, https://www.edcatalogue.com/category/podcast/.

4   Jessica Shelton, "Top 25 Best Mental Health Apps: An Effective Alternative for When You Can't Afford Therapy?," Psycom, April 21, 2018, https://www.psycom.net/25-best-mental-health-apps; Rena Goldman, "Best Eating Disorder Recovery Apps of 2018," Healthline, April 19, 2018, https://www.healthline.com/health/top-eating-disorder-iphone-android-apps; Hannah Nichols, "The Top 10 Mental Health Apps," *Medical News Today*, January 8, 2018, https://www.medicalnewstoday.com/articles/320557.php.

5   Maggy van Eijk, "17 Amazing Apps for People Recovering from an Eating Disorder," BuzzFeed, December 7, 2015, https://www.buzzfeed.com/maggyvaneijk/17-amazing-apps-for-anyone-recovering-from-an-eating-disorde.

Face-to-face therapy is, by far, the best-case scenario. But if you want to investigate these apps because you feel you cannot afford a therapist, then you should. Please use discernment, ask questions, and do a test run. If they help, why not engage?

However, by no means do we suggest apps are a substitute for treatment. If your loved one is in medical crisis, call one of the hotlines listed in the appendix, and go to the nearest hospital.

Recovery Record

This app seems to be the one most talked about and suggested in the eating-disorder field, including a recommendation on the National Eating Disorders Association website.

> Recovery Record [has been found] to be the most comprehensive eating disorder treatment app on the market. It contains features including self-monitoring, personalized coping strategies, social connections, and a portal to connect with the user's clinician. It also contains components of cognitive-behavioral based interventions. Users can enter food, thoughts, feelings, and urges to use compensatory behaviors. The app offers assistance with coping strategies and goal setting in addition to the ability to set reminders. Additional features include meal planning, rewards, affirmations, and the potential to connect with others.[6]

What'sMyM3

"Many people with eating disorders also deal with other mental health conditions, like anxiety and depression. M3 is a research-based screening technique that assigns a number to your risk for depression, anxiety, PTSD, and bipolar disorder. The app lets you take a three-minute screening and gives you a personalized report of how your symptoms may be impacting your life."[7]

---

6   Lauren Muhlheim, "How Apps Can Be Used for Eating Disorder Recovery," Verywell Mind, updated October 1, 2018, https://www.verywellmind.com/apps-and-eating-disorders-the-good-and-the-bad-3878432.

7   Rena Goldman, "Best Eating Disorder Recovery Apps of 2018," Healthline, April 19, 2018, https://www.healthline.com/health/top-eating-disorder-iphone-android-apps.

Rise Up + Recover

"If you're going through cognitive behavioral therapy (CBT), your therapist likely assigned some homework. Rise Up + Recover is designed to make that homework easy to complete. Use the app to log meals, emotions, and behaviors."[8]

Headspace

"The Headspace app makes meditation simple. Learn the skills of mindfulness and meditation by using this app for just a few minutes per day. You gain access to hundreds of meditations on everything from stress and anxiety to sleep and focus."[9]

What's Up

"What's Up is an amazing free app that uses Cognitive Behavioral Therapy (CBT) and Acceptance Commitment Therapy (ACT) methods to help you cope with Depression, Anxiety, Stress, and more. Use the positive and negative habit tracker to maintain your good habits, and break those that are counterproductive."[10]

Happify

"Need a happy fix? With its psychologist-approved mood-training program, the Happify app is your fast-track to a good mood. Try various engaging games, activity suggestions, gratitude prompts and more to train your brain as if it were a muscle, to overcome negative thoughts."[11]

Calm

"Named by Apple as the 2017 iPhone App of the Year, Calm is quickly becoming regarded as one of the best mental health apps available. Calm provides people experiencing stress and anxiety with guided meditations,

8   Goldman, "Best Eating Disorder Recovery Apps of 2018."

9   Jessica Shelton, "Top 25 Best Mental Health Apps: An Effective Alternative for When You Can't Afford Therapy?," Psycom, April 21, 2018, https://www.psycom.net/25-best-mental-health-apps.

10   Shelton, "Top 25 Best Mental Health Apps."

11   Shelton, "Top 25 Best Mental Health Apps."

sleep stories, breathing programs, and relaxing music. This app is truly universal; whether you've never tried meditation before or regularly practice, you'll find the perfect program for you."[12]

Consultant and well-being technology expert Tchiki Davis, PhD, suggests the following four apps. Please see her *Psychology Today* article "The Best Happiness Apps of 2018," in which she compares top science-based happiness apps to reveal their strengths and weaknesses, to help you find the best app for you.[13]

- Happify: Happify.com
- Just One Minute: RickHanson.net
- SuperBetter: SuperBetter.com
- Greater Good in Action: GGIA.Berkeley.edu

The Greater Good in Action app, developed by the Greater Good Science Center at UC Berkeley to help people engage in practices for a meaningful life, caught our attention. This app helps to enhance personal skills like gratitude, empathy, and mindfulness. Please see chapter 14 for more on this topic.

You may have to be creative in obtaining financial help for treatment. Are you comfortable asking family members for money? Do you know an "angel donor" who would give you the money? Are you comfortable asking friends for financial support? If you know you cannot pay them back, be honest. The donation is a gift, and you have to get comfortable with that.

Remember, you're asking for help for your loved one's health and life. Can you separate yourself and ask on their behalf? A good rule of thumb when fundraising is to say to yourself, "If capable, would I give money to this person if they asked?" If the answer is yes, they will most likely give to you. Remember, self-worth is based in one's own perspective. What if we turn it around and think of it as allowing others the gift of giving? You are giving that person the ability to give. Giving

---

12   Shelton, "Top 25 Best Mental Health Apps."

13   Tchiki Davis, "The Best Happiness Apps of 2018," *Psychology Today*, January 4, 2018, https://www.psychologytoday.com/us/blog/click-here-happiness/201801/the-best -happiness-apps-2018.

fulfills purpose and is a wonderful feeling, but you have to be willing to receive.

None of us recommends taking out a loan or a lien again your home mortgage. You might consider talking with a banker, but please do not put yourself and your family in an irreconcilable financial situation. Some of us have had to, and it took years to recover.

Please consider asking your friends and family for help first.

Pause and Write

There is room in *Working by Their Side* to take notes on favorite apps you discover. Keep track of information, and keep your findings from this chapter all in one place.

Does This Feel Familiar?

"We're going to have to sell our house."

"I can't afford the treatment my sick child desperately needs."

"I'm a single parent with a single-income household."

"I am scared; we have no insurance."

Over the years, I have encountered parents who were financially burdened and often in debt because of the cost of their loved one's treatment. My husband and I spend an incredible amount of time fighting with insurance companies, and with each year that passes, both of us are constantly baffled at the cost of treatment. I am neither a doctor nor an eating-disorder specialist, but I am a mom who, over the last fifteen years, has befriended parents whose children have also had to seek treatment for various eating issues. Whether we meet in a support group, intensive outpatient (IOP), or just through word of mouth, it always pains my heart to hear the stories of sorrow and discomfort when a family is in financial distress. It is quite simply unfair and infuriating that treatment is so costly.

Families have moved into one-room apartments; grandparents have moved cities to be closer to their loved one in treatment; a sibling skipped a semester of college because a parent could not afford both; cars have been sold and savings depleted, parents haved worked two jobs, leaving little time for family—the stories go on and on. Furthermore, there is often quite a bit of guilt associated with the lack of financial wherewithal, especially when another sibling in the family will be without.

And yet, I have also witnessed success stories in which patients have received financial assistance or scholarships and have rebuilt their lives after their child completed treatment. These success stories do not come easy, and parents are tasked with the job of helping find financial aid and resources. Does financial strain add to the stress level of an already difficult situation? That is absolutely a solid yes. But the energy spent on finding financial assistance is well worth the effort. In a most ironic and seemingly illogically way, I have also seen relationships be reconciled, families bond, loved ones give of themselves for another, and people rebuild a more meaningful life and actually benefit from the hardest of times. The resilience is awe inspiring. Not all stories end that way, but getting help is possible.

I loved writing this chapter because it offers hope. It has also inspired me to do my own research, dig further into resources and places to start, and even find a voice to connect with on the other end of a phone call.

One of my favorite blogs to read and suggest to others can be found at TheProjectHEAL.org. Liana Rosenman and Kristina Saffran founded Project HEAL with the belief that full recovery is possible and should be accessible. They raise funds for people who cannot afford treatment and created the Treatment Access Program, along with free peer support, mentorship, and a network of chapters that aim to connect with under-represented populations such as low-income communities, LGBTQ communities, communities of color, and male-identified people. One of my favorite aspects of their ideology is that money is just one piece of the complex treatment puzzle; thus, they have devised a model that reaches beyond just giving financial help. When it comes to treatment, the financial mountain is steep, but the climb is not just money alone; it is the stepping-stones toward health, the coping skills learned along the path, the people that walk beside you, and those who offer to help push you up to the top.

I have been following therapist Jennifer Rollin on Instagram for a couple of years now. I often go to her blog, JenniferRollin.com/blog, for knowledge and education as well as for encouragement. Sometimes, the eating-disorder world feels dark, and I need that spark of light and optimism. Through her post "We Need to Get Rid of the Stigma around Mental Health," I was reminded once again that "mental illnesses are *not* choices. The same way that physical illnesses are not choices." Also, sadly, insurance companies "often will cover physical health conditions but deny or shorten coverage of life-saving eating disorder residential treatment stays."[14] Jennifer further explains that many of her clients feel like burdens to their families, and she reminds them that the fact that they are struggling with a mental illness is not their fault. They deserve support, and reaching out for help is not a sign of weakness but, to the contrary, a sign of courage. I believe this is true for all of us caretakers as well. We did not choose to be parents to children struggling with eating disorders—but we are. Our children deserve adequate treatment, and we, too, are courageous when we seek help.

There is no easy answer to affording treatment for our children when money is tight. At times, the torment is brutal, and yet believing with persistence, asking for help, reaching out beyond our comfort zone for assistance, and exerting the extra amount of energy spent researching financial aid is all worth the effort. You will never look back and regret your effort. I know we don't. Whenever I have shared time with parents in desperate need of financial help, our ultimate goal has collectively been the same: we want our children well. We want our children to have the best care possible in hopes of getting back that child we miss, that child we so desperately love. A healthy, resilient, happy child who is able to organically live their life to the fullest.

—An experienced friend who knows seeking help is imperative

---

14 Jennifer Rollin, "We Need to Get Rid of the Stigma around Mental Health," JenniferRollin.com, June 28, 2018, https://www.jenniferrollin.com/blog/we-need-to-get-rid-of-the-stigma-around-mental-health.

14 Therapies, Practices, and Innovative Treatments

[
Be creative, look beyond your boundaries, and
be open minded to new ways of healing.
]

There are new strategies being developed in eating-disorder recovery all the time. The ideas offered in this chapter do not cover everything, so please do your own research, and always check with your licensed professionals and doctors before proceeding with a new treatment.

By "innovative," we mean treatments that are relatively new, out of the box, novel, or sometimes centuries old but from Eastern philosophy. These techniques are designed to work as one part of the whole of a treatment team, often in combination with conventional medicine. Discussed below are some of the options we have found most useful: naturopathic medicine, integrative medicine and doctors, integrative psychiatry, traditional Chinese medicine/acupuncture, yoga, eye movement desensitization and reprocessing (EMDR), extended care and aftercare treatment, solution-focused brief therapy (SFBT), logotherapy, zero balancing (ZB), understanding emotional intelligence (EI/EQ), hypnosis, equine therapy (EAP/EFL), pet therapy (AAT), referenced EEG, targeted nutritional therapy, online therapy and therapy apps, repetitive transcranial magnetic stimulation (RTMS), deep brain stimulation (DBS), and faith practices, meditation, and spiritual healing. We refer to "natural" ways of healing as innovative, but truthfully, many of them have been around longer than traditional medicine. For more detailed information, please refer to the appendix.

Next Steps to Take Now:
Putting One Foot in Front of the Other

Educate yourself on options for healing outside of traditional medical methods. The ideas listed here are a beginning, but you will need to extend your research to find help in the area where you live. These ideas are given in no order of preference or endorsement. If you are already practicing natural healing, we suggest you visit with your doctors and practitioners about their expertise with eating disorders. If they are not experienced in working with eating-disordered patients, ask for a referral. Be both open minded and discerning as you discover new avenues of healing. As always, if you are currently under the care of a doctor, check with them before proceeding with new treatments.

Naturopathic Medicine

Dr. Sheri Lewis, ND, explains naturopathic medicine as follows:

> A naturopath—a licensed doctor of naturopathic medicine—can assess your child scientifically and deal naturally with imbalances in the brain potentially causing depression, anxiety, eating disorders, and physical health issues. In the treatment of eating disorders, it is most effective to work simultaneously with medical doctors, therapists, and naturopaths. Licensed doctors of naturopathic medicine can assess your child scientifically (through blood work) and deal naturally with the imbalances in the brain and body through science. They are also licensed nutritionists.
>
> —Dr. Sheri Lewis, ND, the Nutrition Club

Naturopaths (ND) base their practice on six timeless principles founded on medical tradition and scientific evidence:

- Let nature heal.
- Identify and treat causes.
- Use low-risk procedures and healing compounds.

- Customize each diagnosis and treatment plan to fit each patient.
- Educate patients.
- Encourage self-responsibility, and work closely with each patient.[1]

For more information on naturopathic medicine, please refer to the appendix.

Integrative Medicine

Integrative medicine and therapies treat not just the physical frame of the human body but the mind, body, and spirit all at the same time. This method emphasizes the healing of the entire person (in the biological, psychological, sociological, and spiritual dimensions) by integrating the use of conventional and alternative health care. If you choose to go in this direction, make sure the professional is experienced in eating disorders. Many MDs combine integrative medicine and practices into their traditional work.

To find an integrative doctor close to you, start by researching on the websites of the following organizations: the Academy of Integrative Health & Medicine (AIHM.org), the International Network of Integrative Mental Health (INIMH.org), and the American College for Advancement in Medicine (ACAM.org). Dr. James Greenblatt, MD, is also a good person to learn from. In *Answers to Anorexia*, he speaks about mental illness and eating disorders with an integrative medical approach.[2]

Integrative Psychiatry

Rather than focusing just on the eating disorder itself, integrative psychiatry focuses on an individual's mental wellness while discovering who they are and how they can heal both physically and emotionally. For example, integrative psychiatry promotes natural healing, combines alternative healing modalities, and addresses the origin of symptoms while focusing on mind, body, and environment.[3] To begin a search for

---

1   "What is Naturopathic Medicine?," North Carolina Association of Naturopathic Physicians, http://ncanp.com/what-is-naturopathic-medicine/.

2   James M. Greenblatt, *Answers to Anorexia: A Breakthrough Nutritional Treatment That Is Saving Lives* (North Branch, MN: Sunrise River Press, 2010).

3   Elana Miller, "The 10 Principles of Integrative Psychiatry," *HuffPost*, last updated January

doctors and practitioners in your state, try calling 800-385-7863, or search the internet for additional information.

Traditional Chinese Medicine/Acupuncture

If "stepping out of the box" is a stretch for you or you need a declaration of validation, maybe this is a good place to look back into history. Learning that traditional Chinese medicine has been a part of human practice for thousands of years should give you some peace about using ancient healing practices such as acupuncture, meditation, herbal remedies, and massage. Anxiety and depression are prevalent in eating-disorder cases; acupuncture has been used as a healing force for both. The flow of energy throughout the body is called *chi*. When the chi is blocked, problems are exaggerated, the immune system is weakened, and illness sets in easier. Acupuncture stimulates certain places along the meridian pathway, allowing the chi to flow naturally. This holistic treatment has proven healing in treating both anorexia and binge eating.[4]

Yoga

Why yoga? Because it helps to ground an individual in body, soul, and mind. Yoga is a healthier alternative to compulsive exercise and can help reduce anger, depression, and frustration. Yoga calms compulsive behavior and egocentric thoughts about one's physical beauty.

There are many advocacy groups and hundreds of articles on the internet explaining why participating in yoga is a healthy choice. For example, it lowers cortisol, a chemical that can trigger two side effects from an eating disorder: depression and osteoporosis. Ultimately, yoga affects your mental health as you learn to accept your physical self, to connect with a community, and to thus feel more content and happy.

Despite all of the positive side effects of yoga, however, we must be aware of aggressive yoga practices that are not appropriate for people

23, 2014, https://www.huffpost.com/entry/integrative-psychiatry_n_4074874.

4   "Traditional Chinese Medicine: In Depth," National Center for Complementary and Integrative Health, last modified July 16, 2018, https://nccih.nih.gov/health/whatiscam/chinesemed.htm.

struggling with an eating disorder. Hot yoga, power yoga, and any yoga used specifically for weight loss are not recommended. These types of practices are harmful to the patient both physically and psychologically.

As a therapist for teens and adult women struggling with a range of eating disorders, I recognized that as long as their minds and bodies remained disconnected, true healing and integration would be impossible. I am trained as a clinical psychologist, with postdoctoral training in eating-disorder recovery. Again and again in my private practice, I observed clients who could intellectually understand the root causes of their symptoms as well as the methods of recovery. They knew what to do, but still could not get better. Knowing was not enough. Understanding on a cognitive level did not catalyze true change. In yoga, change happens from the inside out. It is a physical practice, sure, but that, known as asana, is only one of the eight limbs of yoga. Yoga, which means "to unite" or "to yoke," connects the mind and body through the breath. When someone with an eating disorder, whose mind and body have been disconnected as a way of maintaining their symptoms, is asked to get inside of their body, to feel sensation, to experience proprioception, to get present, they are being offered an experience of healing. When someone whose thoughts are merged with their mind is offered the practice of meditation and of distancing thoughts from their mind, they are given a tool that can greatly increase their capacity to be nonreactive and to tolerate frustration. Both the physical practice of yoga and the mental tool of meditation can be powerful healing agents for those struggling to reconnect to their bodies after the severing of mind and body by an eating disorder.

However, yoga can cause great harm if it is being taught and practiced as a way of exercise, of burning calories, or of sculpting the body. For someone who may use these as fuel for their eating disorder, sending them to any yoga class is not wise.

When trying to find a way to offer the therapeutic tools of yoga to someone struggling with a negative body image or an eating disorder, choose a teacher who has their own body confidence and who uses the teachings of yoga, its philosophy, and its practice as an agent of finding sensation, presence, and peace, not as a tool for weight loss or body shaming. Choose a teacher who cues for sensation and for presence rather than celebrating poses or perfection.

—Melody Moore, PhD, E-RYT, licensed clinical psychologist and experienced registered yoga teacher, founder of Embody Love Movement Foundation®

Eye Movement Desensitization and Reprocessing

Eye movement desensitization and reprocessing (EMDR) is a type of counseling that can help change how you react to memories of traumatic experience. EMDR is used in trauma healing and often in helping individuals suffering from PTSD (posttraumatic stress disorder). A trauma can trigger the onset of an eating disorder, and EMDR helps to deal with and then process this issue. For more information on EMDR providers, please refer to the appendix.

Extended Care and Aftercare Treatment

Once someone is perceived as "healthy," terminating therapy or leaving the security of a treatment facility can feel scary. No matter what treatment or therapy you and your loved one have been involved in, following up on their health is critical. Aftercare structure is imperative to preventing a relapse. (Please see the appendix for more information on relapses.)

Recovery should absolutely include follow-up care at home while the patient is reintegrating into their life. Older patients may choose to live near or on the property of the treatment center, depending upon that center's policies about aftercare. Some treatment centers follow their patients anywhere from one to five years posttreatment. This includes, but is not limited to, phone calls, mentorships, crisis management, and timely checkups.

As life evolves, changes, and moves on, it is important to stay mindful of new and innovative coping skills for a life of full and proper healing. You and your loved one should always continue learning new coping skills.

A well-conceived plan for aftercare is essential! Stepping from a cocoon of care and treatment back into a world ridden with angst and triggers is a relapse waiting to happen. Staying on the path of recovery is difficult with any disorder. Because food is necessary to live, the individual struggling with an eating disorder is challenged every day. Having a therapist and dietitian to help you transition into being surrounded by food choices is critical for success. Reinforcing positive, self-loving mantras is also critical. Aftercare programs are set up to support the individual recovering and keep a watchful eye on them not just for accountability but so they don't feel alone.

—A mom

At the very least, one year of aftercare with the patient's doctor or therapist is recommended for individuals once treatment has been terminated. You and your team of doctors will need to determine the best avenue for successful extended aftercare.

Solution-Focused Brief Therapy

SFBT is a therapy that focuses on solutions rather than problems. After thirty years of development, SFBT helps people improve their life and feel more confident and hopeful about the future they are able to achieve. SFBT focuses on finding solutions based on the individual's positive traits and resources that can help build a future of hope. SFBT therapists do not spend a lot of time discussing past or present problems or causes. Consider engaging in SFBT as a component of extended aftercare.[5]

Logotherapy

Viktor Frankl's logotherapy is based on the premise that human beings are motivated by a "will to meaning" and that we have the freedom to find meaning and choose our attitude in any given circumstance. In short,

---

5   Barbara McFarland, *Brief Therapy and Eating Disorders: A Practical Guide to Solution-Focused Work with Clients* (San Francisco: Jossey-Bass, 1995).

logotherapy is the pursuit of meaning in one's life.[6] One of the families helping to write this book is currently experiencing emotional relief and healing in their logotherapy sessions. They feel empowered and say that this type of therapy has allowed them to release fears, be more vulnerable, feel joy, and find purpose.

> I wish we had found this type of therapy earlier. I felt like the therapist actually got me and could understand my desperate need for love and purpose. I was taught three different ways to discover meaning in my life: creating a work or doing a deed, encountering someone, or experiencing something. Also, I get to choose my attitude toward suffering and toward all circumstances. I was empowered to know that it is actually me who gets to make decisions regarding my life!
>
> —A logotherapy fan

The name of this therapy originates from the Greek word *logos*, which in theology means "the Word of God, or principle of divine reason and creative order."[7] That feels grounded and of the soul.

Zero Balancing

> Zero balancing (ZB) incorporates knowledge of Western biomechanics with an understanding of Eastern energy theory, offering a comprehensive, deeply healing return to self. Practiced through clothing, ZB is a gentle form of bodywork. The practitioner evaluates the movement of certain joints, locates and releases bone-held

6   "Viktor Frankl Institute of Logotherapy," Viktor Frankl Institute of Logotherapy, http://www.logotherapyinstitute.org/Home.html.

7   *Oxford English Dictionary*, s.v. "logos," https://en.oxforddictionaries.com/definition/logos.

tension in relation to the joint, and then organizes the ligamentous tension in and around those joints. These techniques treat physical pain in addition to stress. But zero balancing doesn't just reduce stress; it changes how a person experiences stress. The name refers to a concept from Taoist alchemy: all physical manifestation arises from emptiness. Returning to zero allows our truest nature to manifest, transforming all of our orchestrated resistance into effortless momentum.

—Joanna Johnson, certified zero-balancing practitioner, faculty, mentor, CMT, TurningAspens.com

Understanding Emotional Intelligence

For decades, we have assessed intelligence with a score derived from standardized IQ tests. We believe assessing emotional intelligence (EI or EQ) is equally critical, if not more important, to the well-being of human beings. EI is often misunderstood, and we tend to view it as charisma or "the 'it' factor." EI is a nonverbal self-awareness and awareness of those around you. It is the ability to understand and manage our own emotions and also understand what others are experiencing emotionally. Understanding and developing mature emotional intelligence is consequential in the treatment of eating disorders. EI is intangible, yet it monitors our behavior, social skills, and self-awareness.

Many children, teens, young adults, and adults with eating disorders are both blessed and cursed with high emotional intelligence. They feel deeper, hurt deeper, love deeper, are very sensitive, and have an overwhelming sense of heart power that gets confused in our social structure. Often, a child cannot control their EI to guide their own behaviors and thinking; they tend to live in the highest degree of intense feelings. Ever wonder whether the control of an eating disorder is affected by your loved one's EI? So, how can you help your loved one? Here are a few thoughts:

• Listen, without judgment, in hopes that getting the emotions out will help your loved one process through to a more rational side.

- Remind them to access coping skills and learn positive ways to solve problems. One easy coping skill is deep breathing, as it often helps one to calm down.

- Do not overreact in your responses.

- Role-play.

Hypnosis

Among other things, hypnotherapy uses the power of suggestion to retrain thought and patterns. It also includes teaching relaxation techniques and building confidence through guided imagery. There are lots of articles supporting the use of hypnotherapy when treating eating disorders. You will need to research to find a hypnotist familiar with these disorders in your area.

Equine Therapy

Referred to as equine assisted psychotherapy (EAP) or equine facilitated learning (EFL), this treatment utilizes the relationship between a horse and a patient—in our case, the patient being our eating-disordered loved one. The human-horse relationship revolves around emotional healing and growth. There are many articles and websites about the mental and emotional benefits of equine therapy for people struggling with eating disorders.[8]

Pet Therapy

According to the American Humane Association, animal assisted therapy (AAT) can be an effective treatment for those dealing with mental illnesses, low self-esteem, negative body image, and eating disorders.[9]

Led by Shannon Kopp (author of *Pound for Pound: A Story of One Woman's Recovery and the Shelter Dogs Who Loved Her Back to Life*), Dr. Annie Peterson, and Dr. Patricia Flaherty Fischette, SoulPaws is a nonprofit organization that uses the loving connection between humans and animals to inspire change and help women with eating disorders. SoulPaws holds

---

8   For more information, visit EatingDisorderHope.com.

9   Crystal Karges, "Pet Therapy for Eating Disorder Recovery while in College," August 23, 2016, https://www.eatingdisorderhope.com/blog/pet-therapy-eating-disorder-recovery-college.

workshops focusing on recovery both in person and online. For more information, visit SoulPawsRecovery.org.

Referenced EEG

This technology has been used in the treatment of eating disorders for more than ten years. Referenced EEG provides psychiatrists with information to guide them in choosing the medications used for co-occurring emotional issues. There is no medication that cures eating disorders, but stabilizing coexisting illnesses is helpful in the healing process. The individual results of this technology show the psychiatrist what medications have been successfully used.

Targeted Nutrition Therapy

Can vitamin and mineral deficiencies be linked to developing anorexia? Calcium, vitamin B, and omega-3 fatty acids are just three of the nutrients and minerals nutritional therapy targets. For example, zinc deficiency can lead to loss of appetite, weight loss, altered taste, depression, and absence of monthly periods. All five of these characteristics are prevalent in the development of anorexia. Zinc is also one of the most prevalent trace elements found in the human brain. Preteens and teenagers typically eat diets low in zinc. The traditional medical community has been slow to integrate zinc therapy, but if you see a naturopath, they can run a blood test to check your loved one's zinc levels.[10]

Online Therapy and Therapy Apps

Please refer to chapter 13 for a list of online therapy resources and therapy apps. These apps are new and innovative but are not recommended as a substitute for therapy or treatment.

Repetitive Transcranial Magnetic Stimulation

Repetitive transcranial magnetic stimulation (RTMS) is noninvasive magnetic stimulation most commonly used on patients who have suffered with anorexia and binge eating over a long period of years.

---

10   "Vitamins, Minerals and Deficiencies," Something Fishy Website on Eating Disorders, 2019, http://www.something-fishy.org/dangers/vitamins.php.

Recently, 20 patients with severe anorexia or bulimia received targeted, non-invasive magnetic brain stimulation through a procedure called "repetitive transcranial magnetic stimulation (RTMS)." The stimulation was directed toward the region of the brain involved with control of thoughts, emotions and behavior. It is this part of the brain, the frontal lobes, that is essentially "off line" in people with active eating disorders.[11]

Deep Brain Stimulation (DBS)

Deep brain stimulation (DBS) is a more intense neurosurgical procedure that involves implanting a neurostimulator. It is being researched in chronic, extremely ill, treatment-resistant people with anorexia. We cannot recommend DBS treatment for severe anorexia, as it is still in the experimental stages and in clinical trials with the National Institutes of Health (NIH) and organizations in other countries. With advances in neurological disorders, researchers believe there could be an effective treatment involving DBS in the future. Today, the procedure is risky, and the outcome is unclear.

The treatment, still considered experimental, is believed to work by stimulating specific areas of the brain to reverse abnormalities linked to mood, anxiety, emotional control, obsessions and compulsions.[12]

This work shows how modern neuroscience can lead to a new treatment and simultaneously improve understanding of perpetuating factors in a complex, multifactorial disease.[13]

---

11   Kim Dennis, "Utilizing Brain Stimulation in the Treatment of Eating Disorders," Eating Disorder Hope, https://www.eatingdisorderhope.com/treatment-for-eating-disorders/types-of-treatments/eating-disorder-treatment-may-include-magnetic-brain-stimulation.

12   Janice Wood, "Deep Brain Stimulation Shows Promise for Anorexia," Psych Central, last updated August 8, 2018, https://psychcentral.com/news/2013/03/10/deep-brain-stimulation-shows-promise-for-anorexia/52401.html.

13   Ana Sandoiu, "Anorexia: Deep Brain Stimulation May Be an Effective Treatment," Medical News Today, February 24, 2017, https://www.medicalnewstoday.com/articles/316060.php.

Faith Practices, Meditation, and Spiritual Healing

Last but not least—actually, it is most important—is a focus on faith practices, meditation, and spiritual healing in the treatment of eating disorders. We believe these practices are critical, so much so that faith practices deserve their own chapter. For more information, please refer to chapter 16.

It is important to spend a little time detailing one of the most effective forms of spiritual practice: meditation. Meditation is another method for gaining perspective and self-acceptance, and it comes in many forms. Yoga, mantra repetition, prayer, guided meditation, musical trances, and simple focus are all included in the field of meditation. If the concept of sitting still, breathing, and quieting the mind seems unattainable, try doing something you love with extreme focus. This intense focus will bring attention to the present moment and generate mindfulness, leading to a deeper sense of understanding and emotional evaluation. See chapter 5 for more information on ten-minute meditation.

Pause and Write

There is room in *Working by Their Side* to take notes about the suggestions in this chapter. Please keep track of information, and keep your findings all in one place. You might also want to do your own research, keeping notes on what you learn. Check with the professionals you are working with before you proceed with any of the treatments and therapies listed above.

Does This Feel Familiar?

A new way of thinking.

At a very young age, our minds are introduced to certain types of media that cause incredible—sometimes even irreversible—damage. Not only are women in our society faced with a stereotypical look that is thought to represent beauty, we all assume that by achieving this look, life will be easier. The myth that many of us believe—"You can never be too thin"—has caused countless women and men (often teens and young adults) to fall under the abusive spell of anorexia.

Anorexia is crippling, not only to our generation but to people throughout the world. Our society strives to be what the world tells us is beautiful, but beauty should never be defined by size or become a competition. However, we are the victims of our own crimes. We have allowed our personal views and common sense to be altered by the media we willingly allow ourselves to absorb.

It is critical that we find a new way of thinking. Find new, creative avenues of healing. Find a way to only hear the truths.

Living around this devouring disease has allowed me to understand its ways from the inside out. This sickness is one that not only affects the victim but engulfs everyone who is even the slightest bit involved with it. Being in a family that included someone who was enslaved by this hell has allowed me to understand how powerful and truly corrupting this lifestyle is. My family was unwillingly forced to live side by side with the disease of anorexia. Every aspect of our daily lives was affected by it—going out to dinner, having a full-length mirror, keeping secrets from loved ones around us, etc. However, the deepest effect it had on me was my struggle to love the victim. I had to learn to recognize that her actions, which limited my life, were a result not of her selfishness but rather of her disease. I also had to fight to stay connected with my other family members amongst tearing pain. The day she left for treatment, I realized I would have to be more of a parent to my younger sibling and more of a comforter to my devastated parents—roles someone should never have to fill at my age. I learned that many families that live with this disease will live with it for forever. However, my family somehow found the strength to work together, to become whole again, to be a family again.

Although survival was thought to be impossible, I know now it is more than achievable. Over the past six years, I have watched firsthand as my family took down anorexia with love and forgiveness. I have developed a passion to help others learn to love themselves, to see their bodies as beautiful, just as they were created. We have to stop believing what we are fed by the media and find new, novel, and radical ways to not only *hear* the truth but to *believe* in it.

—A child who has witnessed the lies of anorexia

The Bigger Picture? Deepening Your Essential Purpose

Maybe thinking of others before yourself or in equal measure to yourself is the most effective medicine for the unending abuse. For it is hard to hate yourself when you feel connected to another. The amount of time spent obsessing over perfection could be spent being a lover. A friend. An advocate. A daughter. A wife. A sister. A blessing. A teacher. A student. An ally. A researcher. A helper. A caretaker. A giver. An artist. A change maker. That time is precious. Once given away, it will never come back. So here is my Thomas Edison, my invention, my thought. Let me not get caught in the web of lies being fed to me by a media rooted in insecurity. Let my mind be filled with power, might, creativity, and love, not impurity. For every minute I waste trying to perfect myself is a minute less that I could have chosen heaven over hell.

—A diary entry

15

Service to Others

With eating-disorder patients, service to others and volunteer work are most often effective after work has been done to restore brain chemistry and the body is no longer malnourished. Do not start volunteer work before your loved one is of sound mind and truly in recovery. This does not mean they must be fully recovered, but if they are too sick to focus and give of their talents, their service to others means nothing.

Are you interested in volunteering, or do you already serve somewhere? If so, your loved one will witness your efforts and be affected by your choice of action. We suggest you volunteer outside of the eating-disorder world.

With almost all other mental illnesses, we use exercise as a way to refocus by creating a flow of serotonin and a healthy body. This is not possible with eating disorders and thus makes service work a possible alternative. The brain is able to refocus away from the eating disorder and onto something else. This is when a caretaker can create opportunities for the loved one to find someone or something else to serve.

Once your child is stable—when the brain is nourished and the body safe from medical danger—is a great time to start volunteer work. Service work is often a frustrating waste of time if your child is not mentally ready, and you do not want to introduce another feeling of failure or potential relapse.

Although we recommend service work after the brain is stable, we have also witnessed success when service work is introduced early in the diagnosis. Repetition of an experience builds neural pathways in the brain; this is truest if your family is service oriented and volunteer work is a part of your routine. When to begin this work is a personal answer, and you, as the caretaker, have to decide the timing. Sometimes, depending on your experience, it's trial and error. Often, it is a commitment that becomes a purposeful pleasure, sparking new experiences and knowledge.

> I think repetition affects the neural pathways and is most effective combined with cognitive behavioral therapy. When the service fit is right, it gives the child a feeling of positively participating in the world and a break from the selfishness of the eating disorder. I think sometimes that initial selflessness has to be forced, but positive feelings are inevitable when helping someone or something else, and then the brain chemistry changes.
>
> —A mom of four

We have heard it since we were children: "You receive more than you give." It's a simple but well-documented statement that has survived the test of time. Think of it as interchangeable goodness! You, your loved one, your family, and those you aid will benefit.

The more we care for the happiness of others, the greater our own sense of well being becomes.[1]

Cultivating a close, warm-hearted feeling for others automatically puts the mind at ease. It helps remove whatever fears or insecurities we may have and gives us the strength to cope with any obstacles we encounter. It is the ultimate source of success in life.[2]

---

1   Dalai Lama (@DalaiLama), "The more we care . . .," Twitter, May 29, 2010, 2:33 a.m., https://twitter.com/dalailama/status/14965703261?lang=en.

2   Dalai Lama (@DalaiLama), "Cultivating a close . . .," Twitter, June 29, 2018, 2:33 a.m., https://twitter.com/dalailama/status/1012630016683859968?lang=en.

Next Steps to Take Now:
Putting One Foot in Front of the Other

Inquire about what service opportunities are available in your community. There will be something your community needs that will be available and interesting for your loved one. Ask the school counselor, your place of worship, and friends in the neighborhood for referrals. Check the internet for listings.

Why Is Service to Others Important?

- Service to others is service to self.

- Service creates a more compassionate way of living.

- Service can alleviate the pain of personal torment, both exposing and validating the dichotomy of human existence. You are never alone in suffering.

- Service opens the door to a myriad of human emotions, some joyful and some sad. It's this exposure that helps you grow as a person. The experience empowers both yourself and others.

- It is you who repairs, reconciles, expands, and hopefully finds a greater purpose than materialistic desire.

- It is time well spent.

- Service provides global comfort. The up-and-coming generation lives globally, and the sooner we expose our children to the needs of their world, the better equipped they will be as global citizens.

- Service can combat depression, build relationships, and bring fulfillment and fun into your life.

- Service will enhance your current skill set and expand your knowledge.

- Volunteer jobs, though not paid, can teach new job skills and introduce you to new potential fields of career opportunities.

- It helps you become less judgmental and more tolerant as you work side by side in new and unexpected relationships.

- It builds self-confidence. You are worthy, purposeful, and needed by other people.

Service to others has allowed me to grow, to learn, and to strengthen my personal understanding of the world. I'm in college, and I appreciate the gift of an education, yet the gift of experiential, hands-on learning has been just as important to my personal understanding of humanity. At this point, I have been volunteering since I was a little girl, and I am able to reflect back on my experiences and recognize my own self-worth, my reason for being here, and my own importance. We all are important. Service work has taught me to become part of the bigger picture rather than becoming focused only on my life. It has broadened my views and has been a stepping-stone for me to get involved in the lives of other people. This has created space for me to love others and, through that, learn to love myself.

—A social work student

Pause and Write

Please see *Working by Their Side* for ideas on where to volunteer that are not hands on. You might consider a gently encouraging conversation with your loved one about why service to others feels important.

Find the Right Fit

Service does not always include physical manpower, but it does include the way you choose to live your life! Sometimes service is as easy as everyday kindness.

If you and your loved one are not ready to engage in hands-on volunteer work, do not force a commitment. Instead, be open to creatively forging a different service path. For example:

- Sponsor a child in a different country who you are required to write once a month. This commitment most often involves a monthly fee of approximately $20 to $70.00 a month.

- Work at the Society for Prevention of Cruelty to Animals (SPCA). Working with animals enhances a physical, calming, and loving touch.

- Write a letter to a government agency, your school, or your place of worship on behalf of a belief or idea you feel passionate about. Lobby for good.

- Write letters to veterans and soldiers.

- Spend time with the elderly. Offer to teach them to use technology. And most importantly, just be there, and listen to them.

- Use social media to spread the word on positive, newsworthy causes. Utilizing social media is important because it is prevalent in our children's way of life, but with no accountability, it is also easy to become obsessed. Please be careful and wise when choosing a social-media outlet; eating disorders are compulsive behavior, and you don't want to amplify the problem.

Build Your Village of Support

When people from various backgrounds gather to work from the heart, relationships are built on passion, often creating lifelong friendships. Working for good brings out the best in you and the best in others, and together, in the same mind-set of love and service, we actually can change the world for better.

Volunteering broadens your village, helping you find commonality with others of different backgrounds, religions, and political views. The common goals unite a diverse community. Passion gifts you with joy and love, two of the most meaningful human emotions.

Working together for good is a spiritual experience; it moves people beyond thoughts of the self into an understanding of divinity and goodness.

Service helps you realize it actually is possible to feel like an instrument of peace.

> *Lord, make me an instrument of Thy peace. Where there is hatred, let me sow love. Where there is injury, pardon. Where there is doubt, faith. Where there is despair, hope. Where there is darkness, light. Where there is sadness, joy.*[3]

Be an Example

Are you already philanthropy oriented? Be an example to your loved one. When appropriate, invite your loved one and your family to join you. Your volunteerism can be a crucial piece of your own healing. It gets you out of the eating-disorder obsession, and when you choose to be openhearted, you broaden your thinking and experiences. Leading by example helps you become a stronger person. Remember, you affect those you are closest to by just being you.

Include Your Family

Even if you do not really want to serve or if your loved one fights you all the way there, go anyway. Eventually, the act of service will imprint positivity upon your heart and memory. These positive feelings help shape a more favorable view of yourself, the world, and others. They give you the ability to sympathize with and experience empathy for human beings, thus helping you live beyond your own selfish desires. So volunteer for fun, for service hours, to make connections, or any reason at all, and eventually your child, your family, and you will feel the passion.

In this book, we have used the word "lonely" many times. Caretaking a loved one with an eating disorder is lonely. Caretaking in general can be challenging. By serving those less fortunate—and no matter how bad your life seems, there are always others in worse condition—you are given the opportunity to make a choice on how you view life. This is not to undermine your troubles but to recognize that all people have struggles, and each person's struggles are relative to their life. Are you able to be grateful?

---

3   "Make Me an Instrument of Your Peace, Saint Francis Prayer," Catholic Online, last modified 2019, https://www.catholic.org/prayers/prayer.php?p=134.

Are you able to empathize with others? Are you able to steer your thinking and mood toward realistic hope? Are you optimistic? Are you caught in a vicious cycle of obsession with the disorder? If you are, you are normal! All of us have been sucked in by the grip of our loved one's disorder, and it is lonely. It can be very depressing. But what did we do? We broadened our minds and moods by volunteering. Sometimes our children and families joined us, and sometimes we ventured out on our own. Sometimes it was just a day serving hot meals at the shelter, and for some of us, it is our lives' work. Sometimes it was beneficial, and sometimes we had to try again.

Soul Food

Give because giving feeds the soul. Give because in helping others, you help yourself, for in the act of giving, the focus on the self is removed. This shift then allows you to dedicate your attention to others. In turn, your heart and soul are touched and opened, and you can see deep within yourself. Giving requires an open, non-judgmental heart and mind. To look into the eyes of a homeless man, hold the hand of an orphaned child, or share a meal with a family that barely makes ends meet is humbling beyond words. Seeing, feeling, and touching others allows you the opportunity to view life through a different lens. Those less fortunate could be others, or they could be our own children. See your child through a new lens—a perspective you never knew existed or could even imagine. I think that, in the recovery process, there probably comes a time when giving would become a great form of therapy.

More often than not, you will realize that the people you are helping have more than you do. They possess grace, hope, faith, and the belief that everything will be OK. They have enough, and that is all any of us needs: enough. So make the opportunity to give a priority in your life and in your recovery. Maybe the giving is right here in your own backyard, or maybe it's halfway around the world in a country and a culture you know nothing about. It does not matter! Each of us has the ability to get out of our comfort zone, open our heart, extend our hand, and make a difference. I promise that in giving you will receive more than you ever dreamed possible.

Find your tiny corner of the world, and make a difference in just one life. The life of that one person affects the lives of many, and it will help you grow and strengthen like nothing else in this world can.

—A mom and child-appointed court advocate

Look back into history at those who left this world a better place. Those marks were not made without helping others in need—often with pain and suffering, but always with extensive giving and inevitable receiving. Every religion across this planet asks you to help take care of others by loving your neighbor as yourself; it is said in the Torah, the Hindu Vedas, the Bible, the Koran, the Bahá'í Faith, Buddhism, Taoism, Confucianism, and more. Every moral and honorable principal is based on giving to others. Service provides the invaluable possibilities that money cannot buy: contentment, meaningful relationships, the gifts of giving and receiving, love, passion, connection, and purpose. A life beyond yourself can improve your health, your mental state, and your happiness.

I slept and dreamt that life was joy. I awoke and saw that life was service. I acted and behold, service was joy.

—*Rabindranath Tagore*

Pause and Write

Please give service work or volunteerism a fair try. There is never an ideal time to begin or continue, but you will know when it is right. In *Working by Their Side*, list ideas of how you can give service to others a fair chance.

Does This Feel Familiar?

Two versions of myself!

How is it that there are currently two people living in my home who have never experienced running water, are truly illiterate, and have never had enough food, yet all I can manage to think about is how much I don't want to eat? How could I possibly be willing to starve myself when there are people who have literally been starved based on poverty, not privilege? How could I be so selfish? How could I succumb to this level of vanity?

I remember these thoughts echoing through my mind constantly during the time a Haitian family lived in our home with us on my parents' invitation. My parents had very intentionally chosen this time to host the family, as I was in the midst of an eating disorder and in desperate need of purpose outside of my addiction and a commonality that didn't revolve around the brokenness my illness was causing.

I am forever grateful that my generous parents were so willing and so courageous to serve when it was anything but convenient. They were the most beautiful examples of what it meant to truly love without condition and what genuine generosity looked like.

My brother and sister were incredible as well. Intentionality came so easily to them. They were able to connect with the family right off the bat and were eager to forgo birthday parties, plans with friends, and their personal pleasures to ensure that the family staying with us was always more comfortable than they were. They were true examples of servants, able to gain worldly wisdom and perspective with such ease.

This was not the case for me. You see, I was caught between two versions of myself. It wasn't that I didn't want to be like my siblings—generous, kind, and selfless; it was that I wanted that but also wanted my addiction. And you can't have both. I always had the logic to understand that my choices were selfish and that my reasoning was flawed. However, the need to control would override my desire to be the best version of myself, which led me to end up in a cyclical pattern of bad decision-making, leading to negative self-perception.

Service in the midst of an eating disorder can be one of the trickiest subjects of all. It is absolutely critical. However, it is also absolutely dependent upon one's willingness to forgo one's selfish tendencies . . . and there are few things in the world that cause selfishness more than addiction and this type of disease. It is not that we are selfish people at heart; it is that the disease causes us to act selfishly and to have selfish thoughts. At times, it can even feel as if we have no control at all over our inability to think outside of our own minds. We are held captive to the mental monster we are serving, and we are unable to escape.

In order to truly serve, we must be willing to get outside of our own perspective. We must become the person we were meant to be—the person we want to be. You see, within each of us is a deep desire to have purpose, and I have found that purpose most often comes in the form of helping another. We crave this. And, quite frankly, we need this. We are desperate for it.

That is why service is so crucial to recovery and healing. It gives us purpose. It reminds us of the person we want to be and assures us that that is the person we are meant to be. Without service, we stay captive to the voice in our head that keeps us chained to self-loathing and hatred.

In the beginning, we might only get to a place where we are torn—a place where we are able only to see the irrational thinking going on in our clouded minds. However, I can tell you from experience that slowly but surely, through the practice of service, incredible healing occurs. Those two versions of yourself will slowly morph into one clear vision, one clear purpose. The confusion and frustration will transform into a willingness to let go of the vanity and to show up as the human you were made to be.

—A twenty-four-year-old who is now service oriented

16 Faith Practices

We all desire an explanation for the unexplainable. We all desire a place to put our hope. We can only temporarily put our faith in a person or a thing; people eventually pass on, structures break, and the tangible can diminish with time. We all desire to have faith in something that is good and that cannot be taken away. It's an anthropological truth that mankind has always searched for meaning. Civilizations past and present have used gods, religions, faiths, and belief systems to explain their existence and the world around them. Through the wonderment of miracles and the excruciating hardships in our lives, we question: Is there something more?

Religion is everything, and religion is nothing. Religion is life, and religion is death. Religion exists beyond the confines of humanity, for it is a practice of the spirit. No amount of words, action, thought, feeling, or belief can capture its true essence. It is unformed, ever changing, ever evolving beyond the confines of human experience and perception.

—A religious studies student

Have you ever felt this desire for more? Have you asked yourself, "Is there something bigger? What is the meaning of life?" Have you ever wondered about a power greater than ourselves, something words can't even explain? Though no two people are exactly alike, our desire to love and be loved is a profound commonality we all share as part of the human race. It is this common desire that drives us to look beyond our own understanding of humanity. It ignites our search for meaning. Some satisfy this desire through great teachers—Jesus, Buddha, the Dalai Lama, Krishna, Mohammed, etc. Sometimes, those teachers are our own children, our friends, or a stranger. Every individual has to find their own path to this source of love and hope.

For some, it takes loneliness, doubt, or pain to begin a search for teachers who can provide us with meaning. For others, it is those moments of silence, joy, or laughter that satisfy this urge. As a result of an eating disorder's negativity, it is natural for our struggling loved ones to search for self-worth and acceptance in deceptive, transient things, such as societal approval from friends, family, or the media.

> Within us there is an inner, natural dignity. (You often see it in older folks.) An inherent worthiness that already knows and enjoys. (You see it in children.) It is an immortal diamond waiting to be mined and is never discovered undesired. It is a reverence humming within us that must be honored. Call it the True Self, the soul, the unconscious, deep consciousness, or the indwelling Holy Spirit. Call it nothing. It does not need the right name or right religion to show itself. It does not even need to be understood. It is usually wordless. It just is, and it shows itself best when we are silent, or in love, or both. It is God-in-All-Things yet not circumscribed by any one thing. It is enjoyed only when each part is in union with all other parts, because only then does it stand in the full truth.[1]

Our loved ones struggling with an eating disorder can often feel a lack of significance and worthiness. In order to recover from an eating disorder, one must have a sense of purpose and perspective in life. These qualities

---

1   Richard Rohr, *Immortal Diamond: The Search for Our True Self* (San Francisco: Jossey-Bass, 2013).

are often most effectively cultivated through a belief system. No matter whether the practice is labeled a "religion," a "way of life," or simply a "world perspective," the spiritual element of recovery plays a critical role in healing as well as a crucial role in preventing relapse later down the road. Just as Rabbi Harold Kushner says at the top of this chapter, most people desire meaning and a sense that our lives matter. Whether the purpose has been replaced with disordered eating or whether the individual never had a strong sense of purpose in the first place is irrelevant. Purpose can be redefined for the individual when a sense of meaning is attained outside of bodily goals or physical appearance. A different type of healing occurs.

No matter your religious preference or cultural heritage, we believe a belief system and faith practice is critical to recovery. We also believe only you can define what that means. Many people have had unexplainable experiences, whether on a mountain top, in an orphanage of abandoned children, during a call to prayer or a shared Shabbat dinner, in a gospel church, at the river's edge, at the death bed of a loved one, at the birth of a child, or at the foot of the cross. The practice of faith comes in actively seeking those sacred places and satisfies our desire for "more." This place looks different for everyone.

No matter what system of religion you choose, each has a unique way of inviting the individual into a place where focus on the self isn't the only part of connecting to the world. Often, there is a higher power or a higher being of creation that gives us the freedom to exist as our true self. With the stigma of mental illness specifically, it's important to find places where we are allowed to be who we are. It's no one's fault that we struggle with depression, eating disorders, or bipolar disorder. Many times, we can find chemical imbalances that we can begin to treat with proper medication. And if we can find networks inside faith communities able to accept humankind as the proper image bearers of a creator, we can find social healing that works in tandem with physical healing.

It becomes an issue of addressing the *whole* human rather than simply trying to treat one symptom and then move on to another.

Human beings aren't like any other part of our world today. We can't simply change the oil, rotate the tires, change the timing belts, and be on our way. Human beings need holistic ways of looking at the world to climb their way to healing. Faith communities can provide one part.

—Andy Braner, Mediterranean Basin Fellow at the Center for Transatlantic Relations, Johns Hopkins University, Paul H. Nitze School of Advanced International Studies (SAIS)

Belief systems come in a wide variety of forms: reading sacred religious texts, meditation, prayer, journaling, chanting, spiritual ceremonies, communal gatherings, and more. When these practices are effective, experiences of peace, love, hope, and acceptance often occur, and the hope of healing brings us out of the darkest of places.

During the darkest days of my daughter's disease, my faith kept me believing we were going to survive the overwhelming chaos of the healing journey. I often felt alone, defeated, and exhausted. Handing my fears and frustrations over to a higher power in prayer not only gave me relief but enabled me to stay focused on concrete tasks rather than get caught up in the control and secrecy that characterize an eating disorder. Some days, it was only for five minutes, but they were my five minutes, and they empowered me to get through the rest of the day. Don't fight this battle alone! Find partners you can trust with your hopes and fears; journal, meditate, and hang on to your faith. There is great joy on the other side of this disease.

—A parent

Gaining perspective is another component of a spiritual practice. Most practices bring attention to the whole of humanity and the universe. When the mind is filled with a perspective outside of the limited self-perspective, it is able to alter thoughts, patterns, and beliefs. This type of alteration proves highly beneficial, if not essential, in recovery from an eating disorder. When an individual struggling with an eating disorder is able to get outside their own mind, they are then able to view the world with different lenses. Spiritual practices are the lenses by which perspective can be shifted. The nature of an eating disorder is to trick the mind into existing only within the limited perspective of the self. However, through the implementation of a spiritual practice, one is able to gain insight into an alternate viewpoint and move toward a transformation of beliefs and thoughts. Through these practices and the attainment of purpose and perspective, one becomes better acquainted with practices of love as well. Almost all religions and spiritual disciplines emphasize the importance of love for others and love for the self. This concept is critical in recovery for your loved one as well as for yourself.

Matthew Williams is a trauma counselor who restores hope and life to child soldiers in the Congo. Consider his insight.

I have met and counseled few, if any, individuals who dismissed the need for or longing for something transcendent (most often a loving god) when faced with something overwhelming. That overwhelming force might be the result of an eating disorder, war, trauma, abuse, or any number of other circumstances. Faced with such, we humans often recognize—even if for the first time—our need for a higher power, a loving god, or a transcendent purpose. Few have expressed this more poignantly than Viktor Frankl, author of *Man's Search for Meaning*, and few can question that he was qualified to speak to (dare I say) every human's need for self-transcendence. A professor of neurology and psychiatry, Frankl was also a survivor of four World War II concentration camps. Bearing witness to death and life, to horrid traumas and selfless courage, Frankl wrote about a key common denominator in those who have bravely faced the worst conditions, endured suffering with dignity, and ultimately survived. That common denominator he called "the self-transcendence of human existence"—that is, a transcendent purpose greater and more purposeful than one's mere existence. Living for oneself provides no grand motivation to live, much less to overcome. Yet to live with love for another, or to find hope in something greater . . . *That* can empower individuals to overcome the most overwhelming of odds. It may even have the power to restore the psyche—the soul, mind, spirit; breath; life.

—Matthew Williams, MA, counselor and director of operations of Exile International

This chapter utilizes a different format. We are not going to give suggestions on next steps because belief is so personal to each person's own existence that you have to explore and answer your own questions. For many of us, faith communities have been deeply healing. We have had to be diligent about nurturing our faith and making time to meditate, commune, read, pray, and breathe. Often, there is doubt, frustration, and fear. Truths, convictions, meaning, and purpose come to each of us on an individualized path. Faith has helped us strengthen our psyches, our inner beings, and our capacity.

Helping each other tap into our own personal faith and truth is paramount to recovery and to daily living. I have touched the intangible, experienced the unusual, and felt obscurities that have no explanation. And it is in these experiences of another realm that I find rest, quiet, and insight into my own soul. I believe faith is not a learned behavior but rather an internal knowledge innately born in each of us. One just has to be open to that for which we have no words in the human vocabulary to fully explain—that within whose image we are created.

—A mom

Pause and Write

Please take some quiet time to refer to *Working by Their Side* to journal your thoughts and feelings. We have offered some prompts, but only you can find your way. This is a deeply personal chapter, so please find a quiet place to reflect on and contemplate your faith. My faith might look different from yours, yet the yearning for peace in our souls and the belief that there is more to life than the physical is a common thread of familiarity. We sincerely hope you can find that place of love and hope for yourself.

Does This Feel Familiar?

It is well.

When my friend, a mother whose child had fought a nasty eating disorder, asked me to consider writing a piece on faith, I hesitated. "Oh gosh, I'm not a good writer, my story is too deep and perplexing . . ." But I quickly realized that my story is your story. Our pain is shared in the human heart; we are all very similar, and the pain of love has a common thread. The author of the timeless hymn "It Is Well with My Soul" knew that together, by the Grace of God, we can find peace. So please let me tell you why it is well with my soul even in the face of pain and suffering.

Twenty-nine years ago, my then fiancé had a traumatic brain injury that affects every part of his life. He was never and is never going to be the same. Unlike the final scene of a movie in which the protagonist walks out of the hospital healed, our new reality was not a fairy tale. Life would be challenging. He would have to learn how to walk, use a fork, read, write, clothe himself, and talk again. At twenty, you have no idea what that really means!

We married a year after the accident, and it was quite the celebration of life, family, and faith. Yes, faith, because it was my faith that led me to continue our relationship from engaged to married. At twenty-three, you have no idea what that really means.

The emotional toil of caring for a loved one broke me, crushed my dreams, and frustrated me. I was tired. Really tired. I had the burden of financially supporting us and decided to start my own company. Fast forward to 2016. I love my work, and it still sustains me in so many personal ways. Though we learned how to live with the reality of my husband's injury, accepting the physical difficulties was easier than accepting the mental and behavioral ones. Life was challenging, but the good Lord was preparing me for even greater challenges!

We had three beautiful boys. Our sons replaced my loneliness; the love of a child can do that. I had a flexible schedule. I could help the kids and my husband more. I could pay the bills. My mind was being stimulated. It was a win-win. But I battled a lingering guilt about the amount of time that work demanded, and the balance was challenging. Imperfectly fallible, I would fall out of balance and began sinking again. Family members would come to my rescue as I relied on them heavily. I grew up with parents who loved God and ingrained a deep faith. That faith was and still is my lifeline.

I finally began seeing a counselor. I wanted someone to make things normal in our marriage and smooth the balance of motherhood, work, and life. The professionals kept telling me that I was on a slow simmer and my top was going to blow off. From the outside, things looked OK. I could put on a smile, kiss away tears, work full time, keep up with the chores, cook a yummy dinner, and keep my kids happy. Was it really well with my soul? At times, it was, but not always. He was, yet again, preparing me for far harder circumstances that would come.

Our youngest had three back-to-back head injuries, all requiring trauma, hospitalization, and being transferred by ambulance or CareFlite. After the third accident, I remember sitting in the parking lot crying to my sister-in-law. Fear set in, panic set in, and yet again, I was being preparing for far harder circumstances that would come.

Our oldest son started using drugs and alcohol when he was fourteen. A mom will go to desperate measures to change a terrifying situation for their child. We went to a counselor on a regular basis, but the learning did not happen. Instead, more abuse, until it was normal: a daily high, treatment centers, family therapy, psychological testing, evading arrest, homelessness, a suicide attempt, and six constant years of anguish. I wonder whether caretaking a loved one with an eating disorder creates the same fear of losing a child. I think so. The caretaking is similar; the boundaries, tough love, sleepless nights, and consequences require unquantifiable mental strength! The pain of love has a common thread.

Most professionals would ask, "What are you doing for yourself?" It took me years to figure out what they meant. Now I get it, but it doesn't come naturally. I chose to follow a passion and befriended people who have experienced hell on earth: abuse, prostitution, poverty, and little or no support. Yet it is they who became my teachers. They've had a profound effect on every part of my being. To think that even in the midst of the saddest times in my life, I too could still keep going, love others, and have joy. The depth of this universal love is not of the earth; it is the joy of faith in something that makes order out of chaos and peace of out anxiety. It offers rest from worry, rest from being in control, rest from fear, rest from the future.

Many years have passed, and many more chapters in our storybook of life. And guess what? I am still not in control! I am still learning that the mental, emotional, and spiritual side of life affects us much more than the physical. If you are reading this book, my guess is you, too, have felt the pain of loving someone battling addiction, struggling with a mental illness, or battling an eating disorder. The parental worry, the fear of expectations not being met, the loneliness, the prayers not answered the way we wanted them to be, the resentment, the disappointments, the failed efforts or botched experimental treatments with this or that doctor—these feelings and emotions lead us on a journey that brings about a lot of hardship. But look closely, because even if not right this moment, we will eventually experience joy, purpose, and deep empathy. Out of our deepest pain comes purpose.

Across the planet, mankind continues to search for a peace that surpasses all understanding. Who is the Creator of all? Can I depend upon Him for real? Not only *can* you, I dare to say that you *have* to. We are not created to live in solitude. We need each other, and we need the one who abides beyond our human comprehension. God is not going away, even when and if everything else does. Though I can only see in this moment of time, God comprehends a divine order that exceeds our understanding.

So how do I sustain my faith in the face of adversity? I draw inner strength from others, stay grounded in my faith, and, when appropriate, pass it on to others in need. I am grateful for my life. It is the Creator of everything who grants me the peace to feel with my heart and know with my mind that it is well with my soul.

—A mom whose faith sustains her

17

Closing

[
There is no ending to this book. The
story is yours to continue.
]

Your story is intricately unique to you, as it is to your loved one and your family.

One of the challenges with recovering from any eating or mental disorder is that—unlike a medical problem that can be solved with surgery, medication, or physical therapy—the disorder is manipulative and intangible. Therefore, the journey to recovery is complex and unique.

Mental illness—of whatever kind—is so very hard. I honestly have wished my child had cancer sometimes. What mother would ever have such a thought! But cancer you can cut out or treat with strong meds, and it's socially acceptable. Mental illness is sneaky, insidious, and unscrupulous.

Friends and family understand cancer. It is tangible; you can see a tumor, test blood for bad cells. Treatment is definitive. You have something specific to fight, and everyone can sympathize with a cancer patient. Society does not understand mental illness; it is vague and abstract. Even with as much progress as we have made with eating disorders, they are still misunderstood. They creep up on individuals and families and make all of us question who we and the people we love are. Diagnosis is difficult, and treatment is multifaceted and never a quick fix.

And yet, there is always hope. Hope for a better tomorrow. With advancements in technology, psychology, and neuroscience, it is my hope that one day soon, it will be we, the human beings, that imprison mental illness instead of it imprisoning us.

I truly believe that every person afflicted with an eating disorder or any other disorder has very special gifts to share with the world. It is our job as mothers, fathers, family friends, and part of the human race to see these gifts and to help our loved ones identify and use them.

—A mom

If you have fought for your child's life due to an eating disorder or mental illness, you understand the above testimony. When we are brutally honest, every one of us has thought the same thing: Can't this please be an illness fixed with surgery or drugs? Currently, there is no easy fix for an eating disorder via surgery or an exact drug. But there is hope for healing. There is always hope for healing.

How do we know that healing really is attainable? We know because many of our children are the proof. It might look different for each of them, but they share the healing quality of self-love. Loving themselves has set them free to love others and live a fulfilling life.

By tapping into the knowledge of professionals and by learning from all of us—moms, dads, brothers, sisters, aunts, uncles, grandparents, and friends—we pray you are better equipped to move forward in helping yourself and your family.

There is a universal desire to see all eating disorders and mental illnesses cured—not just healed but vanished, totally gone away forever. Is that possible? We don't know, but it is a goal worth working toward.

The worst and darkest times of our lives were when we learned the most about ourselves and about humanity. Going through life's inevitable pain was when we discovered our potential and our gifts. Being the mother of a child with an eating disorder is not a road of choice nor a "club" we choose to be in, but many of us are in that club. And until there is a cure, we will continue the fight. Is it not our job to help our loved ones heal? Help them learn the ultimate earthly gift of being loved, giving love, and loving ourselves—our exquisite human selves?

Pause and Write

Please take some quite time to reflect on what you have learned, and follow the final prompts in *Working by Their Side*.

Thank you for taking the time to read this book. We pray, from the bottom of our hearts, that this book has helped you know the fight is worth it—that you are not only never alone in this struggle but are also capable and competent. You are never perfect, and you're sometimes wrong, but you're always perfectly human. Integrating honesty, love (very often tough love!), and kindness with a commitment to doing the best we can do offers us the potential for full and comprehensive healing. Ask for help; learn from the professionals; and use us as your learning curve. As we have said before, healing might not look exactly like the picture you've painted in your mind, in which all the edges are straight and no colors blend or overlap. There is no perfect picture; however, there is *your* picture.

But you will know, you will feel, and you will be deeply grateful. When asked what it feels like when your loved one has an eating disorder, you will be able to confidently answer and to turn to them and say, "Is there anything I can help you with?"

We leave you with this fiercely passionate poem written by a recovered advocate to all those who are fighting the battle or witnessing the struggle.

Watch Out, Girl . . . I'm Coming For You

Watch out, girl . . . I'm coming for you.

I'm coming to adore you so hard that you will never again think that the cellulite on your thigh is anything less than the markings of a goddess or that the rolls on your tummy are not the story of a life fearlessly and courageously enjoyed. When you look in the mirror, you will want to yell, "*Thank you*," because you will no longer see a body, but a soul . . . and you have a hell of a lot to thank it for.

I am coming to tell you the truth of your magnificence, to erase the lies you used to believe in and replace them with the honesty of your importance, worth, ability, and sheer force. I am coming to grab you and wrap you in my arms so tight that you will never, *ever* feel alone again. Because you are female, and to be female is to be one with all. *We* are a force to be reckoned with . . . You have a fierce army as your tribe.

I am coming to kiss your precious throat and to remind you that—your voice . . . ? It *matters*. Your story, your thoughts, your opinions . . . yes. They are the words that are going to heal this aching world. So scream them at the top of your lungs. Be loud, and show up.

I am coming to beg for that well of intelligence inside your complicated brain. There is an entire world inside of you just waiting to be unlocked, explored, and discovered. It is just waiting to be tapped into. Never underestimate what you have to offer . . . It is millions of years old and barely born. It is freshly unthought of and also soaked in wisdom. Listen to yourself . . . You have a universe in there.

I am coming to crack open that worried heart of yours. I am going to break it so much that every ounce of intuition, service, wisdom, care, compassion, and goodness is made known to you. You will never again use the words "not enough," because that is no longer your name. You don't even know her.

You will be so overwhelmed with the goodness you find in there that you will take on a new name. You will be called Healed. You will be called A Beautiful Mess. You will be called Imperfect. You will be called Generous. You will be called Capable. You will be called Warrior. You will be called Complicated. And you will own it *all*. You will wear every name, for you are everything . . .

. . . So watch out, girl, cause I'm coming for you.

[
Signed,
Your Recovered Self
]

Appendix

Foreword

The foreword was written by Betty K. Armstrong, PhD.

> Dr. Armstrong's training in clinical psychology, her theoretical orientation of behavior analysis, and her over 30 years of experience give her a strong foundation for working with clients who struggle with a wide variety of psychological problems: depression, anxiety, relationship conflicts, eating disorders, and emotional traumas. . . . Everyone in the family is affected in some way by the person who struggles with a psychological disorder. Dr. Armstrong's extensive understanding of psychological problems, particularly eating disorders, enhances her ability to offer support, education, and therapy to family members.[1]

- Dr-Armstrong.com

Chapter 1

The following are the four primary eating disorders discussed in this book.

- Anorexia nervosa (AN)
- Bulimia nervosa (BN)
- Binge-eating disorder (BED)
- Other specified feeding and eating disorders (OSFED)

For definitions of other eating disorders, please refer to FEAST's Eating Disorders Glossary. This glossary of disorders, disturbances, and therapeutic terms is published by Families Empowered and Supporting Treatment of Eating Disorders. Also see "Information by Eating Disorder" on the website of the National Eating Disorders Association.

- Glossary.FEAST-ED.org
- NationalEatingDisorders.org/information-eating-disorder

• • •

For the diagnostic criteria described in the fifth edition of the American Psychiatric Association's

---

1   "Dallas Psychologist Betty K. Armstrong Professional Background," Betty K. Armstrong, Ph.D., https://www.dr-armstrong.com/behavior-therapist/.

Diagnostic and Statistical Manual of Mental Disorders (DSM-5), visit the website of the American Psychiatric Association.

- Psychiatry.org/patients-families/eating-disorders/what-are-eating-disorders

• • •

"There has been an unprecedented growth of eating-disordered individuals in the last two decades. Up to 95 percent of those suffering are between the ages of twelve and twenty-five."[2]

• • •

"The NEDA Parent Toolkit is for anyone who wants to understand more about how to support a family member or friend affected by an eating disorder. You will find answers to your insurance questions; signs, symptoms and medical consequences; information about treatment and levels of care; and questions to ask when choosing a treatment provider."[3]

Chapter 2

Carrie Arnold, *Decoding Anorexia: How Breakthroughs in Science Offer Hope for Eating Disorders* (New York: Taylor & Francis, 2013):

> *Decoding Anorexia* is the first and only book to explain anorexia nervosa from a biological point of view. Its clear, user-friendly descriptions of the genetics and neuroscience behind the disorder is paired with first person descriptions and personal narratives of what biological differences mean to sufferers. Author Carrie Arnold, a trained scientist, science writer, and past sufferer of anorexia, speaks with clinicians, researchers, parents, other family members, and sufferers about the factors that make one vulnerable to anorexia, the neurochemistry behind the call of starvation, and why it's so hard to leave anorexia behind. She also addresses:
>
> - How environment is still important and influences behaviors
> - The characteristics of people at high risk for developing anorexia nervosa
> - Why anorexics find starvation "rewarding"
> - Why denial is such a salient feature, and how sufferers can overcome it
>
>   Carrie also includes interviews with key figures in the field who explain their

---

2   "7 Powerful Statistics about Eating Disorders," Avalon Hills Foundation, February 4, 2015, http://www.avalonhillsfoundation.org/blog/2015/02/7-powerful-statistics-about -eating-disorders/.

3   "Parent Toolkit," National Eating Disorders Association, 2018, https://www.national eatingdisorders.org/parent-toolkit.

work and how it contributes to our understanding of anorexia. Long thought to be a psychosocial disease of fickle teens, this book alters the way anorexia is understood and treated and gives patients, their doctors, and their family members hope.

Chapter 3

Huxing Cui et al., "Eating Disorder Predisposition is associated with *ESRRA* and *HDAC4* Mutations," *Journal of Clinical Investigation* 123, no. 11 (November 1, 2013): 4706–4713, https://doi.org/10.1172/JCI71400.

• • •

Jennifer Brown, "Two Genes Linked to Increased Risk for Eating Disorders," *Iowa Now*, October 8, 2013, https://now.uiowa.edu/2013/10/two-genes-linked-increased-risk-eating-disorders.

• • •

"The Neuroplasticity of the Brain," Emily Program, October 28, 2015, https://emilyprogram.com/blog/the-neuroplasticity-of-the-brain/.

• • •

Founded by Eddie Coker, the Wezmore Project "support[s] young people in honoring their emotional experiences, enhancing psychological resiliency, and encouraging a sense of well-being."[4]

•   TheWezmoreProject.org

• • •

Marcia Herrin and Nancy Matsumoto, *The Parent's Guide to Eating Disorders*, 2nd ed. (Carlsbad, CA: Gürze Books, 2007):

> [*The Parent's Guide to Eating Disorders* by Marcia Herrin] is the first book written by a nutritionist that addresses childhood and teenage eating disorders—with an emphasis on home-based recovery. Herrin focuses on early detection and intervention with effective solutions that begin in the home, at virtually no cost other than a healthy investment of time, effort, and love. This second edition includes new information on family communication, medical consequences, advice for siblings, relapse prevention, food plans, and boys at risk. Unique to this version are four chapters devoted to the Maudsley approach, the highly-successful, parent-assisted method for normalizing eating. Also, the parent of one of the author's anorexic

---

4   "The Wezmore Project, Inc.," North Texas Giving Day, Communities Foundation of Texas, last modified 2019, https://www.northtexasgivingday.org/wezmore.

patients contributed a chapter about her family's experiences in recovery using the techniques described in this book.

For more information on this book and its authors, visit the website below.

- EatingDisorderGuides.com/index.php/marcia/

Chapter 4

Eddie Coker is an award-winning singer, songwriter, and performer, as well as the founder of the Wezmore Project and Okay to Say.

> The deal with kindness is it is really something not to be thought of. It really is something one does. To teach our kids kindness, we first and foremost have to be kind to them, show them how we are kind to others, and then get them to practice it themselves, over and over and over.
>
> —Eddie Coker; EddieCoker.com

Okay to Say was launched by the Meadows Mental Health Policy Institute and our partners to increase awareness that most mental illnesses are treatable and to offer messages of hope and recovery to Texans and their families.

The goal of Okay to Say is to change the conversation and perceptions around mental illness, which ultimately can lead to:

- Growing understanding, advocacy and support for the mentally ill.
- Improving access to community services for diagnosis and treatment.
- Accelerating progress in the quality and delivery of mental health care.[5]

Chapter 5

Miki Johnston, MSW, LCSW, is a mother, wife, daughter, and therapist for teens, adults and families. "With more than 20 years of experience, Miki has had the privilege of working with many diverse populations in a variety of therapy and non-profit settings . . . specializ[ing] in adolescent social and emotional struggles, women's issues, teen dating violence, parent-child conflict, stress management, peer conflict, body image, depression, and anxiety."[6]

---

5   "Our Story," Meadows Mental Health Policy Institute, 2017, okaytosay.org/about/.
6   "Miki Johnston, MSW, LCSW," LinkedIn, https://www.linkedin.com/in/miki -johnston-msw-lcsw-78026aa1.

Everyone faces challenges in life. It's how you learn to overcome them and use them to your betterment that matters most.

—Miki Johnston; MikiJohnstonTherapy.com

Chapter 6

My passion lies in working with children and adults, to reduce stress in their lives and rebuild the family environment. To work together openly and honestly to create a greater understanding of your unique self and your relationships with others, identify attainable short and long-term goals, process emotions, enhance self-esteem, and instill hope through the altering of thoughts and behaviors.

—Mary Grace Mewett, licensed professional counselor, MS, LPC, NCC; marygrace@mewettcounseling.com

Chapter 7

Melody Moore, PhD, RYT is a clinical psychologist, yoga teacher, and the founder of the Embody Love Movement. Her vision of the world is of one in which everyone is able to recognize the inherent worth and value of themselves and of their contributions.

Everyone on earth has a right to be here, a right to be seen and heard, and a right to be completely loved. When we value who we are, we value everyone around us just as much.

—Dr. Melody Moore; DrMelodyMoore.com

The Embody Love Movement's mission is "to empower girls and women to celebrate their inner beauty, commit to kindness, and contribute to meaningful change in the world." The organization conducts transformational workshops and events for children ages seven to eleven, teens ages twelve to eighteen, and adults. They also offer facilitator training and leadership development.

• EmbodyLoveMovement.org

• • •

"Section 10: Therapy," Ethical Principles of Psychologists and Code of Conduct, American Psychological Association, 2017, apa.org/ethics/code/index.aspx.

• • •

The National Eating Disorders Association (NEDA) is a national nonprofit eating-disorders organization. It offers information, referrals, support, prevention, conferences, and newsletters. NEDA's Parent Toolkit is a great reference for information to answer your questions.

- Website: NationalEatingDisorders.org; NationalEatingDisorders.org/find-help-support
- Toll-free information and referral helpline: 1-800-931-2237
- Email: info@NationalEatingDisorders.org

• • •

If you are in crisis and want to immediately text with a trained crisis counselor for free, text "NEDA" to 741741 or (with AT&T, T-Mobile, Sprint, or Verizon) "GO" to 741741.

- CrisisTextLine.org

• • •

EDReferral.com is in partnership with the American Eating Disorder Association. Search for treatment for eating disorders in the area in which you live.

- EDReferral.com

• • •

The National Association of Anorexia Nervosa and Associated Disorders (ANAD) is a national eating-disorder nonprofit organization offering treatment referral, support groups, conferences, education, statistics, and events.

- Website: ANAD.org
- Helpline: 630-577-1330
- Email: anadhelp@anad.org
- Phone: 630-577-1333

Chapter 8

Call the National Eating Disorders Association (NEDA), and ask for a referral in your area. Their toll-free information and referral helpline is 1-800-931-2237.

• • •

The International Association of Eating Disorder Professionals (IAEDP) is also a resource. To find a licensed professional in your area, visit web.MemberClicks.com/mc/directory/viewsimplesearch.do?orgId=iaedp.

• • •

Around the Dinner Table is an online community of parents from all around the world supporting one another. Registration is required, so contact Families Empowered and Supporting Treatment of Eating Disorders (FEAST) online at AroundTheDinnerTable.org.

• • •

Abigail Natenshon, *When Your Child Has an Eating Disorder, a Step-by-Step Workbook for Parents and Caregivers* (San Francisco: Jossey-Bass, 1999):

> *When Your Child Has an Eating Disorder* is the first hands-on workbook to help parents successfully intervene when they suspect their child has an eating disorder. This step-by-step guide is filled with self-tests, questions and answers, journaling and role playing exercises, and practical resources that give parents the insight they need to understand eating disorders and their treatment, recognize symptoms in their child, and work with their child toward recovery. This excellent and effective resource is one therapists can feel confident about recommending to patients.

Chapter 9

Visit the Accreditation Council for Education in Nutrition and Dietetics (ACEND) at EatRightPro.org/ACEND.

• • •

"Anyone can call himself or herself a nutritionist. But, only an RD or RDN has completed multiple layers of education and training established by the Accreditation Council for Education in Nutrition and Dietetics."[7]

• CDRNet.org.

• • •

Visit the International Federation of Eating Disorder Dietitians, and look under the tab labeled "Treatment Finder" to locate a registered dietitian or nutritionist in your area.

• EDDietitians.com

• • •

---

7   "10 Reasons to Visit an RDN," eatrightPRO, Academy of Nutrition and Dietetics, September 22, 2019, https://www.eatright.org/food/resources/learn-more-about-rdns /10-reasons-to-visit-an-rdn.

- Eating Disorder Hope: EatingDisorderHope.com/treatment-for-eating-disorders/therapists-specialists/texas-tx

• • •

A Certified Nutrition Specialist (CNS) is an accredited nutrition expert.

• • •

BMI is the measure of a person's body mass index.

• • •

Refeeding is the act of reintroducing nutrition/food to patients who are severely malnourished. Refeeding is most common in the treatment of anorexia or of a person who suffers from a severe medical issue. It is best to have medical professionals oversee the process, most especially when the patient who has been starved of nutrition, to avoid refeeding syndrome, which is a series of metabolic disturbances and electrolyte/fluid imbalances that negatively affect the body due to starvation.

For detailed information on refeeding and refeeding syndrome, visit NCBI.NLM.NIH.gov or EatingDisorderHope.com.

• • •

Relapse is a deterioration in someone's state of health after a temporary improvement. It is not uncommon with eating disorders. In that context, relapse refers to when a patient falls back into old disordered habits and patterns with food and behavior. For example, a client who has obtained forward progress by restoring their body to a healthy weight and living a positive lifestyle might fall back into old patterns triggered by trauma, depression, negative environmental influences, a sense of failure, etc. For more information on relapses, check out NationalEatingDisorders.org/slips-lapses-and-relapses.

• • •

Intuitive Eating: A Revolutionary Program That Works, 3rd ed., is a helpful resource from Evelyn Tribole, MS, RDN, CEDRD-S, and Elyse Resch, MS, RDN, CEDRD, FIAEDP, FADA, FAND. The authors also have a blog[8] and a new workbook geared toward patients called *The Intuitive Eating Workbook: Ten Principles for Nourishing a Healthy Relationship with Food*. The authors' ten principles of intuitive eating include:

1. Reject the diet mentality.

---

8   Evelyn Tribole, "What Is Intuitive Eating?," Intuitive Eating, https://www.intuitiveeating.org/what-is-intuitive-eating-tribole/.

2. Honor your hunger.
3. Make peace with food.
4. Challenge the food police.
5. Respect your fullness.
6. Discover the satisfaction factor.
7. Honor your feelings without using food.
8. Respect your body.
9. Exercise; feel the difference.
10. Honor your health.[9]

• • •

Visit NationalEatingDisorders.org/neda-navigators to consult with a NEDA Navigator associated with the National Eating Disorders Association. You can also contact NEDA's information and referral helpline by calling 1-800-931-2237, emailing info@nationaleatingdisorders.org, or chatting online with a helpline volunteer via their "Click to Chat" feature.

Chapter 10

Eating Recovery Center is an international center for eating disorders recovery providing comprehensive treatment for anorexia, bulimia, binge eating disorder and other unspecified eating disorders.

We offer healing and hope for a lasting recovery to individuals and families suffering with an eating disorder. Utilizing a full continuum of care, we provide expert behavioral health and medical treatment in an environment of compassion, competence, collaboration and integrity.[10]

• • •

Dr. Stephanie Setliff, MD, CEDS-S, has specialized in the treatment of eating disorders for twenty years and currently serves as regional medical director at the Eating Recovery Center of Dallas.

• • •

Dr. Tyler A. Wooten, MD, is a psychiatrist for children, adolescents, and adults who is certified by the American Board of Psychiatry and Neurology and has been a practicing psychiatrist

---

9   Evelyn Tribole and Elyse Resch, *The Intuitive Eating Workbook: Ten Principles for Nourishing a Healthy Relationship with Food* (Oakland, CA: New Harbinger Publications, 2017).

10 "About Eating Recovery Center," Eating Recovery Center, last modified 2018, https://www.eatingrecoverycenter.com/about-us.

and psychotherapist for two decades. He currently serves as a medical director at the Eating Recovery Center.

- Dallas.EatingRecoveryCenter.com/about-us/meet-our-team
- EatingRecoveryCenter.com
- 972-476-0801

• • •

For additional definitions of types of treatment and therapies, visit EatingDisorderHope.com/ treatment-for-eating-disorders/ types-of-treatments.

• • •

The following sites can help you find a treatment center.

- National Eating Disorders Association (NEDA): NationalEatingDisorders.org/ find-treatment
- Eating Disorder Hope: EatingDisorderHope.com/treatment-centers

• • •

Information on and reviews of treatment centers can be found at the following sites.

- EDTreatmentReview.com/usa-treatment-consumer-reviews/general-comments-and -questions-forum/
- EatingDisordersTreatmentReviews.org
- NYTimes.com/2016/03/15/health/eating-disorders-anorexia-bulimia-treatment-centers. html

• • •

For more information on the Mental Health Parity and Addiction Equity Act of 2008 (MHPAEA), visit CMS.gov/CCIIO/Programs-and-Initiatives/Other-Insurance-Protections/ MHPAEA.html.

• • •

For more information on the Affordable Care Act, visit HHS.gov/healthcare/facts-and-features/ key-features-of-aca/.

Chapter 11

The Patient Protection Affordable Care Act (PPACA) extends to small and individual plans, but you need to try to understand it according to your personal situation. For more information on laws related to insurance, visit the websites below.

- Affordable Care Act: HHS.gov/healthcare/facts-and-features/key-features-of-aca/
- Paul Wellstone and Pete Domenici Mental Health Parity and Addiction Equity Act of 2008 (MHPAEA) and state parity laws: CMS.gov/CCIIO/Programs-and-Initiatives/ Other-Insurance-Protections/mhpaea_factsheet.html

"Mental health coverage offered through the individual market also was notoriously skimpy or nonexistent. Now, anyone who buys a plan through the new online marketplaces will find mental health services covered as one of ten "essential health benefits" and no lifetime limits on services that will be reimbursed."[11]

• • •

Find out the latest news, events, and policy updates via the Mental Health America website at MentalHealthAmerica.net.

• • •

Billing codes are provided by professionals and submitted to insurance companies for reimbursement. Remember to ask the professionals you are working with to provide you with a billing code for services rendered.

> When a service is provided by a doctor or facility, a billing code is needed to obtain reimbursement for services. Certain rules and regulations govern how services must be coded and who can perform these services. Different types of facilities and different healthcare professionals must use codes that apply to that type of facility and health professional. Also, if codes don't exist for certain services delivered in a particular setting, then facilities and health professionals have no way to bill for their services. Codes used for billing purposes are set up by various entities such as the American Medical Association, U.S. Medicare program, and the World Health Organization's International Classification of Diseases.[12]

For more detailed information, check out the simplified billing codes from Magellan Standard Services.[13] You are not responsible for the billing codes, but you are responsible for inquiring about the billing codes when speaking with any and all of your doctors.

---

11   Judith Graham, "New Insurance Policies Must Cover Mental Illness," *Kaiser Health News*, January 9, 2014, https://khn.org/news/mental-illness-an-essential-benefit-sidebar/.

12   "Understanding Insurance Issues for Eating Disorders Treatment," National Eating Disorders Association, 2018, https://www.nationaleatingdisorders.org/toolkit/ parent-toolkit/understanding-insurance.

13   Magellan Health, Inc., *Magellan Standard Services Simplified Billing Codes*, reviewed February 2018, https://www.magellanprovider.com/media/11704/codingsimplified.pdf.

• • •

The following are national websites to consult for insurance coverage information.

- National Association of Anorexia Nervosa and Associated Disorders (ADAD): ANAD.org. Call the helpline at 630-577-1330, or email questions to anadhelp@anad.org.
- National Eating Disorders Association (NEDA): NationalEatingDisorders.org. For more information about insurance issues, visit the NEDA Parent Toolkit at NationalEatingDisorders.org/parent-toolkit.

Chapter 12

The mission of the Elisa Project (TEP) and its student-led program, LEAD (learn, empower, accept, discover), is to use a curriculum of knowledge, case management, and advocacy to combat eating disorders. "The Elisa Project (TEP) serves women, men, adolescents and children of all ages—we even have services for dependents of clients and their caregivers. Our clients include people living with symptoms of unhealthy relationships with food including: disordered eating, obesity, eating disorders, and more."[14]

Visit TheElisaProject.org or call the TEP helpline at 866-837-1999.

> Treatment programs do exist for people who have no money or benefits, but they are often hard to locate. Some agencies that receive public funds do provide treatment, and sometimes that treatment is outstanding. Another way to obtain treatment is through community agencies—sometimes treatment is provided at no cost or with a sliding scale fee. Counseling centers and student health services are another option if your patient is a student on a college or university campus. To get treatment at these locations, you usually pay a student health fee with your tuition.
>
> Many departments of psychiatry within medical schools have low-fee clinics run by psychiatric residents (medical school graduates who have had two or three years of their psychiatric training and are supervised by experienced faculty members). Call the department of psychiatry within the medical school and ask if they have low-fee clinics run by residents and if they will accept a patient with an eating disorder. Be sure to ask about sliding-scale fees and ask about what supervision the medical resident has available to him or her.[15]

• • •

---

14   "Who We Serve," Elisa Project, last modified 2019, https://theelisaproject.org/who-we-serve/.

15   "Insurance Coverage for Eating Disorders," EDReferral.com, https://www.edreferral.com/insurance-coverage.

The Foundation for Health Coverage Education can help determine whether you or someone you know is eligible for free or low-cost health coverage.

- CoverageForAll.org

• • •

- Health Network Group, LLC: HealthNetwork.com
- Obamacare: Obamacare.net

• • •

Call the National Eating Disorders Association (NEDA) Helpline with your questions, and they will guide you through their website if necessary. NEDA's toll-free information and referral helpline is 1-800-931-2237.

• • •

The following are mentor programs and scholarships to explore.

- Mentor Connect: MentorConnect-ED.org
- Manna Fund: MannaFund.org
- Moon Shadow's Spirit: MoonShadowsSpirit.org
- Project HEAL: TheProjectHEAL.org
- The Gail R. Schoenbach FREED Foundation: FREEDStat.org
- Clinical Trials: ClinicalTrials.gov
- Lisa's Light of Hope: LisasLightOfHope.com
- Mercy Multiplied: MercyMultiplied.com
- Eating Disorders Anonymous: EatingDisordersAnonymous.org/join.html

• • •

Around the Dinner Table is an online community of parents from all around the world supporting one another. Registration is required, so contact Families Empowered and Supporting Treatment of Eating Disorders (FEAST) online at AroundTheDinnerTable.org.

• • •

The following platforms can be used for online fundraising.

- GiveForward: GiveForward.com
- GoFundMe: GoFundMe.com
- YouCaring: YouCaring.com
- FundRazr: FundRazr.com
- Kickstarter: Kickstarter.com
- DonationTo: DonationTo.com
- JustGiving: JustGiving.com

• • •

The existence of the internet and smartphones has opened up new ways of delivering psychological treatments, one of which is to digitalise them so that they can be delivered online or via smartphone apps. Digital treatment is new and has only recently become the focus of research. Its use as a means of providing treatment for depression and anxiety disorders is receiving considerable attention, but there has been much less research on its use to help people with eating disorders.

At CREDO we are developing a digital form of CBT-E, termed CBTe. It is designed to be delivered direct to those with an eating problem (via search engines). It is intended for people with recurrent binge eating, and for two groups in particular:

- Those in the early stages of an eating disorder. The goal is to help them break out of it before the problem gets well established.

- Those with an established eating disorder who are unable or unwilling to access face-to-face treatment. This can be for a variety of reasons including reluctance to disclose the problem, lack of local treatment resources, waiting lists, cost of treatment, and practical difficulties attending.

CBTe is designed to be a highly personalised and engaging intervention. It matches the eating problem of the user and adapts itself to his or her progress.[16]

• • •

Rena Goldman, "Best Eating Disorder Recovery Apps of 2018," Healthline, April 19, 2018, healthline.com/health/eating-disorders/top-iphone-android-apps#2.

Chapter 13

As a naturopathic doctor, I believe that personalized preventive care is of the utmost importance in helping people achieve their health goals. I work with each patient on an individual basis, designing therapies to decrease the progressive destruction of tissue and restore normal function. The goal is to assist and support the body in its healing efforts, and the objective is to maintain optimum health. To remain disease-free, the underlying imbalance must be identified and corrected. To do so is the art of naturopathy. The six principles of healing I adhere to come from the Foundation for

16 "CBTe – A Digital Treatment for Recurrent Binge Eating," Centre for Research on Eating Disorders at Oxford, https://www.credo-oxford.com/5.1.html.

Naturopathic Medicine and state: first do no harm; believe in the healing power of nature; treat the whole person; identify and treat the cause; the doctor is a teacher; and prevention is the best cure. When given proper nutrition, pure water, exercise, and rest, the body is allowed to seek its natural balance and maintain a state of health.

—Dr. Sheri Lewis, ND, the Nutrition Club

• • •

There are six timeless naturopathic principles founded on medical tradition and scientific evidence.

- **Let nature heal.** Our bodies have such a powerful, innate instinct for self-healing. By finding and removing the barriers to this self-healing—such as poor diet or unhealthy habits—naturopathic physicians can nurture this process.

- **Identify and treat causes.** Naturopathic physicians understand that symptoms will only return unless the root illness is addressed. Rather than cover up symptoms, they seek to find and treat the cause of these symptoms.

- **First, do no harm.** Naturopathic physicians follow three precepts to ensure their patients' safety:
  » Use low-risk procedures and healing compounds—such as dietary supplements, herbal extracts and homeopathy—with few or no side effects.
  » When possible, do not suppress symptoms, which are the body's efforts to self-heal.
  » Customize each diagnosis and treatment plan to fit each patient.

- **Educate patients.** Naturopathic medicine believes that doctors must be educators, as well as physicians. That's why naturopathic physicians teach their patients how to eat, exercise, relax and nurture themselves physically and emotionally. They also encourage self-responsibility and work closely with each patient.

- **Treat the whole person.** We each have a unique physical, mental, emotional, genetic, environmental, social, sexual and spiritual makeup. The naturopathic physician knows that all these factors affect our health. That's why he or she includes them in a carefully tailored treatment strategy.

- **Prevent illness.** "An ounce of prevention is worth a pound of cure" has never been truer. Proactive medicine saves money, pain, misery and lives. That's why naturopathic physicians evaluate risk factors, heredity and vulnerability to disease.[17]

Find a certified holistic physician through the American Board of Integrative Holistic Medicine (ABIHM) at ABIHM.org/search-doctors.

• • •

Visit the International Network of Integrative Mental Health (INIMH) at INIMH.org.

- Advance a global vision for an integrated whole person approach to mental health care via education, research, networking and advocacy, by bringing together the wisdom of world healing traditions and modern science.

- Re-animate the mental health field with energy, spirit, compassion and joy. We are committed to serving the worthy goal of working toward the cessation of human suffering.

- Create community and opportunities for nurturing personal and professional connections. We honor and respect the unique backgrounds and skills that each person brings to this work, and wish to promote meaningful relationships and connection to a global integrative mental health network.

- Promote evidence-based CAM therapies and the judicious use of modern pharmacotherapies for the betterment of mental healthcare.

- Contribute to the emerging bio-psycho-socio-spiritual paradigm addressing mind, body, and spirit by promoting effective and safe clinical practices. We acknowledge the fundamental importance of an ecological perspective and believe that environmental and transpersonal factors have profound effects on wellbeing and healing.

- Educate, support and inspire integrative practitioners and trainees, at all levels of their careers and in all world regions. Our philosophy is based upon blending the best practices from traditional and modern healing systems. Our focus is on safety and positive outcomes while honoring our patients' unique needs, beliefs, wisdom, and advocacy for therapeutic choices and relationships with practitioners that empower them.

- Facilitate collaborative efforts between researchers and clinicians that extend beyond limited conventional understandings of mental healthcare as it pertains to care of individuals with psychological or psychiatric disorders, to a broader perspective that includes the range of psychosocial, cultural and spiritual factors

17   "Naturopathic Medicine," Quakertown Wellness, 2015, http://quakertownwellness.com/naturopathic-medicine/.

that impact on health, well-being, immune functioning, and physiological integrity.[18]

• • •

"The American College for Advancement in Medicine (ACAM) is a not-for-profit organization dedicated to educating physicians and other health care professionals on the safe and effective application of integrative medicine. ACAM's healthcare model focuses on prevention of illness and a strive for total wellness. ACAM is the voice of integrative medicine; our goals are to improve physician skills, knowledge and diagnostic procedures as they relate to integrative medicine; to support integrative medicine research; and to provide education on current standard of care as well as additional approaches to patient care."[19]

• ACAM.org

• • •

Answers to Anorexia: A Breakthrough Nutritional Treatment That Is Saving Lives by Dr. James Greenblatt offers patients and families new hope for success. Dr. Greenblatt is a leading expert in eating and mood disorders and a pioneer of integrative medicine. He offers a revolutionary approach to improving mental wellness and the treatment of mental illness. To be successful, Dr. Greenblatt explains, treatment needs to correct the physical. His other books include *Finally Focused, The Breakthrough Depression Solution*, and *Answers to Binge Eating*, which offer new hope for appetite control.

• • •

To begin exploring integrative psychiatry, search for doctors and practitioners in your state by calling 800-385-7863 or searching the internet for integrative psychiatrists in your area.

• • •

Traditional Chinese medicine is one of the oldest continuous systems of medicine in history, with recorded instances dating as far back as two thousand years before the birth of Christ. This is in sharp contrast to the American or Western forms of health care, which have been in existence for a much shorter time span . . .

Chinese medicine is quite complex and can be difficult for some people to comprehend. This is because TCM is based, at least in part, on the Daoist belief that we live in a universe in which everything is interconnected. What happens to

---

18   "Consider Joining the International Network of Integrative Mental Health," *Unbound* (blog), March 7, 2012, https://www.saybrook.edu/blog/2012/03/07/consider-joining-international-network-integrative-mental-health/.

19   "ACAM's Mission," American College for Advancement in Medicine, https://www.acam.org/page/AboutACAM.

one part of the body affects every other part of the body. The mind and body are not viewed separately, but as part of an energetic system. Similarly, organs and organ systems are viewed as interconnected structures that work together to keep the body functioning.[20]

For more information on acupuncture and its effects on your healing, visit AcupunctureToday.com or Acupuncture.com.

For in-depth information on Chinese medicine, visit the National Center for Complementary and Integrative Health at NCCIH.NIH.gov/health/whatiscam/chinesemed.htm.

• • •

"EMDR (Eye Movement Desensitization and Reprocessing) is a psychotherapy that enables people to heal from the symptoms and emotional distress that are the result of disturbing life experiences. Repeated studies show that by using EMDR people can experience the benefits of psychotherapy that once took years to make a difference. It is widely assumed that severe emotional pain requires a long time to heal. EMDR therapy shows that the mind can in fact heal from psychological trauma much as the body recovers from physical trauma."[21]

• EMDRIA.org
• EMDRTherapistNetwork.com

• • •

Solution-Focused Brief Therapy (SFBT), also called Solution-Focused Therapy, Solution-Building Practice Therapy, was developed by Steve de Shazer (1940-2005), Insoo Kim Berg (1934-2007) and their colleagues beginning in the late 1970s in Milwaukee, Wisconsin. As the name suggests, SFBT is future-focused and goal-directed. It focuses on solutions, rather than on the problems that brought clients to seek therapy.

The entire solution-focused approach was developed inductively in an inner city outpatient mental health service setting in which clients were accepted without previous screening. The developers of SFBT spent hundreds of hours observing therapy sessions over the course of several years, carefully noting the therapists' questions, behaviors, and emotions that occurred during the session and how the various activities of the therapists affected the clients and the therapeutic outcome of the sessions. Questions and activities related to clients' report of progress were preserved and incorporated into the SFBT approach.

---

20 "The ABCs of Traditional Chinese Medicine and Acupuncture," Acupuncture Today, https://www.acupuncturetoday.com/abc/.

21 "What Is EMDR?," EMDR Institute, Inc., 2019, https://www.emdr.com/what-is-emdr/.

Since their early development, SFBT has become one of the leading schools of brief therapy.[22]

To find a SFBT professional, visit the Solution Focused Brief Therapy Association's website at SFBTA.org.

"Instead of focusing on clients' pathology and character logical deficits, the approach operates on the assumption that eating disorder clients have the necessary internal resources to create unique solutions to their problems. The author believes that clinicians must begin with the least intrusive treatment interventions and work diligently with clients to determine treatment goals that are salient to them."[23]

• • •

Viktor Frankl's Logotherapy is based on the premise that the human person is motivated by a "will to meaning," an inner pull to find a meaning in life. . . .

According to Frankl, "We can discover this meaning in life in three different ways: (1) by creating a work or doing a deed; (2) by experiencing something or encountering someone; and (3) by the attitude we take toward unavoidable suffering" and that "everything can be taken from a man but one thing: the last of the human freedoms—to choose one's attitude in any given set of circumstances."[24]

Frankl's theories were heavily influenced by his personal experiences of suffering and loss in Nazi concentration camps. There is plenty of information on the internet from which you can learn more about logotherapy.

• • •

Emotional intelligence describes one's ability to understand other people, to read others' feelings and signals, and to react appropriately by managing one's own emotions. For more information, please refer to the articles and books below.

- Micheal Akers and Grover Porter, "What Is Emotional Intelligence (EQ)?," PsychCentral, October 8, 2018, psychcentral.com/lib/what-is-emotional-intelligence-eq.

- "5 Steps to Nurture Emotional Intelligence in Your Child," Aha! Parenting, ahaparenting. com/parenting-tools/emotional-intelligence/steps-to-encourage.

---

22   "What Is Solution-Focused Therapy?," Institute for Solution-Focused Therapy, 2019, https://solutionfocused.net/what-is-solution-focused-therapy/.

23   Barbara McFarland, *Brief Therapy and Eating Disorders: A Practical Guide to Solution-Focused Work with Clients* (San Francisco: Jossey-Bass, 1995).

24   "Logotherapy," Victor Frankl Institute of Logotherapy, http://www.logotherapyinstitute. org/About_Logotherapy.html.

- John Gottman with Joan Declaire, *Raising an Emotionally Intelligent Child: The Heart of Parenting* (New York: Fireside, 1997).

• • •

There are always new articles popping up on and offline about using hypnosis as a treatment for eating disorders. The following description comes from one contributed by Tammy Holcomb, LPCS, CEDS, NBCCH, executive director at Carolina House and certified clinical hypnotherapist.

"Hypnotherapy is very helpful for those working on issues around fear and anxiety. . . . Hypnotherapy is meant to be a brief therapy used to create subconscious change in a client in the form of new responses, thoughts, attitudes, behaviors or feelings."[25]

• • •

Equine therapy, also referred to as equine assisted psychotherapy (EAP) and/or equine facilitated learning (EFL), utilizes the relationship between a horse and a patient. For us, the patient is our loved one with an eating disorder. The human-horse relationship revolves around emotional healing and growth. There are many articles and websites about the mental and emotional benefits of equine therapy for people struggling with eating disorders. A good place to begin this study is the Eating Disorder Hope website, EatingDisorderHope.com.

• • •

Read about other new approaches to treating eating disorders at WaldenEatingDisorders.com/beyond-the-basics-new-ap-proaches-to-treatment-of-anorexia-nervosa/.

• • •

Referenced EEG is an innovative new technology that has been used for eating disorder patients for over ten years. Referenced EEG is a technology that provides psychiatrists with objective findings to guide the choice of medications. Referenced EEG utilizes standard electroencephalographic equipment measuring the patient in a resting state. Referenced EEG provides psychiatrists with an individualized report that shows what medications have been successfully used with patients with similar neurophysiology. Over the course of eighteen years, the development of Referenced EEG was based on EEG changes recorded with successful medication changes. Thousands of patients are included in a database that enabled the definition of mathematical relationships for different medications and made possible a report of the likelihood that a patient

25 Tammy Holcomb, "Hypnotherapy in Eating Disorder Treatment," https://www.eatingdisorderhope.com/treatment-for-eating-disorders/types-of-treatments/hypnotherapy-in-eating-disorder-treatment.

with a given abnormality would respond to specific medications. Without adequate research supporting medication choices for patients with anorexia, Referenced EEG reduces the trial-and-error approach to psychopharmacology.[26]

• • •

Anorexia is characterized by severe weight loss from self-starvation, yet signs or symptoms of vitamin and mineral deficiencies are rarely studied or integrated into treatment. Patients with anorexia are profoundly malnourished, although it is rare to find nutrient recommendations beyond a "multivitamin" and calcium.

Research from as early as the 1970's has suggested zinc deficiency may play a role in the development of anorexia. The signs and symptoms of zinc deficiency include decreased appetite, weight loss, altered taste, depression, and amenorrhea. Zinc is one of the most prevalent trace elements found in the brain. Meat and fish are the best sources of zinc, and many plant and wheat products impair absorption of zinc. Adolescents are typically eating diets low in zinc and high in inhibitors of the absorption of zinc. Controlled research studies have supported the use of zinc in the treatment of anorexia, yet the medical community has been slow to integrate zinc therapy as a component of a multifaceted treatment program. Other nutritional deficiencies are prevalent in patients with eating disorders. The Omega-3 fatty acids found primarily in fish cannot be manufactured by the human body and must be acquired through the diet. These Omega-3 fatty acids play a central role in nerve cell membranes from early development through adulthood. Research has supported the relationship between essential fatty acid deficiency and many medical and psychiatric conditions. Depression, attention deficit hyperactivity disorder (ADHD), and bipolar disorders are all thought to be related to essential fatty acid deficiencies. A recent study of anorexia and Omega-3 supplementation showed improvement in patients supplemented with one gram of essential fatty acids in addition to standard treatments.[27]

For more information on supplements, read "Vitamins, Minerals and Deficiencies" at Something-Fishy.org/dangers/vitamins.php.

Chapter 14

Start your search for a suitable volunteer opportunity using the following sites.

---

26   James M. Greenblatt, "Beyond the Basics — New Approaches to Treatment of Anorexia Nervosa," Walden Behavioral Care, 2019, https://www.waldeneatingdisorders.com/beyond-the-basics-new-approaches-to-treatment-of-anorexia-nervosa/.

27   Greenblatt, "Beyond the Basics."

- Volunteer Match: VolunteerMatch.org
- Hands on Network: PointsOfLight.org/handsonnetwork
- Idealist.com: Idealist.org

We suggest you also ask your friends and family for recommendations and do your own research into volunteer opportunities.

• • •

"Andy Braner is a Mediterranean Basin Fellow at the Center for Transatlantic Relations at the Johns Hopkins University Paul H. Nitze School of Advanced International Studies (SAIS) . . . Andy is an internationally recognized speaker, popular blogger and trainer for youth. He has written five books on youth culture, and has over 20 years of experience working with youth."[28]

Andy's books include *No Fear in Love: Loving Others the Way God Loves Us* and *Alone: Finding Connection in a Lonely World.*

- AndyBraner.com
- KIVUGapYear.com

• • •

Matthew Williams, MA, is the director of operations of Exile International and a professional trauma counselor who provides leadership and strategic planning to assist Exile International in restoring war-affected children in the Congo through comprehensive care programs. Matthew and his wife, Bethany, work in America and in the Congo, aiding Exile's leadership team, coordinating with domestic and international partners, developing a domestic support network, and speaking at conferences, universities, and NGOs.

- ExileInternational.org

---

28 Andy Braner, Transatlantic Leadership Network, 2018, https://www.transatlantic.org/mediterranean-basin-middle-east-and-gulf/people/andy-braner/.

About the Author

Lara Lyn Bell represents the collective voice of this book's contributors, who have watched with fear, worry, and hope as their loved ones battled eating disorders. Bell is also comprised of trained professionals with experience in treating eating disorders. From medical doctors to therapists and psychologists, their extensive knowledge rounds out this supportive guide through the darkness of an ED to the light of whole healing. This book's contributors have combined forces because they have found that together is stronger than alone, and they want to offer that strength to anyone else who is fighting this battle.